Evolution and Applications of Quantum Computing

Scrivener Publishing
100 Cummings Center, Suite 541J
Beverly, MA 01915-6106

Publishers at Scrivener
Martin Scrivener (martin@scrivenerpublishing.com)
Phillip Carmical (pcarmical@scrivenerpublishing.com)

Evolution and Applications of Quantum Computing

Edited by

Sachi Nandan Mohanty
*School of Computer Science & Engineering, VIT AP University, Amaravati,
Andhra Pradesh, India*

Rajanikanth Aluvalu
*Department of IT, Chaitanya Bharathi Institute of Technology,
Hyderabad, India*

and

Sarita Mohanty
*Department of Computer Science, Odisha University of Agriculture &
Technology, Bhubaneswar, India*

Scrivener
Publishing

WILEY

Wiley Global Headquarters
111 River Street, Hoboken, NJ 07030, USA

For details of our global editorial offices, customer services, and more information about Wiley products visit us at www.wiley.com.

Limit of Liability/Disclaimer of Warranty
While the publisher and authors have used their best efforts in preparing this work, they make no representations or warranties with respect to the accuracy or completeness of the contents of this work and
specifically disclaim all warranties, including without limitation any implied warranties of merchant-
ability or fitness for a particular purpose. No warranty may be created or extended by sales representa-
tives, written sales materials, or promotional statements for this work. The fact that an organization,
website, or product is referred to in this work as a citation and/or potential source of further information does not mean that the publisher and authors endorse the information or services the organization, website, or product may provide or recommendations it may make. This work is sold with the
understanding that the publisher is not engaged in rendering professional services. The advice and
strategies contained herein may not be suitable for your situation. You should consult with a specialist
where appropriate. Neither the publisher nor authors shall be liable for any loss of profit or any other
commercial damages, including but not limited to special, incidental, consequential, or other damages.
Further, readers should be aware that websites listed in this work may have changed or disappeared
between when this work was written and when it is read.

Library of Congress Cataloging-in-Publication Data

ISBN 9781119904861

Cover image: Pixabay.Com
Cover design by Russell Richardson

Set in size of 11pt and Minion Pro by Manila Typesetting Company, Makati, Philippines

Printed in the USA

10 9 8 7 6 5 4 3 2 1

Contents

12 Problems and Demanding Situations in Traditional Cryptography: An Insistence for Quantum Computing to Secure Private Information 183

D. DShivaprasad, Mohamed Sirajudeen Yoosuf,
P. Selvaramalakshmi, Manoj A. Patil
and Dasari Promod Kumar

Preface

A holistic approach to the revolutionary world of quantum computing is presented in this book, which reveals valuable insights into this rapidly emerging technology. The book reflects the dependence of quantum computing on the physical phenomenon of superposition, entanglement, teleportation and interference to simplify difficult mathematical problems which would have otherwise taken years to derive a definite solution for. An amalgamation of the information provided in the multiple chapters will elucidate the revolutionary and riveting research being carried out in the brand-new domain encompassing quantum computation, quantum information and quantum mechanics. Each chapter gives a concise introduction to the topic.

The book begins with the procedure for designing one of the most important combinational circuits, called the quantum multiplexer with secured quantum gate (CSWAP), that aids in implementing quantum entanglement to provide secured communication. Also provided is a description of the pioneering work being done on the interaction between artificial intelligence, machine learning and quantum computing along with their potential role in the world of big data. Next, the book guides you towards detecting malicious emails and URLs by using quantum text mining algorithms and further helps by teaching the algorithm needed to distinguish between phishing and benign sites. Also included is an interesting chapter on application machine learning to detect phishing URLs and the procedure to implement URL feature extractor. Emphasis is placed on the increasing vulnerabilities a system has to cybersecurity attacks in the chapter on quantum data traffic analysis for intrusion detection system. Furthermore, you will find chapters on interdisciplinary fields like quantum computation in Indian banks, netnomy and vehicular ad-hoc networks, virtual reality in education of autistic children, and quantum computing for identifying bacterial diseases and accelerating drug discovery. The book also touches on the critical domain of traditional classical cryptography and quantum cryptography along with their substantial difference and their role in providing a safe and secure communication system.

Almost every application of quantum computing is covered in this book, so by the end of it you will have an encompassing knowledge about this wide field and its potential offshoots in the digitalized era. Moreover, it is an ideal book for newbies in the field of quantum physics, with simple and lucid language for better understanding. All in all, the updated knowledge on the different dynamics of quantum computing covered in this book will leave you amazed.

The Editors
February 2023

Introduction to Quantum Computing

V. Padmavathi[1], C. N. Sujatha[2], V. Sitharamulu[3], K. Sudheer Reddy[4*]
and A. Mallikarjuna Reddy[5]

[1]Dept. of Computer Science and Engineering, Chaitanya Bharathi Institute
of Technology, Hyderabad, India
[2]Dept. of Computer Science and Engineering, Sreenidhi Institute of Science
and Technology, Hyderabad, India
[3]Dept. of Computer Science and Engineering, GITAM (Deemed to be University),
Hyderabad, India
[4]Dept. of Information Technology, Anurag University, Hyderabad, India
[5]Dept. of Artificial Intelligence, Anurag University, Hyderabad, India

Abstract

Over the past few decades, tremendous growth has been witnessed in cryptography in which different security techniques and concerns were projected and put into practice. The classical methods of cryptography are depended on binary bits, which are susceptible to predicting the key during transit. Hence, moving the classical cryptographic scheme to a new fast, and non-vulnerable scheme is time. The principles of quantum mechanics are applied in quantum computing to enhance security which uses qubits for communication. The advantage of using qubits is that it is impossible to make copies of qubits due to the no-cloning theorem. The computations are performed through photons or qubits produced using the photon's polarization. The qubits are disturbed when measured at an incorrect polarization angle due to the principle of uncertainty. The photons are quantized features used to encode the information. They can be applied in Quantum Key Distribution (QKD), in which distantly apart communicators share a standard secret key.

Keywords: Quantum computing, quantum mechanics, qubits, photon polarization, quantum gates, quantum cryptography, quantum key, Fredkin gate

Corresponding author: sudheercse@gmail.com

Sachi Nandan Mohanty, Rajanikanth Aluvalu and Sarita Mohanty (eds.) Evolution and Applications of Quantum Computing, (1–14) © 2023 Scrivener Publishing LLC

1.1   Quantum Computation

The study of information processing based on quantum mechanics is known as quantum computing and quantum information. Quantum mechanics is a set of mathematical rules used to build physical hypotheses. Building tools to refine the notion of quantum mechanics is one of the objectives of quantum computation [7–11]. There was a debate on whether it was possible to make a duplicate of an unknown quantum state. Quantum mechanics might be used when replication is conceivable to send signals faster than light, which is highly impractical. Wooters and Zurek [3] proved that the theorem of no cloning, was the first result of quantum computation and information. Since then, there have been several improvements.

1.2   Importance of Quantum Mechanics

Quantum mechanics-based communications are safe since they stand on inalienable quantum mechanics concepts. The principles of Heisenberg Uncertainty and Photon Polarization are essential concepts.

The Heisenberg principle of Uncertainty refers to an entity's inability to discern two connected physical attributes [4]. In light of this assertion, two examples are worth considering. The first is the example generally stated: For every P, the momentum and the location cannot be calculated alongside. Second, the photon cannot be measured concurrently on either of it [1, 2, 18], then properties are impacted. According to the theorem of no-cloning [1, 3, 18], replicas of qubits are not feasible.

1.3   Security Options in Quantum Mechanics

Figure 1.1 demonstrates that a bit corresponds to a qubit by polarizing photons and with the help of a rectilinear and diagonal basis. In a rectilinear base, the binary 0 is represented by 0° photon polarization and 45° on a diagonal basis. In Figure 1.2 [4], binary one is represented by 90° rectilinear photon polarization and 135° diagonal photon polarization.

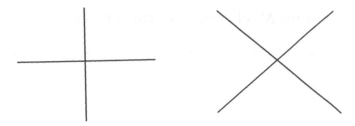

Figure 1.1 Rectilinear, diagonal basis.

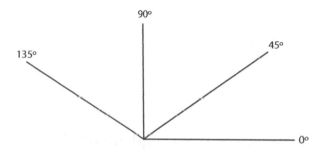

Figure 1.2 Photon polarizations.

1.4 Quantum States and Qubits

Qubit exists in two states, symbolized as $|0\rangle$ and $|1\rangle$ in quantum mechanics. It is stated as a state, a ket, which Paul Dirac created [1, 6]. A bit can be 0 or 1, whereas a qubit can be $|0\rangle$ or $|1\rangle$ state. It also happens in the super-position state that is nothing more than a linear arrangement of the quantum states $|0\rangle$ and $|1\rangle$. The symbol $|\phi\rangle$ indicates a form, and a superposition state is denoted by the symbol $|\varphi\rangle = \alpha|0\rangle + \beta|1\rangle$ where α and β are complex numbers [6].

A qubit exists in superposition state $|0\rangle$ and $|1\rangle$ in most cases, but the state is not calculated. When it is calculated, though, it is either in $|0\rangle$ or $|1\rangle$. The chance of realizing a qubit is either $|0\rangle$ or $|1\rangle$ equals the square of the modulus of α, β. It is stated that in state $|0\rangle$, the likelihood of obtaining $|\phi\rangle$ is $|\alpha|^2$, and in state $|1\rangle$, the likelihood of obtaining $|\phi\rangle$ is $|\beta|^2$. Squaring coefficients yield likelihood of attaining a measurement's result. Thus, $|\alpha|^2 + |\beta|^2 = 1$ [6, 18] is the state.

1.5   Quantum Mechanics Interpretation

The state is shown by the expression $\alpha|0\rangle + \beta|1\rangle$. It can alternatively be represented as a vector or a column. It is represented as a two-dimensional complex unit vector by stacking two complex integers $\begin{bmatrix} \alpha \\ \beta \end{bmatrix}$ [1, 12].

$$|0\rangle = \begin{bmatrix} 1 \\ 0 \end{bmatrix} \text{ where } \alpha = 1 \text{ and } \beta = 0$$

And

$$|1\rangle = \begin{bmatrix} 0 \\ 1 \end{bmatrix} \text{ where } \alpha = 0 \text{ and } \beta = 1$$

$$|\phi\rangle = \cos\theta\,|0\rangle = \sin\theta\,|1\rangle = \begin{bmatrix} \cos\theta \\ \sin\theta \end{bmatrix}.$$

1.6   Quantum Mechanics Implementation

The following notations are used to implement quantum mechanics:

1) $|0\rangle = |-\rangle$
2) $|1\rangle = |\,|\,\rangle$
3) $\dfrac{1}{\sqrt{2}}\,(|0\rangle + |1\rangle) = |/\rangle$
4) $\dfrac{1}{\sqrt{2}}\,(|0\rangle - |1\rangle) = |\backslash\rangle$

In rectilinear basis, 1 and 2 indicates 0° and 90°, respectively. In diagonal basis, the 3 and 4 indicates 45° and 135°, respectively.

1.6.1   Photon Polarization Representation

i)   A binary 0 is represented in rectilinear basis as a 0° state using polarization, as demonstrated below using a linear layout with x and y axes both set to 1. Figure 1.3 depicts the situation.

$$|0\rangle = |-\rangle = \begin{bmatrix} 0 \\ 1 \end{bmatrix} = 1\,|\,x\,\rangle + 0\,|\,y\,\rangle$$

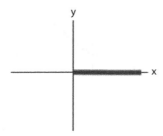

Figure 1.3 Representation of photon polarization.

ii) Using the linear configurations of 0 on the x axis and 1 on the y axis, respectively. Polari-zation isused to represent the binary 1 in rectilinear basis as a 90° state. The illustration is shown in Figure 1.4.

$$| \, | \, \rangle = \begin{bmatrix} 0 \\ 1 \end{bmatrix} = 0 \, | \, x \, \rangle + 1 \, | \, y \, \rangle$$

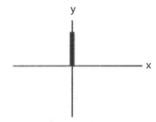

Figure 1.4 Representation of photon polarization.

iii) Using polarization and the linear combinations listed below, a 0 in binary is shown as 45° state on a diagonal basis. Figure 1.5 depicts the situation.

$$| \, / \, \rangle = \begin{bmatrix} \dfrac{1}{\sqrt{2}} \\ \dfrac{1}{\sqrt{2}} \end{bmatrix} \dfrac{1}{\sqrt{2}} \, | \, x \, \rangle + \dfrac{1}{\sqrt{2}} \, | \, y \, \rangle$$

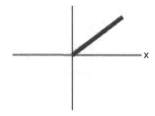

Figure 1.5 Photon polarization in diagonal basis (of binary 0).

iv) Using polarization and the linear combinations listed below, 1 in binary corresponds to 135° in diagonal basis. The representation is shown in Figure 1.6.

$$|\setminus\rangle = \begin{bmatrix} \dfrac{1}{\sqrt{2}} \\ -\dfrac{1}{\sqrt{2}} \end{bmatrix} \dfrac{1}{\sqrt{2}}|x\rangle - \dfrac{1}{\sqrt{2}}|y\rangle$$

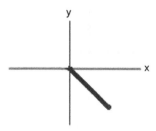

Figure 1.6 Representation of photon polarization.

1.7   Quantum Computation

Quantum computation has led to a new way of thinking about computation. The notion of quantum computation explains changes in state stirring. A classical computer, like a method, is built with the help of an electrical circuit with logic wires and gates, whereas a quantum computer is built with the help of a quantum circuit with quantum wires and gates.

The quantum gates are employed to control or manipulate and act on the quantum bit [5].

The matrix representation is the best way to understand linear combinations. Unitary matrix U is the proper state on the matrix to represent the gate. Specifically, U†U = I, in which U† is the adjoint of U, that is the complex conjugate of the transpose of matrix U, and I is a two-by-two identity matrix. It is simple to validate X†X = I for a gate, for example. Surprisingly, quantum gates are only limited by the unitary check. It denotes the presence of a logical quantum gate [5].

1.7.1 Quantum Gates

Gates are used to carry out computations in quantum computers. Quantum gates are unitary operators with n inputs and outputs that may be expressed using matrices. As a result, they have a 2^n degree. A two-degree matrix is used to represent one qubit. As a result, a two-by-two matrix is required for a quantum gate acting on a qubit. A matrix of 2^2 degrees is used to represent a two-qubit gate. As a result, a four-by-four unitary matrix [5, 6] is used to represent it. As a result, the quantum gates have a temporal complexity of 2^n. It has been proved that exponential complexities are secure. The tensor product is used to obtain the matrix depiction of quantum gates. Tensor product is represented as ⊗.

It creates a single vector space out of two. XY is a space with mxn dimension if X and Y are vector spaces with mxn n dimensions. The components of |x| of X and |y| of Y are the elements of XY, which are linear combinations of these tensor products. The matrix is represented as given if A is an m x n matrix and B is a p x q matrix.

$$
A \otimes B = \overbrace{\begin{bmatrix} A_{11}B & A_{12}B & \cdots & A_{1n}B \\ A_{21}B & A_{22}B & \cdots & A_{2n}B \\ \cdot & \cdot & \cdot & \cdot \\ \cdot & \cdot & \cdot & \cdot \\ A_{m1}B & A_{m2}B & \cdots & A_{mn}B \end{bmatrix}}^{nq} \left.\vphantom{\begin{bmatrix} A_{11}B \\ A_{21}B \\ \cdot \\ \cdot \\ A_{m1}B \end{bmatrix}}\right\} mp
$$

A. One-Qubit Gate

A quantum gate that operates on a single qubit requires a single qubit as input and output. The computation requires a two-by-two unitary matrix. The several forms of one-qubit gates are explained in the following sections [17, 18].

i) H-Gate

The Hadamard gate is represented by H and depicted:

$$H = \frac{1}{\sqrt{2}}\begin{bmatrix} 1 & 1 \\ 1 & -1 \end{bmatrix}$$

ii) Quantum NOT Gate or Pauli X-Gate

The quantum not gate is shown in matrix form as

$$X = \begin{bmatrix} 0 & 1 \\ 1 & 0 \end{bmatrix}$$

iii) Pauli Y-Gate

The gate is depicted as below

$$Y = \begin{bmatrix} 0 & -i \\ i & 0 \end{bmatrix}$$

iv) Pauli Z-Gate

It is portrayed as

$$Y = \begin{bmatrix} 1 & 0 \\ 0 & -1 \end{bmatrix}$$

v) Pauli S-Gate

Pauli S-gate is described:

$$S = \begin{bmatrix} 1 & 0 \\ 0 & i \end{bmatrix}$$

A $|0\rangle$ when operated atop on it returns $|0\rangle$, but when $|1\rangle$ is acted upon, Pauli S-gate returns $i|1\rangle$

B. Two-Qubit Gate

A two-qubit quantum gate accepts two qubits as an input and two qubits as an output. The computation requires a four-by-four matrix. The many forms of two-qubit gates are detailed in the following sections.

i) Controlled NOT

It is well-known as the CNOT gate. The CNOT gate's initial input serves as a control qubit. The target qubit is unaffected if the control qubit is $|0\rangle$. If it is $|1\rangle$, CNOT operates on the qubit by flipping it. $|00\rangle$, $|01\rangle$, $|10\rangle$ and $|11\rangle$ are the states. On two qubits a, b, the function of the CNOT gate is $|a, b\rangle \rightarrow |a, b \oplus a\rangle$.

The CNOT matrix is

$$\begin{bmatrix} 1 & 0 & 0 & 0 \\ 0 & 1 & 0 & 0 \\ 0 & 0 & 0 & 1 \\ 0 & 0 & 1 & 0 \end{bmatrix}$$

ii) Swap Gate Swaps Two Qubits

The Swap matrix is shown as:

$$\begin{bmatrix} 1 & 0 & 0 & 0 \\ 0 & 0 & 1 & 0 \\ 0 & 1 & 0 & 0 \\ 0 & 0 & 0 & 1 \end{bmatrix}$$

iii) Controlled-Z Gate

cZ is another representation for it. The gate's qubits behave in a predictable manner.

The cZ matrix is

$$\begin{bmatrix} 1 & 0 & 0 & 0 \\ 0 & 1 & 0 & 0 \\ 0 & 0 & 1 & 0 \\ 0 & 0 & 0 & -1 \end{bmatrix}$$

iv) Controlled Phase Gate

It is commonly represented as cS gate. The process is identical to that of a Phase gate.

The cS matrix is

$$
\begin{bmatrix}
1 & 0 & 0 & 0 \\
0 & 1 & 0 & 0 \\
0 & 0 & 1 & 0 \\
0 & 0 & 0 & i
\end{bmatrix}
$$

C. Three-Qubit Gate

Three qubits are the input and three qubits are the output of a three-qubit quantum gate. The computation requires an eight-by-eight matrix. The many forms of three-qubit gates are detailed in the following sections.

i) Toffoli Gate

It is a three-qubit quantum gate, as it receives three inputs, produces three outputs a, b, and c out of a total of 2^3 [5]. Figure 1.7 depicts the situation. T gate is the short name for it. The gate operation has no effect on the inputs a, b, the two control qubits. The target is flipped when control qubits is set as 1 or not when the input c is set to 0. T gates have the property of being reversible when applied twice on qubits $|a, b, c\rangle \rightarrow |a, b, c \oplus ab\rangle \rightarrow |a, b, c\rangle$

An eight-by-eight matrix is used to represent it

$$
\begin{bmatrix}
1 & 0 & 0 & 0 & 0 & 0 & 0 & 0 \\
0 & 1 & 0 & 0 & 0 & 0 & 0 & 0 \\
0 & 0 & 1 & 0 & 0 & 0 & 0 & 0 \\
0 & 0 & 0 & 1 & 0 & 0 & 0 & 0 \\
0 & 0 & 0 & 0 & 1 & 0 & 0 & 0 \\
0 & 0 & 0 & 0 & 0 & 1 & 0 & 0 \\
0 & 0 & 0 & 0 & 0 & 0 & 0 & 1 \\
0 & 0 & 0 & 0 & 0 & 0 & 1 & 0
\end{bmatrix}
$$

Figure 1.7 Toffoli gate.

ii) Fredkin (controlled swap) gate

The controlled swap gate is a three-qubit gate. 'a' is the control qubit, and 'b' and 'c' are the target qubits. If control qubit 'a' is set to 1, it swaps target qubits 'b' and 'c,' otherwise they pass through untouched [26, 27].

An eight-by-eight matrix is used to represent it

$$
\begin{bmatrix}
1 & 0 & 0 & 0 & 0 & 0 & 0 & 0 \\
0 & 1 & 0 & 0 & 0 & 0 & 0 & 0 \\
0 & 0 & 1 & 0 & 0 & 0 & 0 & 0 \\
0 & 0 & 0 & 1 & 0 & 0 & 0 & 0 \\
0 & 0 & 0 & 0 & 1 & 0 & 0 & 0 \\
0 & 0 & 0 & 0 & 0 & 0 & 1 & 0 \\
0 & 0 & 0 & 0 & 0 & 1 & 0 & 0 \\
0 & 0 & 0 & 0 & 0 & 0 & 0 & 1
\end{bmatrix}
$$

1.8   Comparison of Quantum and Classical Computation

The operations in the classical computation are based on probability and employ stochastic matrices. In classical computation, the chance of obtaining state i is Pi, where Pi is an actual number. $0 \le Pi \le 1$ and $\sum Pi = 1$. The probability of getting state Y in quantum computation is $|aY|2$, where a is the amplitude and ai as a complex number,

$$0 = |ai|2 = 1, ? i \ |ai|2 = 1.$$

The transition is based on amplitudes in this case. Unitary matrices [5] are used in quantum computation [22–25].

1.9   Quantum Cryptography

The researcher [1], discovered the notion of uncertainty. As a result, the phenomena evolved into Quantum Cryptography, a particularly promising topic for cryptographers. Later, Wiedemann built on this idea by proposing a quantum key distribution mechanism known as QKD [2, 16–21], which follows the laws of quantum physics. Later, the BB84 protocol [4, 22–25] employed for verifiably secure quantum physics concepts.

1.10   QKD

QKD begins by transmitting photons that are generated at random in four quantum states, employing rectilinear and diagonal basis. A rectilinear basis has two states: a 0 in binary is polarized horizontally to 0° and 1 in binary 1 is polarized vertically to 90°. Likewise, the two states of diagonal basis, binary 0 and 1, are polarized at 45° and 135°, respectively [13–15]. QKD starts by sending out a message. For communication, it requires a classical and a quantum channel. Classical messages are sent over a traditional channel, while qubits or polarized photons are sent through a quantum channel.

1.11   Conclusion

The fact that quantum computing techniques are used in cryptography is a good sign in the new research. The objective of quantum computing is made evidently for safe and secure transmission by using quantum mechanics. The qubit is prepared by polarizing photon basis. The computing of classical and quantum computers is investigated. Also mentioned are the limitations of traditional computers. The quantum computer's computations utilize various quantum gates, as indicated. The building blocks are the quantum gates that act on qubits. The introduction to QKD, which follows quantum mechanics laws to provide secure key transfer, is mentioned.

References

1. Wiesner, S., Conjugate coding. *ACM Sigact News*, 15, 1, 78–88, original manuscript written circa 1969, 1983.
2. Wiedemann, D., Quantum cryptography. *ACM Sigact News*, 18, 2, 48–51, Sept. 1986-March 1987.
3. Wootters, W.K. and Zurek, W.H., A single quantum cannot be cloned. *Nature*, 299, 802–803, 1982.
4. Bennett, C.H. and Brassard, G., Quantum cryptography: Public key distribution and coin tossing. *Proceedings of IEEE International Conference on Computers, Systems and Signal Processing*, Bangalore, India, pp. 175–179, December 1984.
5. Nielsen, M.A. and Chuang, I.L., *Quantum Computation and Quantum Information*, Cambridge University Press, University of Cambridge, Cambridge, 2000.
6. McMahon, D., *Quantum Computing Explained*, IEEE Computer Society, Wiley-Inderscience, John Wiley & Sons, Inc., Hoboken, NJ, USA, 2008.
7. NSA seeks to build quantum computer that could crack most types of encryption. *Washington Post*, January 2, 2014. https://www.washingtonpost.com/world/national-security/nsa-seeks-to-build-quantum-computer-that-could-crack-most-types-of-encryption/2014/01/02/8fff297e-7195-11e3-8def-a33011492df2_story.html.
8. https://en.wikipedia.org/wiki/Quantum_computing.
9. World's first silicon quantum logic gate brings quantum computing one step closer. http://gizmodo.com/worlds-first-silicon-quantum-logic-gate-brings-quantum-1734653115.
10. Corcoles, A.D., Magesan, E., Srinivasan, S.J., Cross, A.W., Steffen, M., Gambetta, J.M., Chow, J.M., Demonstration of a quantum error detection code using a square lattice of four superconducting qubits. Nature Publishing Group. *Phys. Rev. Lett.*, 6, 1–10, 2015.
11. Gaudin, S., Researchers use silicon to push quantum computing toward reality, 2014. http://www.computerworld.com/article/2837813/researchers-use-silicon-to-push-quantum-computing-toward-reality.html.
12. Vazirani, U.V., *Quantum Mechanics and Quantum Computation*, University of California, Berkley, 2006, https://www.youtube.com/watch?v=Gfpzke48K9E&list=PL3XnKI-cY52yHBKN3z1n_-hrvjEcmaLW&index=3.
13. Bennett, C.H., Brassard, G., Robert, J.M., Privacy amplification by public discussion. *SIAM J. Comput.*, 17, 210–229, April 1988.
14. Brassard, G. and Salvail, L., Secret-key reconciliation by public discussion in advances, in: *Cryptography—EUROCRYPT'93*, *Lecture Notes in Computer Science*, vol. 765, T. Helleseth (Ed.), pp. 410–423, Springer-Verlag, Berlin, Germany, 1994.
15. Bennett, C.H., Brassard, G., Crepeau, C., Maurer, U.M., Generalized privacy amplification. *IEEE Trans. Inf. Theory*, 41, 6(part 2), 1915–1923, Nov. 1995.

16. Brassard, G. and Crepeau, C., 25 years of quantum cryptography. *ACM Sigact News*, 27, 3, 13–24, 1996.

17. Bennett, C., Bessette, F., Brassard, G., Salvail, L., Smolin, J., Experimental quantum cryptography. *J. Cryptology*, 5, 3–28, 1992.

18. Padmavathi, V., Vardhan, B.V., Krishna, A.V.N., Quantum cryptography and quantum key distribution protocols: A survey. *2016 IEEE 6th International Conference on Advanced Computing*.

19. Padmavathi, V., Vardhan, B.V., Krishna, A.V.N., Provably secure quantum key distribution by applying quantum gate. *Int. J. Netw. Secur.*, 20, 1, 88–94, Jan. 2018.

20. Aluvalu, R., Kamliya, V., Muddana, L., Hasbe access control model with secure key distribution and efficient domain hierarchy for cloud computing. *Int. J. Electr. Comput. Eng.*, 6, 2, 770, 2016.

21. Langaliya, C. and Aluvalu, R., Enhancing cloud security through access control models: A survey. *Int. J. Comput. Appl.*, 112, 7, 8–12, 2015.

22. Chennam, K.K., Muddana, L., Aluvalu, R.K., Performance analysis of various encryption algorithms for usage in multistage encryption for securing data in cloud, in: *2017 2nd IEEE International Conference on Recent Trends in Electronics, Information & Communication Technology*, IEEE, pp. 2030–2033, 2017.

23. Reddy, K.S., Varma, G.P.S., Reddy, S.S.S., Understanding the scope of web usage mining & applications of web data usage patterns. *2012 International Conference on Computing, Communication and Applications*, pp. 1–5, 2012.

24. Ayaluri, M.R., Reddy, K.S., Konda, S.R., Chidirala, S.R., Efficient steganalysis using convolutional auto encoder network to ensure original image quality. *Peer J. Comput. Sci.*, 7, e356, 2021. https://doi.org/10.7717/peerj-cs.356.

25. Kavati, I., Reddy, A.M., Babu, E.S., Reddy, K.S., Cheruku, R.S., Design of a fingerprint template protection scheme using elliptical structures. *ICT Express*, 7, 4, 497–500, 2021. https://doi.org/10.1016/j.icte.2021.04.001.

26. Santhosh Kumar, C.N., Pavan Kumar, V., Reddy, K.S., Similarity matching of pairs of text using CACT algorithm. *Int. J. Eng. Adv. Technol.*, 8, 6, 2296–2298, 2019.

27. Reddy, K.S. and Santhosh Kumar, C.H.N., Effective data analytics on opinion mining. *IJITEE*, 8, 10, 2073–2078, 2019.

Fundamentals of Quantum Computing and Significance of Innovation

Swapna Mudrakola[1]*, Uma Maheswari V.[2], Krishna Keerthi Chennam[3] and MVV Prasad Kantipudi[4]

[1]Matrusri Engineering College, Department of CSE, Hyderabad, India
[2]KG Reddy College of Engineering and Technology, Department of CSE, Hyderabad, India
[3]Vasavi College of Engineering, Hyderabad, India,
[4]Symbiosis Institute of Technology, Symbiosis International (Deemed University), Pune, India

Abstract

Digital transformation has changed the lifestyle of people, business applications, scientific approaches, and communication systems. Data security and protection plays important role in network systems and data repositories. The latest security techniques are being solved by many contemporary attacks. The traditional cryptography techniques applied to binary data, encryption, and decryption use keys. The keys are predicted and broken using hacking methods during the transmission of data. Cryptographic techniques are upgraded using different schemes. The security can be improvised using quantum computing in data transmission of qubits form of data. The property of qubits is liable with the no-cloning theorem, not possible to make no copies. The quantum theory principle can be operated using polarization with qubits and photons. The uncertainty in quantum computing on qubits can be asses at due to wrong polarization angles. The quantized properties are used to encryption of the data using photons. Quantum Key Distribution will share the keys.

Keywords: Quantum computing, qubit, polarization, photon, Hadamard-GATE, quantum cryptography, quantum key distribution, photon polarization

Corresponding author: swapna0801@gmail.com

Sachi Nandan Mohanty, Rajanikanth Aluvalu and Sarita Mohanty (eds.) Evolution and Applications of Quantum Computing, (15–30) © 2023 Scrivener Publishing LLC

2.1   Quantum Reckoning Mechanism

Quantum computing is also known as quantum information uses to process information and known to be the quantum mechanics. The physical theorems are framed using a mathematical formula. The applications are developed using quantum mechanics in the quantum computation process. The notations are also refined to improve the mechanism of Qubit cryptography [7–11]. The unclear statement of whether duplicating the quantum state is possible or not is always unpredicted. The Quantum theory used to translate signals with higher speed and lighter weights is unpractical. Wooters *et al.* [3] have confined there is no cloning in quantum theory and information. Many improvements are done on Quantum.

2.2   Significance of Quantum Computing

Quantum theorems communicate with secure transmission with imaginable quantum computing.

Essential concepts are based on principals of photon polarization and Heisenberg incertitude. The Heisenberg principle of Uncertainty reefed to inadequacy to connect the existing attributes [4]. To Asses, consider using two examples. The first one is for point (p), the location and momentum both can't be calculated against and second example photons are not measured simultaneously [1, 2, 18], then properties are impacted. The quantum theorems are not clonable [1, 3, 18], replicas of qubits are not feasible.

2.3   Security Opportunities in Quantum Computing

A simple demonstration of the qubit by diverging photons in form of quadratic division and corner ways slicing is shown in Figure 2.1. In the

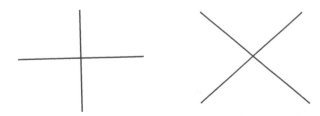

Figure 2.1 Quadratic and corner basis.

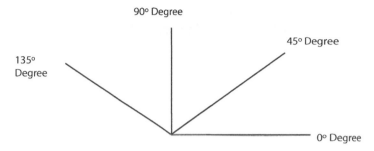

Figure 2.2 Photon polarization.

Quadratic partition the binary 0 specifies the zero degree of photon polarization and in corner slicing (diagonal partition) are 45° angles. The photon Polarization of rectilinear is represented with 90°, and the binary value is 1. The diagonal (corner way) is represented with 135° photon segmentation as shown in Figure 2.2.

2.4   Quantum States of Qubit

In Quantum Computing, Qubit consists of two states and is represented by |0⟩ and |1⟩. These states are represented, and Paul Dirac has represented [1, 6]. The general bit values are 0's and 1's, but qubits are represented by |0⟩ or |1⟩ state. The superposition state will be no more than linear represents |0⟩ and |1⟩ states. The |ϕ⟩ symbol used to indicate a form, The Symbols α, and β are complex numbers is denoted by superposition [6]. In most cases, qubits are represented in superposition |0⟩ and |1⟩ states, but states cannot be calculus. The outcome of the calculation Will is either in the |0⟩ state or |1⟩ state. The qubit is calculated in |0⟩ or |1⟩ states are the square of the Alpha and Beta is the square of the modulus. It is a state |0⟩, it is like getting |ϕ⟩ is |α|2, and it is a state |1⟩, it is like |ϕ⟩ is |β|2. The results are obtained by squaring the coefficients.

2.5   Quantum Computing Analysis

Quantum computing states are expressed in the equation $\alpha|0\rangle + \beta|1\rangle$. Another way of expression is in the form of columns and vectors. The two-dimensional unit vectors are complex by stacking are $\begin{bmatrix} \alpha \\ \beta \end{bmatrix}$ [1, 12].

$$|0\rangle = \begin{bmatrix} 1 \\ 0 \end{bmatrix} \qquad \text{Where?} = 1, \ ? = 0$$

$$|1\rangle = \begin{bmatrix} 0 \\ 1 \end{bmatrix} \qquad \text{Where?} = 0, \ ? = 1$$

$$|??\rangle = \cos? \, |0?\rangle + \sin? \, |1?\rangle = \begin{bmatrix} \cos\theta \\ \sin\theta \end{bmatrix}$$

2.6   Quantum Computing Development Mechanism

Notations are used to implement quantum mechanics are

1) $|0\rangle = |\!-\!\rangle$
2) $|1\rangle = |\,|\,\rangle$
3) $\dfrac{1}{\sqrt{2}}(|0\rangle + |1\rangle) = |/\rangle$
4) $\dfrac{1}{\sqrt{2}}(|0\rangle - |1\rangle) = |\backslash\rangle$

On a quadratic basis, the above two notations 1 and 2 will indicate zero degree and 90°, respectively. On a diagonal basis, another two notations, 3 and 4, indicate 45° and 135°, respectively.

2.7   Representation of Photon Polarization

In quadratic division (rectilinear partition), The binary value zero is represented by Zero-Degree states uses the polarization linear representation of 1 on the X1-axis and 0 is represented on Y1-axis are shown in Figure 2.3.

$$|0?\rangle = |\!-\!?\rangle = \begin{bmatrix} 1 \\ 0 \end{bmatrix} = 1 \, |x1?\rangle + 0 \, |y1?\rangle$$

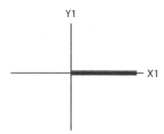

Figure 2.3 Photon polarizations using quadratic basis.

The representation of linear values for zero on x1-axis and one on y1-axis as shown. The binary one value is projected on 90° in quadratic axis has partition. The example is shown in Figure 2.4.

$$\| ? = \begin{bmatrix} 0 \\ 1 \end{bmatrix} = 0 | \ x \ ?+1| \ y \ ?$$

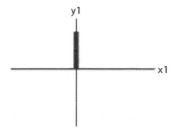

Figure 2.4 Photon polarization in quadrilateral basis.

The Polarization and Linear Lists are used combinable and Zero in Binary form shows at 45° state at diagonal form, as shown in Figure 2.5.

$$| / \rangle = \begin{bmatrix} \dfrac{1}{\sqrt{2}} \\ \dfrac{1}{\sqrt{2}} \end{bmatrix} \dfrac{1}{\sqrt{2}} | x \rangle + \dfrac{1}{\sqrt{2}} | y \rangle$$

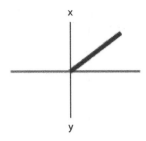

Figure 2.5 Photon polarization in diagonal basis (of binary 0).

In another situation, when polarization and linear lists are combined, I in a binary corresponds to 135° in opposite form, as reflected in Figure 2.6.

$$|\rangle = \begin{bmatrix} \dfrac{1}{\sqrt{2}} \\ -\dfrac{1}{\sqrt{2}} \end{bmatrix} \dfrac{1}{\sqrt{2}}|x\rangle - \dfrac{1}{\sqrt{2}}|y\rangle$$

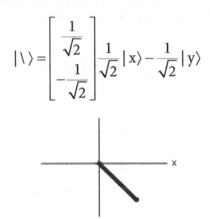

Figure 2.6 Photon polarization in diagonal basis (of binary 1).

2.8   Theory of Quantum Computing

Quantum computing has changed the model of thinking to see problems, solving practices, and creative approaches using quantum principles. The quantum notations in computing will give detailed information about the state changes. Traditional computers are changing their types of components, size, and technology. Earlier the computer components are made up of electric circuit boards with logic and gates, now remodeled computer components are quantum circuits made up of logical wires and gates. The quantum logical gates are asked to be manipulated, controlled, and worked on the quantum bit [5]. The common way to represent the linear combination of a matrix. The Unitary Matrix (U) is a significant state of the matrix using gates. U†U = I is an equation, in which U† is at the joint U, the difficulty of the conjugate of Remodel Matrix U. I is a 2X2 identity matrix and has a validated with X†X = I. In terms of the GATE, Consider an example, Quantum GATES is limited by the unitary check and denoted by logical quantum GATE [5].

2.9 Quantum Logical Gates

In quantum computers, gates are used to carry out the computation task. Quantum gates are used to perform the unitary operators, which have n-inputs and the outputs are represented with matrices. Results have a degree. The $2°$ matrix is use to present the 1-qubit. The 2 x 2 matrix is used to represent one qubit. The 2 x 2 Matrix is used for quantum gates acting on the qubit. The 2 x 2 Matrix with two degrees is used to represent the two-qubit gate. The results are obtained in the 4 x 4 matrix used to represent [5, 6]. The quantum gates gain the temporal complexity of 2n. This complexity is proven to be extreme exponential complex are secure. The obtained study of the quantum gates is the tensor products. They are represented using a combination of two vector spaces into a single one. Now assume P and Q are two vectors space consisting of M x N dimensions, PQ has M x N dimensions. If P and Q are vectors with M x N, n-dimension, then PQ is a vector with M x N dimension. The P⊗Q has a linear combination tensor products |P⟩⊗|Q⟩, variables of |P⟩ of P and |Q⟩ of Q. If P is an M x N matrix and Q is a P x Q are the matrix [5].

$$
A \otimes B = \overbrace{\left[\begin{array}{cccc} A_{11}B & A_{12}B & \cdots & A_{1n}B \\ A_{21}B & A_{22}B & \cdots & A_{2n}B \\ \cdot & \cdot & \cdot & \cdot \\ \cdot & \cdot & \cdot & \cdot \\ A_{m1}B & A_{m2}B & \cdots & A_{mn}B \end{array}\right]}^{nq} \left.\vphantom{\begin{array}{c}a\\a\\a\\a\\a\end{array}}\right\} mp
$$

2.9.1   I-Qubit GATE

The 1-qubit input is required to produce the 1-qubit output; the input is processed using Quantum GATE. The calculations need a 2 x 2 unitary matrix. The qubit gates are discussed in the below section in different forms [17, 18].

2.9.2   Hadamard-GATE

The Hadamard GATE are denoted with 'HG', and obtained matrix is

$$H = \frac{1}{\sqrt{2}}\begin{bmatrix} 1 & 1 \\ 1 & -1 \end{bmatrix}$$

A qubit |0> that is worked on HG gets
A qubit |0 ? operated upon HE gives

$$|0??\quad HE = \frac{1}{\sqrt{2}}(|0?+|1?)$$

A qubit |1? operated upon HE gives

$$|1??\quad HE = \frac{1}{\sqrt{2}}(|0?-|1?)$$

2.9.3   NOT_GATE_QUANTUM or Pauli_X-GATE

The NOT_GATE in quantum is identified as the Pauli_X-GATE, it is represented in the pattern of matrix.

$$X = \begin{bmatrix} 0 & 1 \\ 1 & 0 \end{bmatrix}$$

If qubit |0   ? given as input to Pauli_X-GATE, the result is |1   ?

$$|0??\quad X = |1?$$

If qubit |1? given as input to Pauli_X-GATE, the result is |0?

$$|1??\quad X = |0?$$

2.9.3.1   Pauli_Y-GATE

The Pauli_Y-gate is outlined in the matrix below

$$Y = \begin{bmatrix} 0 & -i \\ i & 0 \end{bmatrix}$$

If the qubit $|0\rangle$ is operated on Pauli Y-gate, then output $i|1\rangle$ is produced

$$|0\rangle \rightarrow Y = i|1\rangle$$

If the qubit $|1\rangle$ is operated on Pauli Y-gate, then the output is $-i|0\rangle$

$$|1\rangle \rightarrow Y = -i|0\rangle$$

2.9.3.2   Pauli_Z-GATE

Pauli_Z-GATE is engraved as

$$Y = \begin{bmatrix} 1 & 0 \\ 0 & -1 \end{bmatrix}$$

When qubit $|0?$ operated on Pauli_Z-gate, it produces $|0?$

$$|0?? \quad Z = |0?$$

When qubit $|1?$ operated on Pauli_Z-gate, it produces $-|1?$

$$|1?? \quad Z = -|1?$$

2.9.3.3   Pauli_S-Gate

Pauli_S-gate is described as:

$$S = \begin{bmatrix} 1 & 0 \\ 0 & i \end{bmatrix}$$

A qubit $|0\rangle$ executed upon Pauli_S-gate it returns the same, but when qubit $|1\rangle$ is acted upon, Pauli S-gate returns $i|1\rangle$

$$|0\rangle \rightarrow S = |0\rangle$$

$$|1\rangle \rightarrow S = i|1\rangle$$

2.9.4   Two-Qubit GATE

The two-Qubit dates are operated with two inputs of qubit and two outputs of qubit. The result required 4 x 4 matrixes after computation process. The forms of two-bit gates are explained in below diagram.

2.9.5   Controlled NOT(C-NOT)

Controlled NOT gate is also known as CNOT GATE. In control qubit, CNOT GATE as an initial input serves. The control qubit is |0> is unaffected with target qubit. The targets Qubit are changed through CNOT GATE, if it is |1>. The possibility of Input states are |11>, |01>, |10>, and |00>. The 2-Qubit inputs X1,Y1 is a function has a CNOT is $|X1, Y1\rangle \rightarrow |X1, Y1 \oplus X1\rangle$.
The Controlled NOT matrix is

$$\begin{bmatrix} 1 & 0 & 0 & 0 \\ 0 & 1 & 0 & 0 \\ 0 & 0 & 0 & 1 \\ 0 & 0 & 1 & 0 \end{bmatrix}$$

2.9.6   The Two-Qubits are Swapped Using SWAP_GATE

The Swap matrix representation shown below

$$\begin{bmatrix} 1 & 0 & 0 & 0 \\ 0 & 0 & 1 & 0 \\ 0 & 1 & 0 & 0 \\ 0 & 0 & 0 & 1 \end{bmatrix}$$

2.9.7   C-Z-GATE (Controlled Z-GATE)

Controlled Z-GATE is other ways of presentation. The GATE's in qubit behaves in general form, with The CZ matrix

$$\begin{bmatrix} 1 & 0 & 0 & 0 \\ 0 & 1 & 0 & 0 \\ 0 & 0 & 1 & 0 \\ 0 & 0 & 0 & -1 \end{bmatrix}$$

2.9.8   C-P-GATE (Controlled-Phase-GATE)

The general it is also known as cS-GATE. Features are similar to the PHASE_GATE.

The cS matrix is

$$\begin{bmatrix} 1 & 0 & 0 & 0 \\ 0 & 1 & 0 & 0 \\ 0 & 0 & 1 & 0 \\ 0 & 0 & 0 & i \end{bmatrix}$$

2.9.9   Three-Qubit Quantum GATE

The three-qubit quantum has three-qubit input and three-qubit output. The calculation needs an 8 x 8 matrix. The three-qubit gates are in the following section in different forms.

2.9.9.1   GATE: Toffoli Gate

Toffoli Gate is a three-Qubit Quantum, it has three inputs and three outputs, with total of 2^3 [5]. Figure 2.7 obtains the situation. Toffoli Gate is also known as T-Gate. The T-Gate operation has no impact on the inputs $a1$, $b1$, and has control qubit is two. The target bits are changed when the stable qubit mark is 1 or not and the input c mark to 0. T gates make reverse when qubit is applied two times.

$$|a, b, c\rangle \rightarrow |a, b, c \oplus ab\rangle \rightarrow |a, b, c\rangle$$

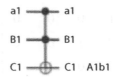

Figure 2.7 Three-Qubit quantum gate.

An 8 x 8 matrix is used to represent

$$
\begin{bmatrix}
1 & 0 & 0 & 0 & 0 & 0 & 0 & 0 \\
0 & 1 & 0 & 0 & 0 & 0 & 0 & 0 \\
0 & 0 & 1 & 0 & 0 & 0 & 0 & 0 \\
0 & 0 & 0 & 1 & 0 & 0 & 0 & 0 \\
0 & 0 & 0 & 0 & 1 & 0 & 0 & 0 \\
0 & 0 & 0 & 0 & 0 & 1 & 0 & 0 \\
0 & 0 & 0 & 0 & 0 & 0 & 0 & 1 \\
0 & 0 & 0 & 0 & 0 & 0 & 1 & 0
\end{bmatrix}
$$

2.9.10   F-C-S GATE (Fredkin Controlled Swap-GATE)

The Swap-Gate Controlled is a three-qubit gate. The disciplined swap gate is a three-qubit gate. 'a1' is the disciplined qubit, and 'b1' and 'c1' are the destination qubits. If disciplined qubit 'a1' made 1, it swaps destination qubit 'b1' and 'c1', if not pass through untouched [26, 27].

The 8 x 8 matrix is as follows:

$$
\begin{bmatrix}
1 & 0 & 0 & 0 & 0 & 0 & 0 & 0 \\
0 & 1 & 0 & 0 & 0 & 0 & 0 & 0 \\
0 & 0 & 1 & 0 & 0 & 0 & 0 & 0 \\
0 & 0 & 0 & 1 & 0 & 0 & 0 & 0 \\
0 & 0 & 0 & 0 & 1 & 0 & 0 & 0 \\
0 & 0 & 0 & 0 & 0 & 0 & 1 & 0 \\
0 & 0 & 0 & 0 & 0 & 1 & 0 & 0 \\
0 & 0 & 0 & 0 & 0 & 0 & 0 & 1
\end{bmatrix}
$$

2.10   Quantum Computation and Classical Computation Comparison

The Probability and Stochastic are the metrics used to classify based on the computation operations. In the classical calculation, the state of l is Pl, where Pl is a real value. $0 \leq Pl \leq 1$ and ΣPl equal to 1. The occurrence of getting Yi in quantum analysis is $|AYi|2$, where a has an amplitude and ai has a complex number [28].

$$0 = |ai|2 = 1, ? i |ai|2 = 1.$$

UM (Unitary Matrices) [5] are designed using quantum theory [22–25]. Transition is based on amplitudes.

2.11   Quantum Cryptography

The uncertainty notations are discovered by the researchers [1]. The results situations are evolved in quantum crypto. Most efficient topic is crypto, after novel cryptographer Mr. Wide designed by quantum key distribution [2, 16–21, 29], and quantum physics laws are followed. After, the BB84 rules [4, 22–25] are deployed to verify the safe quantum concepts.

2.12   Quantum Key Distribution – QKD

Quantum key distribution process starts with transmitting photons in four-quantum states, engaging in quadratic and crosswise basis. The quadratic basis has two-state, Zero in horizontal polarized to zero degree and one in vertical to 90°. The Binary Zero polarized at 45° and Binary One polarized at 135° [1, 4, 13–15]. QKD is sending messages. The general communication is classical and latest communication channel is quantum channel. The messages are sent and received using channels Classical Messages using Traditional channel and Qubit is sent through quantum

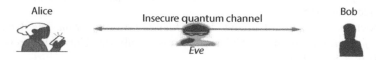

Figure 2.8 Insecure quantum channel communication.

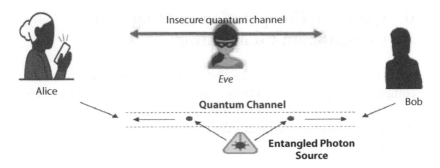

Figure 2.9 Secure quantum channel communication.

channel. Insecure and secure quantum channel communication is shown in Figures 2.8 and 2.9.

2.13 Conclusion

The quantum computing approaches are efficient methods in crypto for novel researchers. The core objective of quantum computing is to provide the secure transmission of data and safe data utilizing the quantum computing. The quantum computing and classical computers are investigated. The limits of traditional computer are discussed, as well as the quantum gates, qubits, and the QKD, laws and secure key.

References

1. Wiesner, S., Conjugate coding. *ACM Sigact News*, 15, 1, 78–88, original manuscript written circa 1969, 1983.
2. Wiedemann, D., Quantum cryptography. *ACM Sigact News*, 18, 2, 48–51, 1987.
3. Wootters, W.K. and Zurek, W.H., A single quantum cannot be cloned. *Nature*, 299, 802–803, 1982.
4. Bennett, C.H. and Brassard, G., Quantum cryptography: Public key distribution and coin tossing. *Proceedings of IEEE International Conference on Computers, Systems and Signal Processing*, Bangalore, India, pp. 175–179, December 1984.
5. Nielsen, M.A. and Chuang, I.L., *Quantum Computation and Quantum Information*, Cambridge University Press, Cambridge University Press, New York, USA, 2000.

6. McMahon, D., *Quantum Computing Explained*, IEEE Computer Society, Wiley-Interscience, John Wiley & Sons, Inc., Canada, 2008.
7. Szikora, P. and Lazányi, K., The end of encryption?–The era of quantum computers, in: *Security-Related Advanced Technologies in Critical Infrastructure Protection*, pp. 61–72, Springer, Dordrecht, 2022.
8. https://www.washingtonpost.com/world/national-security/nsa-seeks-to-build-quantum-computer-that-could-crack-most-types-of-encryption/2014/01/02/8fff297e-7195-11e3-8def-a33011492df2_story.html.
9. https://en.wikipedia.org/wiki/Quantum_computing.
10. Kumar, A., Dadheech, P., Singh, V., Poonia, R.C. and Raja, L., An improved quantum key distribution protocol for verification. *J. Discrete Math. Sci. Cryptogr*, 22, 4, pp. 491–498, 2019.
11. Corcoles, A.D., Magesan, E., Srinivasan, S.J., Cross, A.W., Steffen, M., Gambetta, J.M., Chow, J.M., Demonstration of a quantum error detection code using a square lattice of four superconducting qubits. Nature Publishing Group, Macmillan Publishers Limited, Germany, 6, 2015.
12. Padamvathi, V., Vardhan, B.V. and Krishna, A.V.N., February. Quantum cryptography and quantum key distribution protocols: A survey. In *2016 IEEE 6th International Conference on Advanced Computing (IACC)*, pp. 556–562, IEEE, 2016.
13. Vazirani, U.V., *Quantum Mechanics and Quantum Computation*, University of California, Berkley, 2005, https://www.youtube.com/watch?v=Gfpzke48K9E&list=PL3XnKI-cY52yHBKN3z1n_-hrvjFcmaLW&index=3.
14. Bennett, C.H., Brassard, G., Robert, J.M., Privacy amplification by public discussion. *SIAM J. Comput.*, 17, 210–229, April 1988.
15. Brassard, G. and Salvail, L., Secret-key reconciliation by public discussion in advances, in: *Cryptography – EUROCRYPT'93, Lecture Notes in Computer Science*, T. Helleseth (Ed.), vol. 765, pp. 410–423, Springer-Verlag, Berlin, Germany, 1994.
16. Bennett, C.H., Brassard, G., Crepeau, C., Maurer, U.M., Generalized privacy amplification. *IEEE Trans. Inf. Theory*, 41, 6(part 2), 1915–1923, Nov. 1995.
17. Brassard, G. and Crepeau, C., 25 years of quantum cryptography. *ACM Sigact News*, 27, 3, 13–24, 1996.
18. Bennett, C., Bessette, F., Brassard, G., Salvail, L., Smolin, J., Experimental quantum cryptography. *J. Cryptology*, 5, 3–28, 1992.
19. Padmavathi, V., Vardhan, B.V., Krishna, A.V.N., Quantum cryptography and quantum key distribution protocols: A survey. *2016 IEEE 6th International Conference on Advanced Computing*, 2016.
20. Padmavathi, V., Vardhan, B.V., Krishna, A.V.N., Provably secure quantum key distribution by applying quantum gate. *Int. J. Netw. Secur.*, 20, 1, 88–94, Jan. 2018.
21. Aluvalu, R., Kamliya, V., Muddana, L., Hasbe access control model with secure key distribution and efficient domain hierarchy for cloud computing. *Int. J. Electr. Comput. Eng.*, 6, 2, 770, 2016.

22. Langaliya, C. and Aluvalu, R., Enhancing cloud security through access control models: A survey. *Int. J. Comput. Appl.*, 112, 7, 2015.

23. Chennam, K.K., Muddana, L., Aluvalu, R.K., Performance analysis of various encryption algorithms for usage in multistage encryption for securing data in cloud, in: *2017 2nd IEEE International Conference on Recent Trends in Electronics, Information & Communication Technology*, pp. 2030–2033, IEEE, Bangalore, India, 2017.

24. Reddy, K.S., Varma, G.P.S., Reddy, S.S.S., Understanding the scope of web usage mining & applications of web data usage patterns. *2012 International Conference on Computing, Communication and Applications*, pp. 1–5, 2012.

25. Ayaluri, M.R., Reddy, K.S., Konda, S.R., Chidirala, S.R., Efficient steganalysis using convolutional auto encoder network to ensure original image quality. *Peer J. Comput. Sci.*, 7, e356, 2021. https://doi.org/10.7717/peerj-cs.356.

26. Kavati, I., Reddy, A.M., Babu, E.S., Reddy, K.S., Cheruku, R.S., Design of a fingerprint template protection scheme using elliptical structures. *ICT Express*, 7, 4, 497–500, 2021. https://doi.org/10.1016/j.icte.2021.04.001.

27. Santhosh Kumar, C.N., Pavan Kumar, V., Reddy, K.S., Similarity matching of pairs of text using CACT algorithm. *Int. J. Eng. Adv. Technol.*, 8, 6, 2296–2298, 2019.

28. Reddy, K.S. and Santhosh Kumar, C.H.N., Effective data analytics on opinion mining. *IJITEE*, 8, 10, 2073–2078, 2019.

29. Maheswari, V.U., Aluvalu, R., Mudrakola, S., An integrated number plate recognition system through images using threshold-based methods and KNN, in: *2022 International Conference on Decision Aid Sciences and Applications (DASA)*, pp. 493–497, IEEE, Chiangrai, Thailand, March 2022.

3

Analysis of Design Quantum Multiplexer Using CSWAP and Controlled-R Gates

Virat Tara[1], Navneet Sharma[1]*, Pravindra Kumar[1] and Kumar Gautam[2]†

[1]Thapar Institute of Engineering and Technology, Quantum Computing Department, Quantum Research and Centre of Excellence, New Delhi, India
[2]Quantum Computing Department, Quantum Research and Centre of Excellence, New Delhi, India

Abstract

Multiplexing is a technique used widely in electronics and networking to use a common channel or wire to transmit information between circuits or communicating agents on a network. Multiplexing is also economical as it saves the need for multiple transmission channels for different data pins. On the receiver end, a demultiplexer is used to divide the information from the common channel back to multiple data pins. To design a quantum multiplexer, this paper proposes two circuit designs using controlled SWAP (CSWAP) and controlled-R gates. A quantum circuit consists of combinations of quantum gates applied to one or more qubits in order to change or manipulate their quantum state. Here in this paper, we propose circuits for multiplexing multiple qubits. Generalized synthesis is done to construct higher-order multiplexers. Applications based on the proposed circuit design are also discussed along with the limit on the information that can be transferred using a quantum multiplexer which is presented as a corollary to the Holevo's Theorem. Holevo's theorem provides an upper limit to the amount of information that can be extracted from a qubit. It states that a qubit can encode only one bit of information. Later in this paper, we will see how this bound affects the design of a quantum multiplexer. Lastly, we also discuss and compare the complexities of the circuits that we have proposed.

Keywords: CSWAP quantum gates, controlled phase gates, Holevo's theorem, unitary quantum gates, quantum computation

---

**Corresponding author*: navneet.sharma@thapar.edu
†*Correponding author*: kumar.gautam@qrace.org

Sachi Nandan Mohanty, Rajanikanth Aluvalu and Sarita Mohanty (eds.) *Evolution and Applications of Quantum Computing*, (31–44) © 2023 Scrivener Publishing LLC

3.1   Introduction

The demand for high-speed complex computational processes has drastically increased in the past few years. It is increasingly becoming difficult for the classical circuits to maintain the growth required [1] seen previously in terms of the number of transistors in a dense integrated circuit. Further reduction in transistor size towards the size of a single atom transistor will involve overcoming quantum effects like quantum tunneling. The need to harness computation from quantum particles and research new computational models is becoming more and more imperative. Different computing techniques are under active research like Quantum computing, Optical computing [2], and Ising machines [3]. All of these aim at using quantum particles to perform computation and have a common goal of pushing the limits of conventional computers to produce a case against the Extended Church-Turing thesis [4]. Richard Feynman first proposed the idea of creating machines based on the laws of quantum mechanics instead of classical physics in 1982 [5]. Quantum computers since then have been theoretically proven to be more powerful in terms of time complexity at some tasks [6, 7] compared to classical computers. Quantum computation is based on the laws of quantum mechanics, which is the behavior of particles at the sub-atomic level. Application of the law of quantum mechanics to computation usually involves some sort of finite-dimensional truncation of infinite-dimensional Hilbert spaces. The basic principle is that the quantum properties of particles can be used to represent and structure data. The fundamental idea behind many quantum algorithms is to couple the system state with another state (like an entangled state) using the tensor product, act upon the resulting state with unitary operators and then make measurement via a positive operator valued measurement (POVM) on some point of the state or follow up with a partial trace.

The basic unit of quantum information is a qubit, analogous to a classical bit. Where a classical bit can only take 0 or 1 as a value at a given point of time, a qubit can be represented as a linear combination of $|0\rangle$ and $|1\rangle$ often called superposition as $|\psi\rangle = \alpha|0\rangle + \beta|1\rangle$), $|0\rangle$ and $|1\rangle$ are known as computational basis states and α, β are the complex numbers. At the time of measurement of the qubit, the result will be 0 with probability $|\alpha|^2$ and result 1 with probability $|\beta|^2$ with the constraint $|\alpha|^2 + |\beta|^2 = 1$. The state of a single qubit can be visualized using a Bloch sphere. Interactions of n qubits probe a Hilbert space of 2^n, so with increase in the number of qubits it will be harder to simulate quantum computers on a classical computer since storage of complex amplitudes and performing operations on them requires a large amount of memory. This has resulted in the building of new type of computers using elements that show quantum phenomena. A classical bit and its 0-1 states can be represented using a transistor or vacuum tubes, similarly qubit can be built using different techniques, two of the most prominent designs being superconducting qubit such as Transmon [8] in which a Josephson junction is used as the quantum mechanical element and ions in a Trapped ion quantum computer [9]. Although there's still not a clear winner as to which architecture is the best among the two, one major drawback of superconducting qubits is that there is limited inter-connectivity between qubits otherwise needed to implement multiple qubit gates or complex circuits. A workaround to this is to use additional SWAP gates such as shown in [10] and break multiple qubit gates to smaller two qubit or single qubit quantum gates [11]. Similar to classical gates, quantum computers have their own set of gates. A gate in quantum computing is a unitary operation performed on a qubit or set of qubits. The gate operation is performed differently depending upon the architecture of the computer like microwaves are used to perform gate operations on transom qubits whereas trapped ion quantum computers use lasers. To read the state of a qubit a measurement operation is performed which collapses the wave function of the qubit and thus is an irreversible operation compared to gate operations. Although a qubit can store more than 1 bit of classical information, the amount of classical information that can be retrieved from a single qubit is limited to 1 by Holevo's theorem [12]. Even extracting lesser than n bits of information in a way that does not violate Holevo's bound from an n qubit quantum state containing m bits of information with $M \geq n$ is also highly limited by Nayak's bound [13], such types of codes are also known as quantum random access codes. Figure 3.1 shows a multiplexer and demultiplexer.

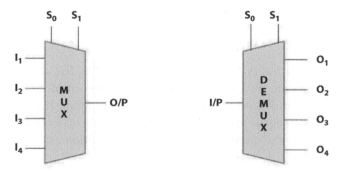

Figure 3.1 A multiplexer and demultiplexer.

The rest of this chapter is organized as follows: Section 3.2 discusses the basic mathematical background of quantum circuits. The working principle of general universal quantum gates is also explained here in this section. In Section 3.3, the proposed method for designing a quantum multiplexer is described and explained in detail. A complete analysis of the stated methodology is discussed in Section 3.4. Section 3.5 discusses the complexity and cost of the proposed circuit. In the end, Section 3.6 gives the conclusion of the presented work.

3.2   Mathematical Background of Quantum Circuits

It is worthwhile to mention here that the below points must be considered in designing a quantum circuit. First, the circuit as a whole should be reversible, which implies that no information should be lost after the application of the circuit. Due to this, the number of output and input lines of the circuit must remain the same and the output of the circuit must be read from one of the existing inputs or an ancilla qubit. Another way to put this would be, for every input combination the output combination must be unique. Since only then it would be possible to backtrack the input given the output. Secondly, an arbitrary complex quantum state cannot be copied. Whereas, computational basis states $|0\rangle$ and $|1\rangle$ can be copied. Quantum gates are represented using unitary matrices.

3.2.1   Hadamard Gate

One of the most important gates in Quantum computing, the Hadamard gate (H) with the following matrix:

$$H = \left(\frac{1}{\sqrt{2}} \right) \begin{bmatrix} 1 & 1 \\ 1 & -1 \end{bmatrix} \tag{3.1}$$

The H gate is unitary since $HH^\dagger = I$. Where $H^\dagger$ is the conjugate transpose of H. The gate puts qubits in a superposition of all possible states. Measuring a qubit in computational basis after applying H gate will result in a $|0\rangle$ or $|1\rangle$ with equal probability. Applying H gate on a qubit with initial state $|0\rangle$ results to the qubit being set to a superposition as:

$$\left(\frac{1}{\sqrt{2}}\right)\begin{bmatrix}1 & 1\\ 1 & -1\end{bmatrix}\begin{bmatrix}1\\ 0\end{bmatrix}=\left(\frac{1}{\sqrt{2}}\right)\begin{bmatrix}1\\ 1\end{bmatrix} \tag{3.2}$$

The state $\frac{1}{\sqrt{2}}|0\rangle+\frac{1}{\sqrt{2}}|1\rangle$ of the qubit after application of Hadamard gate. The probability of getting a $|0\rangle$ or $|1\rangle$ can be calculated by squaring the amplitude of the corresponding state. For a qubit in given state of $\alpha|0\rangle + \beta|1\rangle$ the probability of measuring the qubit in state $|0\rangle$ or $|1\rangle$ is $|\alpha|^2$ and $|\beta|^2$ respectively. Also, $\alpha^2 + \beta^2 = 1$ holds true always for a closed system. So, with Hadamard gate the final probability of finding the qubit in state $|0\rangle$ or $|1\rangle$ is $\frac{1}{2}$.

3.2.2 CSWAP Gates

The CSWAP or Fredkin gate consists of three input pins, one being the control pin (S_0). The states of the other two inputs (I_0, I_1) are swapped if the control qubit is $|1\rangle$. The Table 3.1 below depicts the behavior of a CSWAP gate on corresponding inputs of the control pin (S_0).

To show that the Fredkin gate inherently works as a 2:1 MUX, taking the first input pin (I_0) in Figure 3.2 as the pin from which output will be read, from the table, it is clear that when the select input (S_0) is $|0\rangle$ the output at I_0 is $|I_0\rangle$ and when the state of S_0 is $|1\rangle$ the value of I_0 at output is $|I_1\rangle$. The matrix and circuit for a CSWAP gate are given as:

Table 3.1 Truth table of CSWAP gate.

Input			**Output**		
$\lvert S_0\rangle$	$\lvert I_0\rangle$	$\lvert I_1\rangle$	$\lvert S_0\rangle$	$\lvert I_0\rangle$	$\lvert I_1\rangle$
$\lvert 0\rangle$	$\lvert I_0\rangle$	$\lvert I_1\rangle$	$\lvert 0\rangle$	$\lvert I_0\rangle$	$\lvert I_1\rangle$
$\lvert 1\rangle$	$\lvert I_0\rangle$	$\lvert I_1\rangle$	$\lvert 1\rangle$	$\lvert I_1\rangle$	$\lvert I_0\rangle$

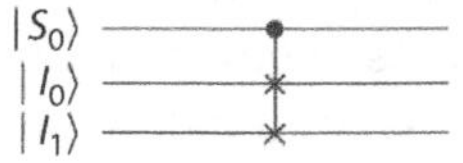

$$= \begin{bmatrix}1&0&0&0&0&0&0&0\\0&1&0&0&0&0&0&0\\0&0&1&0&0&0&0&0\\0&0&0&1&0&0&0&0\\0&0&0&0&1&0&0&0\\0&0&0&0&0&0&1&0\\0&0&0&0&0&1&0&0\\0&0&0&0&0&0&0&1\end{bmatrix}$$

Figure 3.2 Circuit representation and matrix of a CSWAP gate.

Figure 3.3 Circuit and matrix representaion of controlled-R gate.

3.2.3   Controlled-R Gates

The controlled-R gate uses a control qubit to add a phase shift of $\exp(i\phi)$ to the target qubit if the control qubit is in the state $|1\rangle$. In computational basis it maps the combined state of the controlled and target qubits from $\alpha|00\rangle + \beta|01\rangle + \gamma|10\rangle + \delta|11\rangle$ to $\alpha|00\rangle + \beta|01\rangle + \gamma|10\rangle + \exp(i\phi)\delta|11\rangle$. The matrix and circuit representation of a Controlled-R gate is given in Figure 3.3.

3.3   Methodology of Designing Quantum Multiplexer (QMUX)

The function of a QMUX will be the same as that of a classical multiplexer, which is to select one qubit from given n qubits using select pins that tell the index of the qubit to be selected. In this paper, we design QMUX using two different approaches. In the first approach, CSWAP gates are used where the output of the multiplexing operation is read from the first input qubit. The CSWAP gates preserve the information as a whole of the system. The states of the qubits to be multiplexed are interchanged in between them and not destroyed or lost. The second approach uses Controlled-R gates with an ancilla qubit for output and no select qubits. The input qubits are taken in simple states of $|0\rangle$ and $|1\rangle$. The states are then copied on to an ancilla qubit using Controlled-R operations.

3.3.1   QMUX Using CSWAP Gates

As shown in Table 3.1, a single CSWAP gate inherently works as a 2:1 multiplexer. Similarly, a 4:1 mux is created using three CSWAP gates in Figure 3.3. The most significant qubit tells if the input to be selected is in the first half or second half of the circuit (of all the input lines ordered in ascending order as per their index). If the value of most significant qubit is $|1\rangle$ then it means the input to be selected lies in the second half. Operations are performed to swap the states of lower half inputs with that of the corresponding upper half inputs, depicting CSWAP operations as CSWAP($CONTROL$, $INPUT_1$, $INPUT_2$) we can write the above operations as, CSWAP(S_0, I_0, I_2)

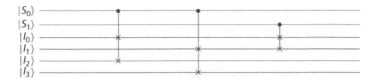

Figure 3.4 Circuit representation of a 4:1 QMUX.

and CSWAP(S_0, I_1, I_3). These operations narrow down the scope to the first half of the circuit, now the least significant qubit dictates whether the input to be selected is in the remaining first half or remaining second half of the circuit with CSWAP(S_1, I_0, I_2).

3.3.1.1   Generalization

The number of select lines is denoted by k then the generalized formula for a 2^k: 1 mux can be given as:

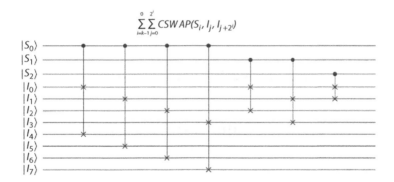

Figure 3.5 Circuit representation of a 8:1 Mux using CSWAP gates.

3.3.2   QMUX Using Controlled-R Gates

In this section the multiplexer is designed using controlled-R gates. The state of the qubits to be multiplexed ($|I_x\rangle \in [|0\rangle, |1\rangle]$) to an ancillary qubit $|q_1\rangle$ initialized to $|0\rangle$. We apply Controlled-R gate to the ancilla qubit with the qubits to be multiplexed as control. A shifted Controlled-R gate is applied, shifted by 'k' (the index of the qubit one wants to select, where $k \geq 1$). So if R_x means a phase shift of exp $(i/2x)$ then R_{x-k} means a phase shift of exp $(i/2x - k)$. For a 4 qubit system and k = 2 the circuit is shown in

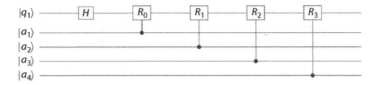

Figure 3.6 Circuit to encode qubits to be multiplexed in q_1.

Figure 3.5. This is followed by a series of controlled-R inversions with the exception of R_1 as shown in Figure 3.6.

The state transformation of $|q_1\rangle$ is given as:

$$|q_1\rangle \overset{H}{\rightarrow} 1/\sqrt{2}(|0\rangle + exp(0.0)|1\rangle) \tag{3.4}$$

$$|q_1\rangle \overset{R_0}{\rightarrow} 1/\sqrt{2}(|0\rangle + exp(a_1.0)|1\rangle) \tag{3.5}$$

$$|q_1\rangle \overset{R_1}{\rightarrow} 1/\sqrt{2}(|0\rangle + exp(a_1.a_2)|1\rangle) \tag{3.6}$$

$$|q_1\rangle \overset{R_2}{\rightarrow} 1/\sqrt{2}(|0\rangle + exp(a_1.a_2a_3)|1\rangle) \tag{3.7}$$

$$|q_1\rangle \overset{R_3}{\rightarrow} 1/\sqrt{2}(|0\rangle + exp(a_1.a_2a_3a_4)|1\rangle) \tag{3.8}$$

The following is the inversion circuit:

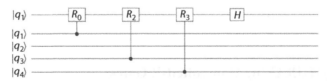

Figure 3.7 Inversion circuit to get output state of q_1 same as the selected qubit.

The state transformation of $|q_1\rangle$ after application of the inversion circuit is given below:

$$|q_1\rangle \overset{R_0}{\rightarrow} 1/\sqrt{2}(|0\rangle + exp(0.a_2a_3a_4)|1\rangle) \tag{3.9}$$

$$|q_1\rangle \xrightarrow{R_2} 1/\sqrt{2}(|0\rangle + exp(0.a_2a_3)|1\rangle) \qquad (3.10)$$

$$|q_1\rangle \xrightarrow{R_3} 1/\sqrt{2}(|0\rangle + exp(0.a_2)|1\rangle) \qquad (3.11)$$

$$|q_1\rangle \xrightarrow{H} cos(\pi*0.a2)|0\rangle + sin(\pi*0.a_2)|1\rangle \qquad (3.12)$$

Finally, we get the final state of $|q_1\rangle$ as $|a_2\rangle$.

It is worthwhile to mention here that the inversion circuit can skip phase shift R_0 since:

$$1/\sqrt{2}(|0\rangle + exp(a_1.a_2a_3a_4)|1\rangle) \equiv 1/\sqrt{2}(|0\rangle + exp(0.a_2a_3a_4)|1\rangle$$

$$(3.13)$$

These instructions suffice to scale the method for multiplexing n qubits, without any specific changes. With the assumption that the system is noiseless and of infinite precision.

3.4   Analysis and Synthesis of Proposed Methodology

Here, we analyze the two methods of constructing a multiplexer discussed in Section 3.3 and some possible applications of a QMUX. The first method is related to the SWAP gates. Although a MUX can be constructed using CCSWAP (4:1) gates or CCCSWAP (8:1) gates as shown in [14], depending upon the number of select lines. A MUX constructed using this method uses the same number of gates as in our implementation in Section 3.1 (which uses only CSWAP gates) but with a higher gate complexity when multiple control SWAP gates are decomposed into two qubit gates. Superconducting transmon qubit processors have a major drawback that not all of its qubits are interconnected, unlike trapped ion quantum processors [15]. MUX implementation using multiple control SWAP gates would require all of the select qubits in a $2^n : 1$ MUX to be interconnected or intermediary SWAP operations [10] would be required. An efficient way to reduce the number of qubits would be to use classical registers as select pins; this is possible when a quantum computer uses classical control systems. A corresponding circuit of CSWAP operation is shown below in Figure 3.8, where S_0 is read from a classical register.

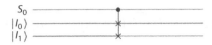

Figure 3.8   QMUX with classical register as select pin.

The purpose of the second method in Section 3.2, where we construct a MUX using Controlled-R gates, was largely to study implications of using phase encoding in the design of a multiplexer.

The technique works only with qubits in $|0\rangle$ or $|1\rangle$ state. The benefit of such a multiplexing method is that there's no need for select pins explicitly although they may be required to control the phase in the gate operations depending upon the hardware implementation. Another advantage is, after performing a MUX operation the qubits don't get shuffled among themselves, like in the previous method where if the qubit to be selected is in the second half of the input pins then all the qubits of the second half are swapped with their corresponding qubits in the first half as shown in Figure 3.4. An important observation made while designing was that the state prepared after encoding values of input qubits (a_1 to a_4) to the ancillary qubit (q_1) in Figure 3.5 can't be used to transfer information to the receiver of all the input qubits by only transferring $|q_1\rangle$.

One way it might seem possible to transfer information like this is to prepare $|q_1\rangle$ as

$$\frac{1}{\sqrt{2}}(|0\rangle + \exp(0.a_1a_2a_3a_4)|1\rangle)$$ and then send it to the receiver where

the receiver would perform a unitary operation on $|q_1\rangle$ and four new qubits (A_1 to A_4) such that the qubits A_1 to A_4 take the values a_1 to a_4 respectively as shown in Figure 3.9.

The idea is to convert a non-orthogonal input state ($|q_1\rangle$) to orthogonal state by increasing the Hilbert space at the receiver end and without knowing how the input state was prepared. Doing so, would make it possible

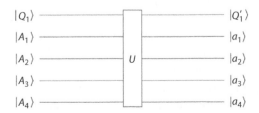

Figure 3.9   An information decoder circuit at the receiver end that violates Holevo's Theorem.

to transfer more than 1 classical bit of data using a single qubit and thus would violate Holevo's bound [12]. This gives us an important corollary of Holevo's theorem that it is not possible to convert a non-orthogonal state to orthogonal state for the purpose of extracting information encoded in the non-orthogonal state. If the message encoded isn't in an orthogonal state, there's no way to retrieve information safely at the receiver. A receiver who doesn't have any information of the quantum state received can't convert a non-orthogonal state to orthogonal, not even by increasing the Hilbert space. Receiver can only do so if the transmitter provides it with adequate information of how the state was prepared in the first place and that would mean transferring information indirectly thus defeating the purpose of efficient communication.

Applications: One of the most obvious use cases of quantum mux would be at the interface of a quantum processor and a quantum wire [16] which would be used to deliver the qubit to another distant Quantum computer or for the applications of quantum internet. Another interesting use of a QMUX could be inside the quantum processor to have a common qubit readout for all or a section of qubits. A qubit with built in readout will act as the output of the multiplexer. The rest of the qubits then can be applied as input. This can reduce the circuitry inside the processor plus the number of read out pins.

3.5   Complexity and Cost of Quantum Circuits

The cost of the QMUX is calculated depending upon the number of two qubit gates required to implement the circuit. The multiplexer design in Section 3.1 uses only CSWAP gates. A CSWAP gate can be implemented optimally using 5 two qubit gates [17, 18]. The number of CSWAP gates required for construction of a $2^n : 1$ MUX are $2^n - 1$ as studied in Section 3.1.1. With each CSWAP gate decomposable into 5 two qubit gates the total cost is of the order of $5 * (2^n - 1)$. The design discussed in Section 3.2 uses only two qubit gates namely, Hadamard and Controlled rotation. The number of gates required for construction of a n:1 mux are of the order of $n + 1$, n gates for each of the input qubits and an extra Hadamard gate to put the ancilla qubit in a superposition state.

3.6   Conclusion

This chapter discusses two methods for multiplexing qubits using realizable gates. While discussing the limits of information that can be transferred via a QMUX we propose a corollary to Holevo's Theorem. Quantum computing (QC) technology development in the various sectors, which has proven to be most challenging, yet demanding over the time. This field has extensive potential for Commercialization due to the fact that we are living in an era where everyone is contributing towards environmentally sustainable approach. The emergence of new strategic investors/business partners in the recent years has opened up innovative opportunities for Quant-tech entrepreneurs in terms of novel commercialization models.

References

1. Thompson, N.C., Greenewald, K., Lee, K., Manso, G.F., *The Computational Limits of Deep Learning*, arXiv e-prints, July 2020, arXiv:2007.05558.
2. Sawchuk, A.A. and Strand, T.C., Digital optical computing. *Proc. IEEE*, 72, 7, 758–779, 1984.
3. McMahon, P.L., Marandi, A., Haribara, Y., Hamerly, R., Langrock, C., Tamate, S., Inagaki, T., Takesue, H., Utsunomiya, S., Aihara, K., Byer, R.L., Fejer, M.M., Mabuchi, H., Yamamoto, Y., A fully programmable 100-spin coherent ising machine with all-to-all connections. *Science*, 354, 6312, 614–617, 2016.
4. Copeland, B.J., The church-turing thesis, in: *The Stanford Encyclopedia of Philosophy*, Summer 2020 edition, E.N. Zalta (Ed.), Metaphysics Research Lab, Stanford University, 2020.
5. Feynman, R.P., Simulating physics with computers. *Int. J. Theor. Phys.*, 21, 6, 467–488, 1982.
6. Shor, P. W., Polynomial-time algorithms for prime factorization and discrete logarithms on a quantum computer. *SIAM J. Sci. Comput.*, 26, 5, 1484–1509, 1997.
7. Grover, L.K. A fast quantum mechanical algorithm for database search. in: *Proceedings of the 28th Annual ACM Symposium on the Theory of Computing*, New York, 212–219, 1996.
8. Koch, J., Yu, T.M., Gambetta, J., Houck, A. A.. .Schuster, D. I., Majer, J., Blais, A., Devoret, M. H., Girvin, S. M., Schoelkopf, R. J., Charge-insensitive qubit design derived from the cooper pair box. *Phys. Rev. A*, 76, 042319, Oct. 2007.
9. Bruzewicz, C.D., Chiaverini, J., McConnell, R., Sage, J.M., Trapped-ion quantum computing: Progress and challenges. *Appl. Phys. Rev.*, 6, 2, 021314, June 2019.

10. Li, G., Ding, Y., Xie, Y., Tackling the qubit mapping problem for nisq-era quantum devices, in: *Proceedings of the Twenty-Fourth International Conference on Architectural Support for Programming Languages and Operating Systems, ASPLOS 2019*, Iris Bahar, Maurice Herlihy, Emmett Witchel and Alvin R. Lebeck, (eds.), 1001–1014, Providence, RI, USA, April 13-17, 2019.
11. Nielsen, M.A. and Chuang, I.L., *Quantum Computation and Quantum Information: 10th Anniversary Edition*, Cambridge University Press, 2010.
12. Holevo, A.S., Bounds for the quantity of information transmitted by a quantum communication channel. *Probl. Peredachi Inf.*, 9, 3, 3–11, 1973.
13. A. Nayak, Optimal lower bounds for quantum automata and random access codes, *40th Annual Symposium on Foundations of Computer Science (Cat. No.99CB37039)*, 1999, pp. 369-376, 1999.
14. Roy, A., Chatterjee, D., Pal, S., Synthesis of quantum multiplexer circuits. *IJCSI*, 9, 3, 67–74, 2012.
15. Linke, N.M., Maslov, D., Roetteler, M., Debnath, S., Figgatt, C., Landsman, K.A., Wright, K., Monroe, C., Experimental comparison of two quantum computing architectures. *Proceedings of the National Academy of Science*, 114, 13, 3305–3310, March 2017
16. Oskin, M., Chong, F.T., Chuang, I.L., Kubiatowicz, J., Building quantum wires: The long and the short of it, in: *30th Annual International Symposium on Computer Architecture, 2003. Proceedings*, pp. 374–385, 2003.
17. Smolin, J.A. and Di Vincenzo, D.P., Five two-bit quantum gates are sufficient to implement the quantum Fredkin gate. *Phys. Rev. A*, 53, 2855–2856, Apr 1996.
18. Yu, N. and Ying, M., Optimal simulation of deutsch gates and the Fredkin gate. *Phys. Rev. A*, 91, 032302, Mar. 2015.

4

Artificial Intelligence and Machine Learning Algorithms in Quantum Computing Domain

Syed Abdul Moeed*, P. Niranjan† and G. Ashmitha‡

Department of Computer Science & Engineering, Kakatiya Institute of Technology & Science, Warangal, Telangana, India

Abstract

Quantum information and artificial learning systems, for example, are cutting-edge technologies that could have a significant impact on our civilization in the future. The difficulties and challenges associated with quantum information, for example, differ significantly from those associated with artificial intelligence, machine learning, and other related fields. These issues have mostly been tackled separately until now. Many researchers are beginning to wonder whether or not these professions can learn from one another. Quantum computing theory is exploding right now, as is the classical machine learning theory of learning from experience. Researchers have recently looked into the possibility that quantum computing could aid in the improvement of current machine learning methods. Hybrid quantum machine learning makes use of quantum physics as well as classical and quantum algorithms. Quantum procedures, rather than classical data, can be used to analyze quantum states. Quantum algorithms, on the other hand, have the potential to improve classical data science techniques by an order of magnitude. We'll go over the fundamental concepts of quantum machine learning right now. The methods we offer combine classical machine learning algorithms with quantum computing techniques. Using IBM's quantum processor, this paper demonstrates how to implement a multiclass tree tensor network. We also present a quantum tomography problem method based on neural networks. It is possible for us to forecast the quantum state without taking noise into account thanks to our tomography technology. In many investigations, a

*Corresponding author: abdulmoeed.cse@kitsw.ac.in
†Corresponding author: pnr.cse@kitsw.ac.in
‡Corresponding author: ga.cse@kitsw.ac.in

Sachi Nandan Mohanty, Rajanikanth Aluvalu and Sarita Mohanty (eds.) Evolution and Applications of Quantum Computing, (45–66) © 2023 Scrivener Publishing LLC

classical-quantum technique can uncover latent dependence between input data and output measurement results.

Keywords: Machine learning, quantum computing, quantum neural network, quantum algorithms, artificial intelligence

4.1   Introduction

Quantum computing technology provides fundamentally different answers to computational issues and allows for faster problem solving than standard methods. It's possible that commercially viable quantum computers will be available within the next few years, given the positive experimental results. Shor's prime factorization algorithm [1, 2] is a well-known demonstration of quantum computing capabilities. The Rivest–Shamir–Adleman (RSA) algorithm's record-breaking speed illustrates the quantum computing power gap. Solving this computational task in a typical computing environment would take billions of years, but a quantum computer might theoretically do so in a matter of hours. These algorithms were responsible for the quantum computing "big bang" that started all subsequent developments in quantum computing technology as well as assessments of quantum computers themselves in 1994 [4]. Despite the fact that the functional aspects of quantum computers (such as registers and gates) are comparable to those of ordinary computers, the physical layer structures of classical and quantum systems are fundamentally different (see, for example, the difference between a CPU and a storage device). When designing a quantum computer architecture, quantum registers are used to perform quantum operations. A quantum register has quantum superposition, but a quantum circuit has quantum states that are interconnected. As a result of these occurrences, a computer now has characteristics that are quite distinct from classical computers. New circuit design methods are required because of quantum hardware constraints such as no-cloning theorem, which states that a quantum state can never be present simultaneously at two or even more discrete quantum gates. Quantum computers with reversible gates operate on quantum systems as a single unit. There have only been a few experiments in the lab with quantum computers, despite their operational status today [6]. To be sure, new disciplines and promising outcomes have just appeared, and these advancements have a good chance of getting much better. Small quantum computers connected via a quantum bus in a distributed context can become huge quantum computers. There will be new technologies that allow these enormous quantum

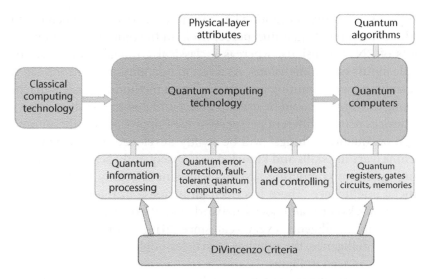

Figure 4.1 The figure shows how conventional computing technology evolves into quantum computing technology. Results integrated by quantum computing technologies are used in quantum computers.

computers to be scaled down to the size of a smartphone in the next few years. Both in terms of size and performance, the scenario resembles previous phases in the history of classical computers.

There's a lot of buzz around quantum computing right now because it holds the potential of a revolution in computing performance due to the massive parallelism that can be accomplished by "interfering, super-positioning, and entangling" distinct kinds of information. This shift in focus from quantum mechanics simulation efficiency to "quantum advantage" or "quantum supremacy," which refers to the design of quantum algorithms that are significantly faster than the best possible algorithms on classical computers, is intended to spur new breakthroughs in various application fields such as chemistry, medicine, and finance, according to the researchers. Anyone interested in implementing well-established quantum algorithms like Shor's and Grover's algorithms [7] or designing new quantum algorithms can currently access and program real quantum computers through the Internet. Because quantum computing isn't just a science fiction concept anymore, this work is crucial. It's been proven that quantum algorithms for machine learning can solve AI-related problems better than classical versions thanks to an onslaught of ever-more-complex findings [8]. Due to quantum computing's exponential increase in the number of dimensions it can process over classical machine learning techniques, quantum computing has a significant advantage when used for machine learning. A quantum perceptron, on the other hand, can process inputs of 2N dimensions, whereas a classical artificial neuron can only handle inputs of N dimensions. As a result, quantum perceptrons can significantly speed up training and classification methods. Classical machine learning techniques could be used to detect and design quantum materials and devices using a different perspective. New approaches to the automatic design of "quantum things" will be swiftly developed using conventional machine learning skills and knowledge. Consequently, scientists agree that future quantum computing systems will benefit greatly from the use of artificial intelligence. There has been an increase in the number of conferences, workshops, and social network activity on quantum computing and artificial intelligence every year since 2014. In the area of quantum machine intelligence, the number of articles published has grown rapidly since 2012, as seen in Figure 4.2.

Quantum computers can be classified as universal or non-universal, depending on their use. While universal quantum computers aim to solve all problems, non-universal quantum computers focus on a single problem rather than solving many problems at once (e.g., optimization of machine learning algorithms). Quantum computers with suitable error correction

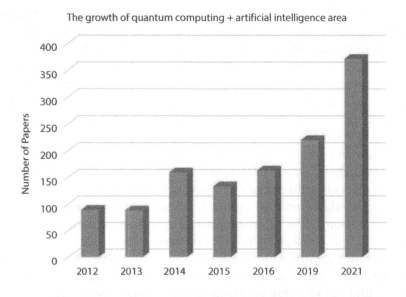

Figure 4.2 The increase in papers published on quantum machine intelligence since 2012 is shown in the graph.

include IBM's 17-qubit universal quantum computer and the D-2000+ Wave non-universal qubits [6]. For the time being, the best universal quantum computer is IBM's quantum computer [7, 8]. Quantum computers from D-Wave and IBM are both available for research on the internet. There was also a debut of the 17-qubit worldwide quantum computer by Intel and QuTech in October of 2017 [7].

It is a field where a specific machine recognizes various components or elements from the input data and as a result, the machine makes some predictions depending on the inputs provided. Computers utilize Machine Learning to predict and process output based on input, combining Artificial Intelligence with Data Statistic. I don't know what to call it. There are now two types of machine learning: supervised and unsupervised, each with their own set of traits and features. For example, in supervised machine learning, an example is supplied and the computer is expected to arrive at an optimal output by evaluating, measuring and computing various factors contained in the example [5]. Several factors influence the accuracy of the prediction, including the type of Dataset used as inputs, biasing and labeling settings, and more. It also heavily relies on the Algorithm employed to alter the input. We can use either a Discriminative or a Generative technique to turn the Machine around [9]. Many researchers believe that the Generative technique is superior to the Discriminative method in terms of relevance and accuracy when analyzing the output. Unsupervised Machine Learning teaches the system to locate a meaningful entity from random input. Supervised and unsupervised machine learning vary in that the output of the machine can be evaluated in some way in supervised learning. Figure 4.3 illustrates the principle of machine learning [10].

In order to extract important information and make predictions about new data samples, machine learning algorithms are tasked. Other mathematical techniques develop and update models based on unknown data; these algorithms do the opposite (training dataset). For example, spam filtering, image processing, widespread social influence (such facial recognition and object recognition), object recognition and signal processing can all be done using machine learning approaches [1–3].

Quantum algorithms have been shown to be faster than their conventional analogues in recent years, thanks to breakthroughs in quantum information processing [4, 5]. Quantum techniques to classical machine learning have been found to generate similar outcomes. With such a combination of quantum computing power and machine learning theories, quantum information science would get a huge boost and new practical solutions to present machine learning challenges might be evaluated.

Among the many varieties of Quantum Learning Algorithms, Quantum Reinforcement Learning Algorithm is one. When this technique is used, the machine gets rewarded for each quantum prediction it produces [11]. With the help of these incentives, the machine can see how well it did in making the forecast. With reinforcement learning, the fundamental goal is to discover the best possible reward for every prediction made. When using Quantum Reinforcement Learning, a particular element of the algorithm interacts with a classical environment and provides results that can be undone in a quantum environment. Time complexity issues with the Brute Force or Classical Probabilistic Methods are no longer present. So that it may accurately predict the outcome, the algorithm must be programmed to understand certain features or concepts related to the problem. In order for the method to work properly, the learning and processing phases must be carried out in parallel.

When it comes to multi-dimensional systems and multi-variable statistical analysis, quantum computing offers an edge [10, 11]. The curse of dimensionality makes it difficult to represent classical systems with many degrees of freedom [12]. Unfortunately, this difficulty cannot be avoided by the quantum parallelism effect. quantum computing resources are therefore extremely beneficial in solving various issues with an extremely large number of dimensions.

Computing data analysis is linked to a wide range of approaches. Quantum approaches, such the k-means algorithm, can be used in principle component analysis, like the k-nearest neighbor methodology (variational autoencoders, associative adversarial networks and etc.). These studies show that quantum information approaches may be used with both linear and nonlinear algorithms.

Most branches of physical science have been influenced by quantum theory. In fields that deal with sufficiently small scales, this influence can range from slight tweaks to substantial overhauls. When it came to engineering jobs in the second half of the 20th century, it became clear that actual quantum effects may also be used. These effects allow for better performance than is possible with solely classical systems. Lasers, transistors, and nuclear magnetic resonance spectrometers were all invented during this wave of engineering. Scientists are investigating the prospect of harnessing quantum effects, which gained traction in the 1980s, for a wide range of occupations that involve the large-scale processing of information. Quantum information science, for example, is currently the common language for research in the disciplines of cryptography, computing, sensing, and measurement. The results of transdisciplinary research are frequently exceptional. There are a number of well-established research areas, such as quantum computation, communication, cryptography and metrology that have changed the way we view information and how it is processed.

For some time now, it's been clear that combining quantum information processing with artificial intelligence and machine learning raises a number of interesting issues and possibilities. Even in the early days of quantum computing, the first ideas were already there, and despite the fact that they are just now receiving wider attention, we have made an attempt to fully recognize such visionary efforts.

4.1.1 Quantum Computing Convolutional Neural Network

They are named after the classical counterparts they are based on, which are now widely used in image processing. Figure 4.3 shows a schematic representation of one of these networks, which processes inputs through a sequence of layers known as convolutional and pooling. First, a translationally invariant quasi-local transformation is used to extract significant information from the input, and then a compression technique is used to reduce the dimensionality of that information. To assess the network's output, traditional techniques like fully connected feedforward NNs are used after several iterations have occurred. Quantum states undergo a convolution layer consisting of a parametrized unitary operation on individual subsets of qubits, similar to quantum convolutional NNs, and then a pooling mechanism obtained by measuring part of the qubits is utilized [4, 5]. It is necessary to repeat this process until only a few qubits remain on the computer. When used for quantum applications like phase detection and error correction, this approach performed exceptionally well. It is

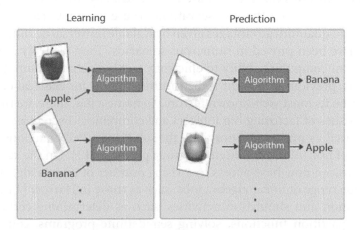

Figure 4.3 Example for machine learning prediction.

also necessary to use just logarithmically numerous parameters in order to train efficiently and effectively on near-term devices.

The following is a breakdown of the paper's structure: To better understand how quantum algorithms help with machine learning, Section 4.2 presents a literature review of QML and other well-known methods. Only for data with extremely enormous dimensions do quantum algorithms outperform classical ones.

Section 4.4 described a quantum classification circuit known as a tree tensor network (TTN). For multiclass classification, we give the TTN generalization here. Data with any number of classes can be predicted using this method, which is built on the SoftMax function concept. Section 4.5 shows the real-world outcomes of the IBM online quantum processor's real-world approval.

Section 4.6 discusses neurotomography, a form of quantum tomography based on classical artificial neural networks. The output quantum state is predicted using a neural network model that excludes noise from the quantum system. Reconstructing the right quantum state can be done with high probability using such an approach in genuine experimental systems. Section 4.7 summarizes the paper's conclusion and future directions.

4.2   Literature Survey

The theory and practice of computation have been transformed by Quantum Computing. According to [11], it may be impossible to calculate some features of quantum systems as they evolve in time, but the quantum systems themselves execute the hard computation by simply evolving. This discipline arose from these observations. These early QC concepts have spread, and quantum advantages given by scalable universal quantum computers have been proved in numerous scenarios. They are truly available. A quantum computer's ability to efficiently tackle algebraic computational problems, previously thought to be insurmountable for classical computers, may be its most well-known feature. To name a few, there are the well-known issues of factoring big integers and computing discrete logarithms [12], as well as numerous more like the solution of Pell equations, and a number of non-Abelian hidden subgroup problem [13]. On the subject of speed-ups, we now have access to a rising number of quanta algorithms6 for a wide range of linear algebra jobs, such as those in Harrow [14]. Many optimization and simulation activities, such as determining certain features of partition functions, solving semidefinite programs, conducting approximate optimization, and, of course, simulating quantum systems, can be improved with quantum computers, as well [15]. Sub-routines and databases can be used more efficiently, which has advantages. This is studied using a black-box object with well-defined input-output relations, and the quantity of calls to an oracle is of relevance here. When used in this way, Oracle abstractly represents anything related to information processing, such as a database or a sub-routine.

To illustrate quantum advantages, consider Grover's search technique, which improves unordered search by a factor of four (where the oracle is the database). New 'cheat sheet method' results [16] and different quantum-walk-based algorithms have led to better-than-quadratic increases in a variety of other contexts, including spatial search [17]. Communication complexity can be reduced for various information sharing protocols by using oracular computational models, which can be used both to mimic computation and communication and minimize the number of communications rounds. Quantum computers may be able to help with sampling issues. A sample from an implicitly specified distribution can be useful for optimization and certain types of algebraic tasks. Markov Chain Monte Carlo methods, for example, are developed to handle sampling jobs and may often be applied to address other types of issues. They are undoubtedly the most prolific group of computational methods in natural sciences. Sample capacity from Gibbs distributions is a common essential method in statistical physics for computing partition function features. For many quantum sampling issues, quantum improvements to Markov Chain techniques are the primary focus [18]. As we'll discuss in a moment, sampling jobs have gotten an increasing lot of attention in the QIP community. A few conventional models of computing exist for quantum computers, most of which are computationally equal in strength. While numerically similar, the two models differ conceptually. Consequently, for a certain class of applications, some are better-suited or more natural. For theoretical and computability-related reasons, the quantum Turing machine was historically favored as the first formal model. For algebraic problems, the quantum circuit model [19] is conventional. When dealing with graph-related challenges, the measurement-based QC (MBQC) paradigm may be the most effective option (for example: multi-party tasks, distributed computations, and blind QC). These techniques for topological error-correction and fault tolerance are strongly related to topological QC [22] and other knot-theoretical algorithm [23].

Several approaches have been put up to prevent or at the very least slow the spread of barren plateaus around the globe. The process known as layerwise learning [24] can be used to initialize and train parameters in batches. It's also an option to lower the circuit's effective depth by randomly initializing only a fraction of its total parameters, with the rest picked so it can perform an identity check [25]. Other researchers have explored lowering the overall complexity of the parameter space by introducing correlations between the parameters in different QNN layers [26]. A good initialization heuristic for parameters has been found using traditional recurrent neural networks (RNNs), which starts the network close to its minimum value. Selecting the appropriate cost function and entanglement scaling between hidden and visible units is crucial in order to prevent reaching barren plateaus, as previously mentioned.

Traditional neural networks are trained using backpropagation algorithms because they combine the derivative chain rule with intermediate layer values saved to produce accurate gradient estimates. An analogous approach will not work in a quantum context because quantum computations require measurements to get intermediate values, which upset the quantum states involved [6]. As a result, classical optimizers employing gradient-based or gradient-free numerical approaches are frequently employed. Some cases allow for quantum considerations to be included, resulting in optimization strategies such as the parameter shift rule, quantum natural gradients, and closed updating formulae that are specifically adapted to the quantum domain. Last but not least, although an all-coherent quantum rewrite of the parameters sounds intriguing, it's simply not possible on current hardware due to the qubit count and circuit depth limitations.

Today's field of artificial intelligence (AI) covers a vast range of subfields in its overall scope. Overwhelmingly, these sub-fields are concerned with deriving and realizing certain human capacities that we call intelligent in machines. The origins of artificial intelligence can be traced back to seminars held at Dartmouth College in 1956 [26]. These conferences are often considered to as the birthplace of AI. At the conferences, the goal was to discover new methods for teaching machines to communicate using language, build abstract concepts, solve problems that were previously only solved by humans, and improve themselves. The history of artificial intelligence has been rocky due to divergent viewpoints on how the technology should be implemented. In the first 30 years of the field, there were two major competing and opposing views on how AI can be realized, for example: computationalism (which believes that the mind operates by performing purely formal operations on symbols, similar to a Turing machine; see, for example, Newell and Simon [32] and connectionism (which views mental and behavioral phenomena as emergent processes from basic interconnected networks, reproducing the AI techniques are strong. Even if one adheres to a particular philosophy, the realization of "true AI" has been said to be "only a few years away" for most of the history of AI. This is something opponents of the field have even attributed to quantum computers. In the case of artificial intelligence, such irrational optimism had a disastrous impact on the field, especially when it came to funding (resulting in the so-called 'winters of AI'). While artificial intelligence had a bad reputation by the late 1990s, there was no agreement on why AI had failed to create human-level intellect even in retrospect. There were a number of important reasons for the division of the field into numerous sub-fields, each of which focused exclusively on specific activities and appeared under a distinct name.

According to Brooks, one of the most important perspectives on artificial intelligence, known as nouvelle or embodied AI, intelligence arises from (basic) embodied systems that interact with their environments and learn via learning. Brooks' theory was widely adopted. As an alternative to traditional AI approaches, Nouvelle AI emphasizes learning rather than preprogrammed qualities, as well as the actualization of AI entities rather than abstract ones like chess programs. Physics students may recall the "rallying cry of quantum information theory" when they hear this concept that intelligence is physically embedded. Perception, mobility, and navigation are all important in robotics because machines use sensors like computer vision and machine hearing to sense the outside world. These embodied methods (critical in, e.g., automated cars). Additionally, AI also covers human-computer interfaces, such as the ability for machines to deduce meaning from human speech, as well as machine-to-machine communication, such as text to speech and voice-to-text. Several well-studied capacities of intelligent beings are also general characteristics of AI [27]. Choosing strategies (i.e., sequences of actions) to attain a goal while keeping costs to a minimum is a challenge in decision theory. NP-complete12 travelling salesman issue is included as a particular example even in the simple class of so-called off-line planning assignments, when the task, cost function and set of potential actions are known in advance (TSP). In recent times, TSP is no longer considered a genuine AI issue, but it serves as an illustration of how tough even extremely specialized, simple AI subtasks may be nowadays. Additionally, there are on-line analogues of more general planning issues, where not everything is known in advance (for example: in TSP, where some roads might be missing from the map owing to traffic jams or rerouting and one must travel to uncover good options). Reinforcement learning, which will be covered in more detail later in this section, has some overlap with online planning. Inherent in intelligent entities is the ability to solve problems.

The principles of quantum computations and information may be found in [17] and [14, 15]; quantum communication networks can be found in [9], with the latter providing an overview of the key features. [24] contains Deutsch's seminal work on quantum theory and the concept of a universal quantum computer. With respect to the subject of whether or not regular computers can simulate quantum computations, see [25] for Feynman's article. See [26] for further information on the 'no-cloning' theorem. See [27] for information on quantum computation challenges. See Unruh's 1995 paper [28] for a study of quantum computer coherence maintenance methods and properties. [29–31] is a seminal paper in quantum coding theory. See [30] for an analysis of the benefits and drawbacks of quantum computing. The author discovers a foundational article on quantum complexity theory. DiVincenzo's foundational quantum computing study from the year 2000 can be found at [21]. To learn more about Shor's groundbreaking work on quantum computer prime factorization, check out [11]. There is an excellent review of quantum algorithms available. See [3] for more information on quantum algorithms for algebraic problems. Quantum algorithms have made some recent advances and Quantum-computational speedup is explained in [5], which discusses the role played by entanglement.

When a charge crosses a quantum resistor, it has an effect on how much resistance it has. This is described in detail in [6]. The suggested model's decoherence mechanism is controlled using a continuous-measurement feedback technique. Superconducting circuits have shown to be great tools for incorporating memory effects in practice, too. Quasi-memristors can be utilized to develop neuromorphic quantum computers and quantum simulations of non-Markovian systems, according to the researchers' findings. They're quantum memristors, which are resistive quantum elements that retain information about their previous dynamics in the form of voltage. The authors of [7] examined the implementations of quantum memristors based on superconducting circuits. When supercurrents are cancelled, a quantum device with memristive behavior is introduced by the authors. A model for quantifying quantum memory retention has been developed and concluded that hysteretic behavior can be achieved by currently implementable measuring approaches in superconducting quantum circuits. Memcaps and meminductors with qubit-based memory are being investigated in [8]. Because of their unique features, capacitive and inductive devices are good tools for quantum processing, according to the findings (superconducting charge and phase qubits are quantum versions of memory capacitive and inductive systems). This work shows that memcapacitors and meminductors based on qubits have unusual hysteresis curves for specific unique inputs. According to the study's findings, quantum devices based on qubits can be built using the same memcapacitive and meminductive principles already used in classical devices.

Quantum memories can be realized in a variety of ways, according to the research. Topological quantum memory is an intriguing method. It uses a torus-like array of quantum states to achieve this goal. Stable logical quantum systems are created by entwining these quantum systems in certain ways.

There is more work to be done on enhancing the lifetime of quantum memories' physical implementations. The outcomes, on the other hand, are positive. Large-scale quantum computer architecture with atomic memory and photonic interconnects has been proposed with a room-temperature, one-second quantum bit memory.

Quantum random access memory (QRAM) is being discussed here. For the purposes of addressing any quantum superposition of memory cells, a qRAM employs n qubits. The authors came up with a design that drasti cally minimizes the number of memory calls needed. The results, according to the authors, enable for the development of a more resilient qRAM technique and lead to a decrease in addressing power that is exponential. The project came to a close with the development of a quantum optical system.

The capacity of associative memory is increased exponentially through quantum annealing recall. As demonstrated by the authors in this paper, quantum annealing for recall tasks gives associative memory models (which in some theoretical models may store a sublinear quantity of memories) exponential storage capacity. The Dwave processor, which featured a programmable quantum annealing mechanism, was used to show how the authors' scheme could be put to use.

Using a quantum bus, the functional elements of a quantum computer communicate with each other in quantum CPUs. Quantum CPUs can be approached from a computing perspective by quantum adders, the building pieces that formulate them. To implement quaternion processing in multiple architectural models, a variety of reversible quantum adder types have been defined, such as the quantum Fourier-transform adders, linear time adders, and quantum carry save and lookahead adders [20–22]. Quantum adders with reversible structures and parallel implementations can be created from quantum counterparts of classical adders for use in quantum calculations. They use ancilla quantum states and are all reversible, but they have distinct operating methods and circuit depths and latencies and performance. This creates a number of unresolved challenges when trying to realize their cooperation [6, 7].

4.3   Quantum Algorithms Characteristics Used in Machine Learning Problems

First, we'll go over the fundamental quantum algorithms that will be put to use in machine learning situations.

4.3.1   Minimizing Quantum Algorithm

Discrete function minimization issues can be solved using a quantum method [16]. A quantum iterations circuit can be used to symbolize it because Grover's search is at the core of it (Figure 4.4).

In the beginning, we choose point at random and set the threshold at using the reduced f. After that, we'll use Hadamard gates on the zero register (see Figure 4.4). After that, we iterate Grover times and take measurements on the first n qubits. We can adjust the threshold value based on the measurement findings. The second iteration begins as follows: threshold is updated again, Hadamard gates and Grover's iteration are applied times, the first qubits are measured, and the iteration is completed as follows: This iteration procedure's convergence is achieved by constantly searching through all potential input states in order to reach the global optimum.

4.3.2   K-NN Algorithm

KNN is a well-liked and straightforward classification method. The dataset T contains feature vectors and the related class labels are used to train the model. For each new input vector, the algorithm selects the class label that appears most frequently among its k nearest neighbors (Test Dataset D). Close feature vectors have comparable class labels, which is how this idea came to be. This holds true in a wide range of situations. Figure 4.5 depicts the T and D modeling datasets that were employed.

Using SWAP-test and QMA, quantum KNN computes all scalar products between feature vectors encoded in quantum states (3). (To get k closest neighbors for each test vector). How efficient the quantum method is depending on the number of SWAP-test iterations and quantum

Figure 4.4 The quantum minimization algorithm's quantum circuit.

multiplicative arithmetic iterations (n_{QMA}). Figure 4.6 shows the results of our modeling (for the datasets indicated in Figure 4.5). The accuracy of classification is proven by employing a confusion matrix with various values of n ST and n_{QMA}.

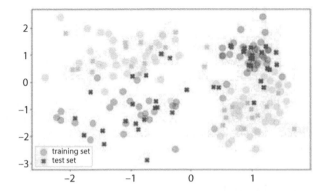

Figure 4.5 Datasets for training and testing the quantum KNN algorithm (four classes).

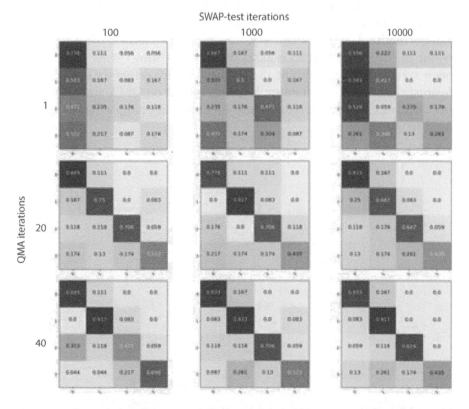

Figure 4.6 For various SWAP-test and QMA iterations, confusion matrices are generated.

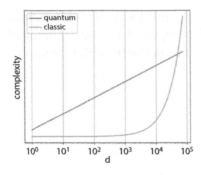 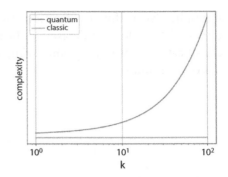

Figure 4.7 Complexity of the KNN algorithm's calculations. As in the previous example, left k< d and right k > d only when d exceeds 5.10_4 can the quantum technique lead to an efficient calculation (Figure 4.7, left picture). Thus, the quantum KNN technique may be used to solve problems with enormous spatial dimensions.

4.3.3   K-Means Algorithm

Unsupervised machine learning techniques such as the classical k-means algorithm are at the very foundation of machine learning in general. To categorize the data into k clusters, we employ a collection of vectors with no labels. This set of vectors is iterated until all existing cluster vectors have been averaged, at which point all the labels on the vectors are shifted to the nearest centroid label. quantum k-means is built on QMA and SWAP-test (to calculate closest centroid). Figure 4.8 shows an example dataset that we used in our analysis.

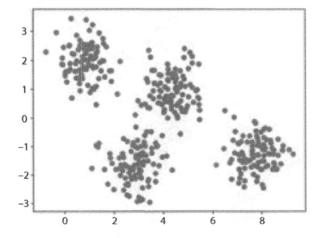

Figure 4.8 Four classes in an unlabeled dataset.

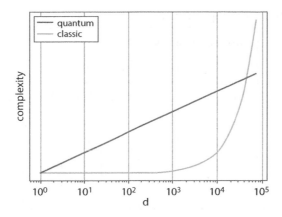

Figure 4.9 The K-means algorithm's computational complexity.

4.4   Tree Tensor Networking

Tree tensor networks (TTN) are quantum circuit architectures based on binary trees [17]. To begin, the TTN circuit applies unitary transforms to the pairs of qubits. After that, one of the qubits in each pair is discarded. We use two-qubit gates again on the remaining qubit pairs in the following circuit layer. This cycle is repeated until there is only one remaining qubit. Figure 4.10 shows such a design with eight input qubits.

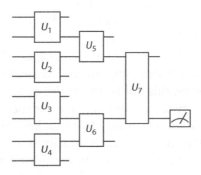

Figure 4.10 TTN quantum circuit architecture.

Table 4.1 IBM TTN implementation.

	Number of shots							
	1	2	6	10	28	57	302	1004
Setosavs Versicolor	0.92	0.97	0.79	0.92	0.96	0.91	1	1
Setosavs Virginica	0.77	0.88	1	1	1	1	1	1
Versicolorvs Virginica	0.62	0.70	0.70	0.80	0.90	0.91	0.95	0.92

4.5   TNN Implementation on IBM Quantum Processor

An IBM online quantum processor can run this circuit (Figure 4.10) using the parameters we've determined (ibmqx4). For each qubit in encoding technique (4), a single-qubit rotation U3 is used (Table 4.1).

4.6   Neurotomography

The process of reconstructing the quantum state from measurement findings is known as quantum tomography [18–20]. This paper introduces a quantum state tomography strategy based on neural networks for imaging quantum states in the brain. To translate measurement findings to pure one-qubit state parameters, we trained our fully connected neural network (polar and azimuth angles on the Bloch sphere).

This work developed fundamental tomography algorithms (based on MLE) in our lab [21, 22] that outperform the neural network approach (Figure 4.11a). However, this holds true in the case of quantum ideal systems. Neurotomography also enables the reconstruction of quantum state amplitudes in noisy quantum systems (without knowing the noise model). Using noisy data (104 quantum states uniformly distributed around the Bloch sphere) and a neural network, On the other hand, as illustrated in Figure 4.11, the neural network outperforms the traditional tomography method. Systematic error is shown in Figure 4.11b, while random error or amplitude-phase relaxation is shown in Figure 4.11c and Figure 4.11d.

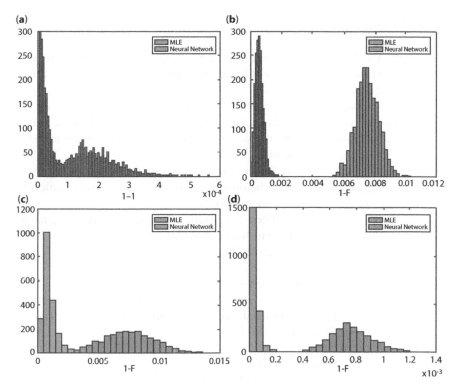

Figure 4.11 Comparison of Neurotomography with MLE tomography. There was a total of 2,000 trials conducted. Size of the sample: 10^5. (a) neural network approach, (b) systematic error, (c) random error, (d) amplitude-phase relaxation.

Using a neural network, the hidden connection between quantum states and noisy measurements is revealed.

4.7 Conclusion and Future Scope

This study's findings describe many methods to quantum machine learning algorithmic design. We use the tree tensor network quantum circuit as a binary classifier (TTN). This dataset (Fisher's Iris) demonstrates the efficacy of our methods. Tree Tensor Network (TTN) method is also demonstrated on IBM quantum processor. Here, we show how to use neural networks to do quantum tomography. In many investigations, a classical-quantum technique can reveal latent dependencies between input data and output measurement results by utilizing this approach.

References

1. Smith, J.S., Isayev, O., Roitberg, A.E., ANI-1: An extensible neural network potential with DFT accuracy at force field computational cost. *Chem. Sci.*, 8, 3192–3203, 2017.
2. Smith, J.S., Nebgen, B.T., Zubatyuk, R., Lubbers, N., Devereux, C., Barros, K., Tretiak, S., Isayev, O., Roitberg, A.E., Approaching coupled cluster accuracy with a general-purpose neural network potential through transfer learning. *Nat. Commun.*, 10, 2903, 2019.
3. Zubatyuk, R., Smith, J.S., Leszczynski, J., Isayev, O., Accurate and transferable multitask prediction of chemical properties with an atoms-in-molecules neural network. *Sci. Adv.*, 5, eaav6490, 2019.
4. Zubatyuk, R., Smith, J., Nebgen, B.T., Tretiak, S., Isayev, O., Teaching a neural network to attach and detach electrons from molecules. *ChemRxiv, Nat. Commun.*, 12, 1, 1–38, July 28, 2020.
5. Feynman, R.P., Leighton, R.B., Sands, M., *Six Easy Pieces: Essentials of Physics Explained by Its Most Brilliant Teacher*, Basic Books, New York, 2011.
6. Sherrill, C.D. and Schaefer, H.F., The configuration interaction method: Advances in highly correlated approaches, in: *Advances in Quantum Chemistry*, vol. 34, pp. 143–269, 1999.
7. Bishop, R.F., An overview of coupled cluster theory and its applications in physics. *Theor. Chim. Acta*, 80, 95–148, 1991.
8. Hohenberg, P. and Kohn, W., In homogeneous electron gas. *Phys. Rev.*, 136, B864–B871, 1964.
9. Löwdin, P.-O., Nature of quantum chemistry. *Int. J. Quantum Chem.*, 1, 7–12, 1967.
10. Wold, S., Sjöström, M., Eriksson, L., PLS-regression: A basic tool of chemometrics. *Chemom. Intell. Lab. Syst.*, 58, 109–130, 2001.
11. Hornik, K., Stinchcombe, M., White, H., Multilayer feedforward networks are universal approximators. *Neural Netw.*, 2, 359–366, 1989.
12. Chen, T. and Chen, H., Universal approximation to nonlinear operators by neural networks with arbitrary activation functions and its application to dynamical systems. *IEEE Trans. Neural Netw.*, 6, 911–917, 1995.
13. Bishop, C.M., *Neural Networks for Pattern Recognition*, Oxford University Press, Inc., New York, 1995.
14. Blank, T.B., Brown, S.D., Calhoun, A.W., Doren, D.J., Neural network models of potential energy surfaces. *J. Chem. Phys.*, 103, 4129–4137, 1995.
15. Lorenz, S., Groß, A., Scheffler, M., Representing high dimensional potential-energy surfaces for reactions at surfaces by neural networks. *Chem. Phys. Lett.*, 395, 210–215, 2004.
16. Behler, J. and Parrinello, M., Generalized neural-network representation of high-dimensional potential-energy surfaces. *Phys. Rev. Lett.*, 98, 146401, 2007.

17. Bartók, A.P., Payne, M.C., Kondor, R., Csányi, G., Gaussian approximation potentials: The accuracy of quantum mechanics, without the electrons. *Phys. Rev. Lett.*, 104, 136403, 2010.
18. Rupp, M., Tkatchenko, A., Müller, K.-R., von Lilienfeld, O.A., Fast and accurate modeling of molecular atomization energies with machine learning. *Phys. Rev. Lett.*, 108, 058301, 2012.
19. Balabin, R.M. and Lomakina, E., II, Support vector machine regression (LS-SVM)-an alternative to artificial neural networks (ANNs) for the analysis of quantum chemistry data? *Phys. Chem. Chem. Phys.*, 13, 11710, 2011.
20. Dral, P.O., Quantum chemistry in the age of machine learning. *J. Phys. Chem. Lett.*, 11, 2336–2347, 2020.
21. Schmidhuber, J., Deep learning in neural networks: An overview. *Neural Netw.*, 61, 85–117, 2015.
22. Smith, J.S., Nebgen, B., Lubbers, N., Isayev, O., Roitberg, A.E., Less is more: Sampling chemical space with active learning. *J. Chem. Phys.*, 148, 241733, 2018.
23. Bartók, A.P. and Csányi, G., Gaussian approximation potentials: A brief tutorial introduction. *Int. J. Quantum Chem.*, 115, 1051–1057, 2015.
24. Bartók, A.P., De, S., Poelking, C., Bernstein, N., Kermode, J.R., Csányi, G., Ceriotti, M., Machine learning unifies the modeling of materials and molecules. *Sci. Adv.*, 3, e1701816, 2017.
25. Shapeev, A.V., Moment tensor potentials: A class of systematically improvable interatomic potentials. *Multiscale Model. Simul.*, 14, 1153–1173, 2016.
26. Hansen, K., Biegler, F., Ramakrishnan, R., Pronobis, W., von Lilienfeld, O.A., Müller, K.-R., Tkatchenko, A., Machine learning predictions of molecular properties: Accurate many-body potentials and nonlocality in chemical space. *J. Phys. Chem. Lett.*, 6, 2326–2331, 2015.
27. Christensen, A.S., Bratholm, L.A., Faber, F.A., von Lilienfeld, O.A., FCHL revisited: Faster and more accurate quantum machine learning. *J. Chem. Phys.*, 152, 044107, 2020.
28. Behler, J., Perspective: Machine learning potentials for atomistic simulations. *J. Chem. Phys.*, 145, 170901, 2016.
29. Artrith, N., Morawietz, T., Behler, J., High-dimensional neural network potentials for multicomponent systems: Applications to zinc oxide. *Phys. Rev. B Condens. Matter Mater. Phys.*, 83, 153101, 2011.
30. Hellström, M. and Behler, J., Neural network potentials in materials modeling, in: *Handbook of Materials Modeling*, pp. 661–680, Springer International Publishing, Cham, 2020.
31. Devereux, C., Smith, J. S., Huddleston, K. K., Barros, K., Zubatyuk, R., Isayev, O., Roitberg. A. E., Extending the applicability of the ANI deep learning molecular potential to sulfur and halogens, *J. Chem. Theory Comput.*, 16, 7, 4192-4202, 2020.
32. Augusto, L. M., From symbols to knowledge systems: A. Newell and H. A. Simon's contribution to symbolic AI. *Journal of Knowledge Structures & Systems (JKSS)*, 2, 1, 29–62, 2021.

5

Building a Virtual Reality-Based Framework for the Education of Autistic Kids

Kanak Pandit[1], Aditya Mogare[1], Achal Shah[2], Prachi Thete[2] and Megharani Patil[1*]

[1]*Department of Computer Engineering, Thakur College of Engineering &Technology, Mumbai, India*
[2]*Department of Information Technology, MVP's KBTCOE, Nasik, India*

Abstract

Autism spectral disorder (ASD) is a developmental disorder that affects communication and social life skills. It is estimated that worldwide about one in 160 children has an ASD. Considering its resemblance to a learning disability, autism can be challenging to the daily life of children especially in the fields of education. In school, autistic kids may not grasp as much as other kids do which hampers their ability to apply the skills they learn in the classroom to real-life situations. In such cases, technology comes as a boon for such children that could assist them in their education. To assist children who are on the autism spectrum, there is a need for assistance in learning in a caring environment that would enable them to grasp concepts. Such children must be given the mimic of the real world. This chapter provides the significance of the impact of machines on the human mind. Various researches are carried out to develop a framework for understanding the mechanisms related to cognition that support human-computer interactions. Some frameworks like virtual reality have been proved instrumental to enable the connection between the mind and the machine. This chapter discusses the implementation of virtual reality and its mechanism to immerse them in the virtual world. Virtual reality becomes more immersive when the sensor extracts data with both the quality and the quantity which proves that perception needs to be data-oriented to increase the human-computer interaction. Our methodology consists of building a virtual

Corresponding author: megharani.patil@thakureducation.org

Sachi Nandan Mohanty, Rajanikanth Aluvalu and Sarita Mohanty (eds.) Evolution and Applications of Quantum Computing, (67–92) © 2023 Scrivener Publishing LLC

environment using A-Frame and neural style transfer. A-Frame is a web framework for building a virtual reality. Based on HTML, A-Frame is not just a 3D scene graph but could also be described as an entity-component-system (ECS) framework. On the other hand, Neural style transfer (NST) is used to blend two images and is therefore an optimization technique where the output image generated is to match the content statistics of the content image and the style statistics of the style reference image. It is based on a pre-trained convolutional neural network and gives 3d touch to the virtual environment. Based on the implementation of such techniques, a special setup in the star topology network could be made to closely observe the change in behavior of autistic kids using the ZigBee Module. It has been observed that the number of transmitting nodes should be minimized to enhance the network performance.

Keywords: Virtual reality, A-Frame, neural style transfer, backpropagation, Zigbee module, convolutional neural networks, star topology

5.1   Introduction

What is autism: Autism spectrum disorder, also called as autism is a variety of challenging conditions that occur in humans and impacts social and communication skills. The Centers for Disease Control and Prevention (CDC) states that 1 in 64 children are affected by autism in the United States today. We know that there is no single autism but many subspecies, which are strongly influenced by genetics and nature. Autism is a spectrum disorder because every victim has his/her own set of strengths and shortcomings. There are autistic individuals who can think over a problem and solve it easily while there are even some individuals who cannot solve a problem due to its difficulty level. Some autistic kids need a lot of assistance and support in their day-to-day life while others may need little support and they can even do things independently in their lives [1]. A few factors may contribute to the ASD development and are known to have been associated with sensory and medical issues such as gastrointestinal problems, sleep disturbances, fainting and challenges on mental health such as anxiety and depression.

Six eras of machine modulation:

    i.   First Generation: Reducing Equipment The first unthinkable machine is the hand ax, the Lateral power converter.

The handle is the visible connector for accessing this tool. A long, smooth round piece of wood is used to ensure a good grip.

ii.   Second Generation: Display Equipment These machines calculate wind speed, temperature, time, etc. It showed people how to read. The presentation of data to the user can be called its interface. The units of measurement, shape, and size of the indicators, color, scale, etc. have made a difference in the ease of use of the machine. The first known machine of this type sundial in the beginning only the pillar of the gro mon fa straight) was used. Gradually a dial was built on which gnomon was inserted. The accuracy required for numbering the dial area determines the accuracy of the read time. Gradually the dialing included various data such as directions, star charts, etc.

iii.   Third Generation: Machines that have provided an answerable result The answer is the consent received by the user on the machine when his action is registered. Most household appliances such as fans, lamps, TV, mixer, microwave oven, washing machine, coffee makers, fans, etc., fall under this category Example, when a user presses the switch on the TV remote control channel, the user can see the change of channel on the screen. The user can quickly see the effect of his action Here the interface is the part where the user can make the system do something like switch, knots, remote controls, etc. product usability. We can see in our homes how each of our machines has changed over time, as well as its usefulness. Electric switches are safer and softer to hold, knots are easy to work with, TV remote controls are standardized, etc. Most of us are familiar with such devices. We used an older version when we were kids, and now we have a modern one. With a keen eye, you can see how the links between these devices have changed over time.

iv.   Fourth Generation
Powerful Computer Devices The invention of computers has encouraged research in various fields, Previously providing performance itself was a challenge, and it has been a field of research. For example, in the past people read DOS

computer instructions Today no one puts much effort into learning how to use the program. They just switch to an easy-to-use system. Human-Computer Interaction is a field of research that has emerged as a result of this competition. Here the focus is on reducing the connection between the user and the computer. Previously only text-based screens were available. With the introduction of photography, the scope of creativity in collaborative environments has grown. Technology is changing rapidly, and we have new computer devices every day. From the mainframe computers, we have reduced ourselves to smart watches, with the same skills! Today's biggest challenge is to present all the functionality in that limited display space.

v.   Fifth Generation: Smart Machines

With the ingenuity of making it in the boom, traditional input methods seem inadequate. We make machines that can get people used to continuing to learn. These programs require the freedom to learn locally. Here the user does not have to learn to use the program. Instead, these programs learn how the user will use the system. These programs can access inputs independently, as well as self-paced learning. Most guessing systems, smart business plans, tracking system sensors, etc. Intelligent. By traditional methods, these programs cannot provide the desired results. Vehicles with obstacle sensors Input is taken directly from the environment and is not marked in or identified by anyone. Consider the default air conditioner. It scans the room to find the number of people, downloads the outside temperature, and automatically adjusts its temperature to the correct value. In such systems a keyboard, mouse, or touch screen restricts machine learning Indigenous language processing is a future field that allows people to speak freely with a computer in their own language, and the computer will interpret. These programs also learn about people in their actions. The limitation of holding the device in his hand and giving the input in some way will not help the machine to read. With the insertion of voice, body touch, or brain signals, all such limits are removed, and there is a wide range of machine learning. With the word Uls, Ki user communicates with the computer completely through his voice. Gesture UTs on the other hand take inputs into body sesame. While the brain-computer Uls, can use systems with just brain signals Users do not have to provide any external output anyway.

vi. The future

The facts about the unpopularity of tax collectors Indigenous language processing This idea is contrary to reality. You may have encountered many games including building a new city, farm or house, and family. This is a reality when the real world is being replaced by the physical world. In the reality of the unpopularity of tax-payers we see, the virtual world is brought to the reality of the user) We watch sci-fi movies where one can get into a video game, or one of the game characters gets into our real game [2].

5.2   Literature Review

This paper reports a survey on virtual reality (VR) and its perception of the human mind. We have considered the autism aspect of our research as well. In our world virtual reality (VR) is defined as a three-dimensional simulation that is generated by the computer which is immersive enough. The person using virtual reality use equipment like gloves with sensors to sense the effects. It is still not clear when virtual reality actually originated due to the difficulty that occurred in creating a different concept of an alternative existence [3]. The concept has been witnessed during the age of Renaissance in Europe which created depictions of non-existent (artificial) worlds. The technique of virtual reality was also seen as early as in 1860s. Antonin Artaud, a French writer and a visual artist believed that the illusion created was not different from the reality and that the viewers should treat the virtual world they are experiencing as a reality. The current context of virtual reality is referred from science fiction. As we have already mentioned about autism we are just giving this information as a reference. This spectrum condition brings challenges like changes in behavior and effect on communication. Although attention issues bring an impact on their lives, they still have their own preferences like others. In the 1990s, Virtual reality has been a technique

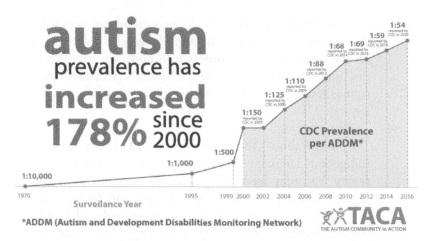

Figure 5.1 Autism statistics. https://tacanow.org/wp-content/uploads/2020/05/TACA-Occurrence-Graph-2020_c-copy-1536x875.jpg accessed on 18-02-2022.

which was initiated by various researchers to aid autistic people in several ways. The therapists and researchers strived to create virtual environments to provide an experience to people with such condition to face stressful situations thereby preparing them for a life that the world faces. The partnership of Yale University's School of Medicine and BrainHealth Center was successful enough to assist autistic adults to make themselves independent and achieve socio-economic stability in their lives through real-life situations like interviews and dating. Figure 5.1 illustrates the prevalence and rise of autism from 1970 to 2016.

The industry of virtual reality played an immense role to help and support autistic community to connect with each other, be in touch with each other, and navigate. On the other hand, it can also assist the community which is not suffering from ASD to get more insights about it.

The most essential purpose of this organized review was to evaluate and explain key outcomes related to the successful use of programs related to virtual reality to treat the community including the young and adolescents suffering from autism. There are thirty-one research papers that are published in the span of 8 years starting from 2010. These papers are available on various websites where they are analyzed and reviewed.

Depending on the attributes of the community who participated, the age of the enrolled study subjects ranged from 5 to 15.5 years. However, the 8 to 14 years old age group was more focused on subjects (only two subjects that do not include children in this list) as observed in Graph 5.1. As expected for children with ASD, participants were boys, and the average boy and girl population observed in the study was 4: 1 (85.15% of the sample).

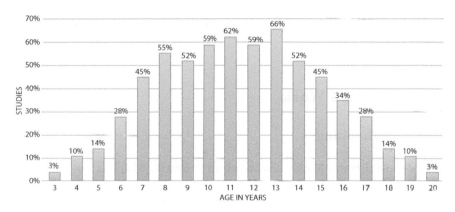

Graph 5.1 Age wise participation in VR program.

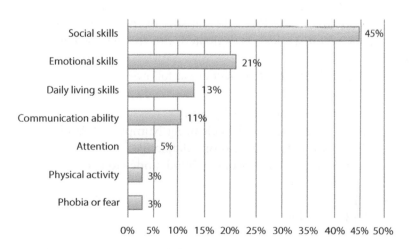

Graph 5.2 Characteristics of autistic kids surveyed.

Autistic kids were surveyed and attempt to identify their characteristics was made. As observed in Graph 5.2, around 45% of the autistic kids have social skills while 55% of them lack these skills. Only 21% of the autistic kids have emotional skills which is important for maintaining positive relationships and making responsible and 13% of them have daily living skills. Shockingly, only 11% of them have communication skills, 5% of them have attention and grasping ability. Only 3% of the autistic kids surveyed can perform some physical activities and the same percentage of such kids have the fear of having crowd around them.

5.3   Proposed Work

5.3.1   Methodology

The proposed framework consists of an A-Frame which is not just a 3D scene graph but could also be described as an entity-component-system (ECS) framework [4]. Being a web framework, it has a big contribution to the building of a virtual reality environment. This framework provides a 360-degree view of the virtual environmental visible area to users. To make the visuals more artistic, neural style transfer can be used as an efficient technique to blend two images which are, therefore, an optimization technique where the output image generated is to match the content statistics of the content image and the style statistics of the style reference image. The behavior of autistic kids is evaluated with the help of ZigBee module setup [5].

The tools required for the project are as follows:

1. Programming language-Python
2. Software libraries for data cleaning-Numpy and Pandas
3. Library for data visualization-Matplotlib
4. Deep Learning framework to build model-Keras
5. Google Colab
6. A-Frame
7. ZigBee Module

5.3.2   Work Flow of Neural Style Transfer

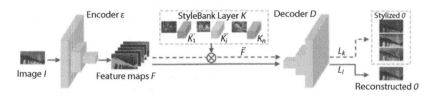

Figure 5.2 Flow of work. Available at https://sunshineatnoon.github.io/posts/2017/05/blog-post-1/" accessed on 04-03-2022.

Figure 5.2 shows the flow of work of how stylized image is obtained from content image using neural style transfer.

5.3.3   A-Frame

The following steps are followed to implement the prediction of Object Detection:

- o Setting up the virtual world and adding components
- o Adding interactivity through Raycasting
- o Animating the components
- o Web animation

5.3.3.1   Setting Up the Virtual World and Adding Components

Setting up the scene is the base of creating the A-Frame which creates a stage for turning on the WebGL (Web Graphics Library) and the camera. WebGL Library is a JS API that provides 2D and 3D interactive components to add to the A-Frame scene. Inside the scene, we place components that we call "entities" which act as basic building blocks of A-Frame. A-Frame works on an Entity component system as it generates less code and performs powerful functionalities to provide a cleaner design. We can add components like a cube, sphere, cylinder, etc. [6].

While adding components, we can use attributes like primitive, type, color, intensity, etc.

Table 5.1 describes the A-Frame entity description where events occurring in A-Frame are described.

Table 5.1 A-Frame entity description.

Event	Description
Child-attached	The entity was attached to by a child entity and are synchronized.
Child-detached	The entity was detached from child entity and both execute independently.
Component changed	One of the entity's components was modified. This event is throttled. Do not use this for reading position and rotation change.
Component initialized	One of the entity's components was initialized.
Component removed	One of the entity's components was removed.
Loaded	The components are first attached to the entity after which it is initialized by the entity.
Object3dset	An entity was set on by the Object3D base class in three.js
Pause	After an entity turns inactive, it is paused with dynamic behavior.
Play	After an entity becomes active, it plays with dynamic behavior.
State added	The new state was taken up by an entity.
State removed	The state was no longer taken up by an entity.
Schema changed	The component which had its schema was altered.

5.3.3.2   Adding Interactivity Through Raycasting

After components are added to the scene, we need to make components interactive. To do this, we use a technique which is called raycasting. Raycasting is modifying the data which comprises less information into a 3D projection. It involves the propagation of light from the origin and sending it to a row of entities. Raycasting examines where the light intersects the entities and thus will emit events on the entity when it will intersect the entity. To initiate raycasting, we use the raycaster component. Different events which are incorporated in raycasting are raycaster-intersected,

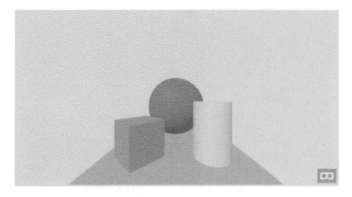

Figure 5.3 A-Frame components.

raycaster-intersected-cleared, raycaster-intersection, and raycaster-intersection-cleared. Raycaster-intersected is when the entity is intersected by the raycaster. This causes event and event details to be known to an entity, raycasting entity, and component containing data about the inter section. Raycaster-intersected-cleared is when a raycaster is emitted on a raycasting entity. In this process, the entity is no longer intersected with a raycaster. Raycaster-intersection is when the raycasting entity is emitted on. It involves raycaster intersecting on single or multiple entities. Raycaster-intersection-cleared is when the raycaster is emitted on a raycasting entity just like Raycaster-intersection. In this process, the entity is no longer intersected with the raycaster. We even use multiple parameters like far, interval, near, objects, and recursive.

Figure 5.3 shows the A-Frame components that are added. Any autistic kid who wants to learn about different 3D shapes like cube, sphere, and cylinder could better visualize through such virtual reality platforms.

5.3.3.3   Animating the Components

Animating the components gives final touch to them. For that, we use A-Frame-animation-component which can tweak values with component values like position and the component property values like light intensity. The component's base name is animation. More than one animation can be attached to an entity by name-spacing the component with double under-scores. We can even use the property like "easings" which initializes the speed and acceleration throughout the cycle of an animation. We can con-figure various animation components from JS by calling setAttribute() on an animation-element.

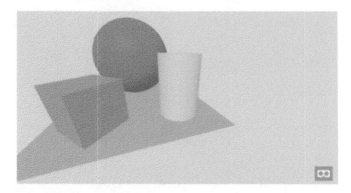

Figure 5.4 A-Frame components from other angle.

A-Frame has the powerful capability of changing the angle the user moves his/her neck for better visualization and the ability to get different types of perspectives [7]. As seen in Figure 5.4.

5.3.4   Neural Style Transfer

Neural-style Transfer (NST) is an enhancement technique which captures content and style image (For Example: a masterpiece by a popular artist) is stitched together to make the resulting image resemble a content image, but "painted" with a reference style image [8].

This is used for optimizing the output image to shape the content material facts and reference fashion records. These figures are extracted from images using a convolutional network [9].

Using this concept as a tool to help such kids, NST uses a pre-trained neural network (CNN) to transfer styles from a given image to another. This is done by defining a loss function that attempts to reduce the difference between a content image, a style image, and a generated image. With the help of NST you will be able to produce amazing art as below [10].

The intention of NST is to offer the Deep Learning model the potential to distinguish between the style representations and content image [11].

NST uses a Convolutional Neural network that is pre-trained with the function of additional losses to change the style from one image to another and combine the newly produced image with the feature it wants to add.

Style transfer activates the neurons in a particular manner, such that the output image and the content image need to fit particularly within the content, while the style image and the favored output image must suit in texture, and seize the equal fashion traits inside the activation maps.

These two goals are combined with a single loss formula, where we can control how much we care about style redesign and content redesign [12]. Here are the inputs required for the image style transfer model:

1. Content Image - an image in which we want to convey style
2. Style Image - the style you want to convey to the content image
3. Input Image (generated) - the ultimate combination of content and style image

The following steps are followed in neural style transfer:

5.3.3.1 Choosing the content and style image
5.3.3.2 Generation of a random image
5.3.3.3 Model Design
5.3.3.4 Loss Calculation
5.3.3.5 Model Optimization

5.3.4.1   Choosing the Content and Styling Image

Neural style transfer powerfully blends content and styled images by applying styles from the styled images to the content images [13]. The content image is defined as the image to which the style is transferred and the style image is defined as the image that transfers its style to the content image to provide the desired output image. Activation of neurons is an important step in this process as the system ensures that the output image and content image are identical in terms of data while the output image and style image are identical in terms of appearance [14].

Figure 5.5 is the content image on which style has to be applied on.

Figure 5.6 is the style image that will transfer its style to the content image to produce an output image.

5.3.4.2   Image Preprocessing and Generation of a Random Image

For producing an output image with enhanced quality, it is important to preprocess the input images. Opening, resizing, and formatting images into appropriate tensors is an essential step in this process [15].

Image preprocessing is followed by the creation of a random image where the same image is subsequently modified so that it retains the material from the input (material) image and texture from the style image. The size of the output image is equal to the size of content image and style image [16].

Figure 5.5 Content image.

Figure 5.6 Style image.

5.3.4.3   Model Design and Extraction of Content and Style

The next step after the collection of data in the form of images is to send it to neural networks. Transfer learning is used in this process. Transfer Learning is getting knowledge from an object recognition problem and applying the same knowledge to a similar problem.

In our case of neural style transfer, we use the VGG-19 model which is pretrained on a large image dataset - ImageNet. VGG stands for "Visual Geometry Group" which is a structure based on the deep Convolutional Neural Network (DeepCNN). So the model consists of multiple layers with VGG-19 CNN having 16 convolutional layers and three fully connected layers. It also has 3 × 3 filters in each convolutional layer. These layers are used for extracting the elements and are divided into five groups with each group having a maximum pooling layer at the last of each group. The features, including the content and style, are extracted from the image and are stored in the model in the form of weights. The final layers are not used for neural style transfer as image classification is not applicable here [17].

5.3.4.4   Loss Calculation

Total loss function is the weighted sum of subject matter and styles loss with the mathematical expression as follows:

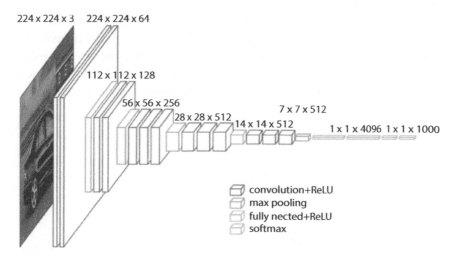

Figure 5.7 Architecture of VGG-19. Available at https://inst.eecs.berkeley.edu/~cs194-26/fa20/upload/files/projFinalAssigned/cs194-26-aco/vgg16.PNG accessed on 26-02-2022

Figure 5.7 depicts the architecture of VGG-19 which is a 19 layers deep CNN.

$$Ltotal(p, a, x) = \alpha L + \beta Lstyle(a, x)$$

where α is the weight of content loss and β is the weight of style loss.

Backpropagation (Backward Propagation of errors) is one of the most important methods used in neural networks to minimize the loss function and increase the accuracy of the model. With the help of chain law it corrects neural network weights depending on the degree of error in the previous by calculating the gradient loss function of a single unit/weight [18]. As it indicates, Backpropagation actions returned from the output layer to hidden layer, thereby requiring no parameters to adjust the weight and prior information of the neural network [19].

x denotes the input values in the neuron. As observed in the Figure 5.8, three inputs of one entity are fetched to the neuron. For example, the shape (rectangle), length (10m), breadth (5m) of just one shape (rectangle) at a time can be inputted into the neuron at a time.

a denotes the output of the neuron and is also called as activation. The entries of an entity that a neuron gets forms a basis of prediction that neuron makes and that prediction is called activation. In the case of a rectangle, prediction could be area.

w denotes the weights of the neuron. The input feature of vector x has different weights w.

b denotes the bias of the neuron where every neuron has only one bias.

y denotes the true value of the output of the network. In the network, the weights w and the bias b are changed to bring a as much close to y as possible.

Loss L depicts the closeness of a to y. Gradient descent has been one of the most efficient techniques to minimize the loss in the network.

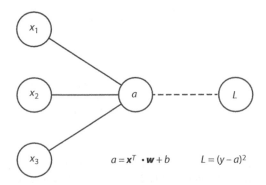

Figure 5.8 Backpropagation.

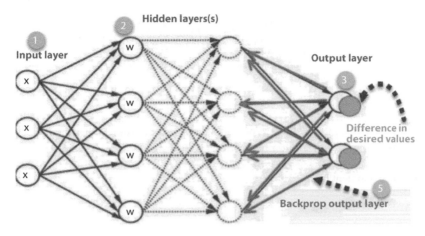

Figure 5.9 Backpropagation algorithm working. Available at https://www.niser. ac.in/~smishra/teach/cs460/2020/lectures/lec19_1/ accessed on 13-03-2022.

1. Inputs X traverse the path that is connected earlier as seen in Figure 5.9.
2. The input is worked on using real weights W which are randomly selected.
3. Computed the output/result from the input layer of all neurons present in the network to the hidden layers to the output layer.
4. Calculate the error/loss in the outputs
5. Move back from the output layer to the hidden layer (backpropagation) to make changes in the weights such that there is a decrease in the error which is referred to as backpropagation.

As discussed earlier, total loss function depends on the weight of content loss and style loss.

Content loss is defined as the pixel difference between the content image and the output image. It is calculated as the Euclidean distance between the feature representation of content and outgoing images at every layer in the convolutional neural network (CNN) model. The filter response of lower layers looks close to the content image and the filter representation of the VGG net's higher layers takes in the high-level content data [20].

Let us consider hidden layer "L" in VGG-16 network to determine the loss. Let "C" and "G" be subject image and output image and C[i] and G[i] be feature representation of the images in layer L of C and G respectively. Hence, the content loss is calculated by formula as shown in Figure 5.10:

$$\mathcal{L}_{content}(\vec{p}, \vec{x}, l) = \frac{1}{2} \sum_{i,j} (F_{ij}^l - P_{ij}^l)^2$$

$\vec{p}$ The original image
$\vec{x}$ The generated image
l Layer
F_{ij}^l Activation of the ith filter at position j in the feature representation of $\vec{x}$ in l
P_{ij}^l Activation of the ith filter at position j in the feature representation of $\vec{p}$ in l

Figure 5.10 Content loss.

Along with content loss, style loss is also taken into consideration while calculating the total loss. We cannot make comparisons between features of both the images to compute the style loss. Hence, we require a new term to calculate the style loss called "gram matrices" [21]. Just like content image, style loss is also measured using squared loss function. Gram matrix is used to get the style of each matrix and helps to determine the style features in an image. This shows how the features are distributed in a particular layer. This also shows the correlation of features between layers.

There are different loss functions that are computed during the process of neural style transfer. Table 5.1 describes the important loss functions that need to be considered. In general, these loss functions help to generate similarity between content and stylized image.

5.3.4.5 *Model Optimization*

After getting the total loss, we need to perform gradient descent through optimizer to modify the generated image in such a way that the total loss decreases after every iteration. As discussed earlier, back-propagation is one of the optimization techniques and can be considered as the subset of gradient descent. Stochastic Gradient Descent is another optimization algorithm that trains such models. At times, both Stochastic Gradient Descent and back-propagation can be used to calculate the gradient. We can call this as "Stochastic Gradient Descent with Back-propagation". Table 5.2 describes the important loss functions that needs to be considered.

Table 5.2 Description of NST loss functions.

Sr. no.	Loss function	Overview
1	Gram Loss	The style loss based on Gram-based style representations.
2	Perceptual Loss	Content loss based on perceptual similarity (certain cognitive subjectivity) of images for training feed-forward neural networks.
3	Mean-subtraction Gram Loss	Loss obtained on calculating the difference between the mean of representations needed for feature detection and then calculating the Gram Loss.
4	Transformed Gram Loss	Calculating Gram Loss over translated feature representations-vertically and horizontally.
5	Batch Normalization	Achieving comparable quality with Gram Loss.
6	Laplacian Loss	The mean-squared distance between the two Laplacians and the loss brings in more similarity between the content and stylized image.
7	Semantic Loss	Segmentation masking over MRF Loss.
8	MRF Loss	Works better when the content and style image is similar in visibility and shape.
9	Histogram Loss	Matching the histogram of feature representations. Removes variability of Gram Matrices.
10	Adversarial Loss	Depends on the probability of the generator fooling the discriminator. Works better at keeping significant textures in complex images.
11	Disparity Loss	Devised for stereoscopic style transfer. Enforces the bidirectional disparity constraint in non-occluded regions.
12	Depth Loss	Calculates the difference in depth between both images-content and style.

Figure 5.11 Output image.

Figure 5.11 depicts the output image that has been obtained from content image by styling it through style image.

5.4 Evaluation Metrics

Autistic kids must be given the mimic of the real world. Developing games for autistic kids will reduce their boredom and can increase their interaction in the game. A crucial component is necessary for tracking their eye movement which can be achieved by an eye tracker such as Tobi Pro Glasses 2. The data fetched from the Tobi Pro Glasses 2 would be analyzed by GlassViewer. This data also includes pupil size, gyroscope, accelerometer, and TTL input which would later be comprehended in a better way by MATLAB software. We can get the time taken by the autistic kid spent on gazing at any object in virtual world with the generation of heatmaps by the software. Even jobs can be created in the market through the evolution of Extended Reality which comes up with the use of AjnaLens and Jio Tesseract. This will improve the social skills of autistic kids and give them the instructions while crossing the road, etc.

It is found that the eye gaze and recognition of sound can determine the state of autism of the individual. There can be a system design with transmitter and receiver.

The transmitter Section helps to extract the response data which includes the voice signals from the autistic kid. Figure 5.12 explains the process of conversion of data into radio frequency. This section includes PC and voice recognizer Integrated Circuit connected to a micro-controller which observes eye and voice identifier respectively. RFID (Radio-Frequency Identification) reader used to make sure than the individual is not prone to accidents and mishaps. Along with these components, additional components like SD card can be used to store waveform data as a result of which the file is saved with an extension .wav. LCD is used to display the output of the individual data. By using ZigBee module, especially of high power transmission type such as ZMN2405HP which is a cheap, wireless mesh network, the data can be sent to the computer which can be viewed on the computer through GUI (Graphical User Interface). ZigBee module uses the CC2430 transceiver IC, a device that can both transmit and receive data which is integrated with high performing 8051 microcontroller. The voltage regulator of 5V is connected to ZigBee module to keep the voltage stable [22].

Figure 5.13 shows the receiver section of the system. The receiver section consists of the Global System for Mobile Communications (GSM) interfaced with the microcontroller to send the output. ZigBee baseboard is used to connect the ZigBee node and the computer via USB (Universal

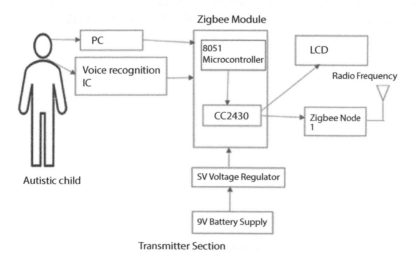

Figure 5.12 Transmitter section.

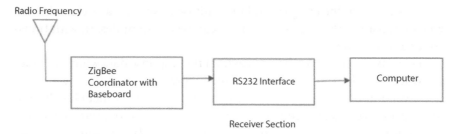

Figure 5.13 Receiver section.

Serial Bus). The ZigBee Coordinator with Baseboard is connected to RS 232 for serial communication transmission of data which is then fetched by the computer.

To briefly access data from a number of ZigBee nodes connected to a common output (hub), star topology can be used. Figure 5.14 shows the star topology network to access data from various systems. Star topology has various. Star topology has various components like hub, bridges, switches, and routers. OPNET Modeler simulator is the best simulator-based approach for star topology in a small network because it calibrates the number of nodes a server can withstand. Even NS-2 being an open-source network simulator can be used. However, it is difficult to use and users can take time to learn it whereas, in OPNET, a GUI is provided making users learn it faster and get acclimatized to it at a quicker pace [23]. The hub can be a PAN coordinator which is a sink node that gets the data pushed from the other nodes that sense the data. The data of every autistic kid would be recorded automatically to the database from GUI.

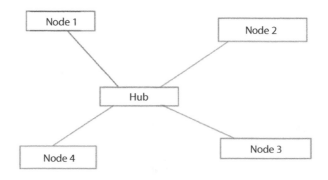

A star network topology

Figure 5.14 A star network topology.

5.5   Results

5.5.1   A-Frame

A-Frame doesn't require any additional installation but just involves usage of HTML files. A-Frame makes sure that the VR is setup including 3D boilerplate and standard controls. HTML is one of the most standardized markup language which is easy to use and powerful three.js framework like A-Frame works on it easily. Even developers have easy access to JavaScript, three.js and DOM APIs making it a composable entity-component structure.

A-Frame also has its own inbuilt visual inspector which can help autistic kids to get a different view of the scene along with visual effects. Hence, autistic kids can visualize better as they get the opportunity to get a better view of the virtual world.

Various metrics are considered to improve the A-Frame Framework like Power of texture dimensions, asset limit, measurement overhead, FPS, and geometries. To ensure optimal memory use, using texture dimensions that are a power of two is preferred. Loading too many assets (more than 70 MB) for a single web page can cause delays in scene loading which can cause browser to crash. Hence, Firefox's performance tool has a feature called Allocations Recorder which can be used to check memory used in the scene. To check on-device performance, WebIDE was used and it was found that CPU was found to be used at around 10% to 25% to render the scenes. This proved the fact that GPU is responsible for scene rendering. Frames per second (FPS) is an important parameter while using the framework. A stable 90 with the WebVR

Table 5.3 Performance metrics of A-Frame.

Sr. no.	Performance metrics	Observations to improve metrics
1	Power of texture Dimensions	2
2	Asset Limit	Allocations recorder in Firefox
3	Measurement Overhead	Scene rendering is done on GPU
4	FPS	stable 90 fps with the WebVR 1.0 API
5	Geometries	A lower count suggests less memory being used by the scene

Table 5.4 Result of NST.

Result	Value
Accuracy (%)	0.84
Precision	0.83
Recall	0.85
F1 Score	0.84
Style Loss	5.36
Content Loss	25.86
Loss	649767393.0

1.0 API. The number of three.js geometries suggest the use of memory in the scene. Table 5.3 describes the performance metrics along with the observations to improve metrics. Table 5.4 describes the result of neural style transfer.

5.5.2   Neural Style Transfer

Neural Style Transfer helps autistic kids to see different stylized sceneries which gives them artistic thoughts and increase their creativity skills. Neural Style Transfer follows some steps to convert the content image to style image like choosing the content and style image, generation of a random image, model Design, loss Calculation and model Optimization [24]. Neural Style Transfer works on videos too and adds style to them which can give autistic kids better visuals of the virtual world.

After carrying out the neural style transfer on an image, it was found that the accuracy was 84.3% while the precision, recall and F1 Score was around 83.58%, 85.73% and 84.64%, respectively. Also, loss was calculated in the process. The style loss was found to be 5.364360 while the content loss was found to be around 25.864335. Hence, the total loss is 649767393.0.

5.6   Conclusion

Richard Coyne, an author who has inferred on Information technology and design in his numerous books, believed that VR becomes most immersive when data both of quality and quantity is perceived by the senses of the

VR user which means that the perception needs to be "data oriented" to increase the human-computer interaction.

Computers came into existence in the last decade and it observes an evolution that is desirable for human-machine interaction. Earlier, desktop metaphor which formed a basis of graphical user interface could be said as a primary component of human-machine interaction. The biggest drawback observed here is that this is restricted to two-dimension. However, for development of three-dimensional applications, the knowledge of two-dimensional input devices is crucial as the insufficiency in two-dimensional input devices become the source of motivation in development of features like 3-D modeling, motion control, surface modeling, etc. At times, due to lack of adaptation to 3-D based applications which is caused by the lack of 3-D motion specification capabilities of the mouse, It will be noteworthy if we develop new device layout and UI analogies that help the users to work in a 3D based virtual environment. Virtual prototyping methods such as architectural walkthrough, natural interaction with digital mock-ups has formed the basis of further research in the fields of virtual engineering.

Educating autistic kids with complete technological use will yield the best result. This should not only include the headset but also the special haptic vest and shoes for better immersion in the virtual world.

References

1. Didehbani, N., Allen, T., Kandalaft, M., Krawczyk, D., Chapman, S., Virtual reality social cognition training for children with high functioning autism. *Comput. Hum. Behav.*, 62, 703–711, 2016.
2. Strickland, D., Virtual reality for the treatment of autism, in: *Virtual Reality in Neuro-Psycho-Physiology*, 1997, 1998.
3. Kutey, E.N. and Mali, S.N., Virtual reality based adaptive response technology for autistic children. *Int. J. Eng. Res. Technol.*, 4, 985–986, 2015.
4. Delporte, B., Perroton, L., Grandpierre, T., Trichet, J., Accelerometer and magnetometer based gyroscope emulation on smart sensor for a virtual reality application. *Sens. Transducers*, 32–47, 2012.
5. Chellappa, M.R., Madasamy, S., Prabakaran, R., Study on zigbee technology. *3rd International Conference on Electronics Computer Technology (ICECT)*, vol. 6, 2011.
6. Gill, A., AFrame: A domain specific language for virtual reality: Extended abstract. *The 2nd International Workshop*, 2017.
7. Sinthong, P. and Carey, M., AFrame: Extending dataframes for large-scale modern data analysis. *IEEE International Conference on Big Data*, 2019.

8. Jing, Y., Yang, Y., Feng, Z., Ye, J., Yu, Y., Song, M., Neural style transfer: A review. *IEEE transactions on visualization and computer graphics*, 26, 11, 3365–3385, 2020.
9. Li, Y., Wang, N., Liu, J., Hou, X., Demystifying neural style transfer. *Proceedings of the Twenty-Sixth International Joint Conference on Artificial Intelligence (IJCAI-17)*, pp. 2230–2231, 2017.
10. Desai, S., Neural artistic style transfer: A comprehensive look, 2017.
11. Dumoulin, V., Shlens, J., Kudlur, M., A learned representation for artistic style. *ICLR*, 2017.
12. Gupta, A., Johnson, J., Alahi, A., Fei-Fei, L., Characterizing and improving stability in neural style transfer. *ICCV*, 2017.
13. Jing, Y., Yang, Y., Feng, Z., Ye, J., Yu, Y., Song, M., Neural style transfer: A review. *IEEE Trans. Vis. Comput. Graph.*, 26, 11, 3365–3385, Nov. 1, 2020.
14. Johnson, J., Alahi, A., Fei-Fei, L., Perceptual losses for real-time style transfer and super-resolution, in: *European Conference on Computer Vision*, 2016.
15. Tanno, R. and Yanai, K., Conditional fast style transfer network. *ICMR*, 2017.
16. Kutey, E.N. and Mali, S.N., A review paper on: Virtual reality based adaptive response technology for autistic children. *Int Res J Eng Technol.*, 4, 02, p. 1 February-2015.
17. Krizhevsky, A., Sutskever, I., Hinton, G.E., Imagenet classification with deep convolutional neural networks, in: *Advances in Neural Information Processing Systems*, F. Pereira, C.J.C. Burges, L. Bottou, K.Q. Weinberger (Eds.), vol. 25, pp. 1097–1105, Curran Associates, Inc, New York, United States, 2012.
18. Choromanska, A., Henaff, M., Mathieu, M., Arous, G.B., LeCun, Y., The loss surfaces of multilayer networks, in: *AISTATS*, 2015.
19. Chauvin, Y. and Rumelhart, D.E. (Eds.), *Backpropagation: Theory, Architectures, and Applications*, Lawrence Erlbaum Associates, Inc. Publishers, 365 Brodway, Hillsdale, New Jersey, 1995.
20. Liu, K., Zhong, P., Zheng, Y., Yang, K., Liu, M., P_VggNet: A convolutional neural network (CNN) with pixel-based attention map. *PloS One*, 13, 12, e0208497, 2018.
21. Zhu, Q., Li, X., Conesa, A., Pereira, C., GRAM-CNN: A deep learning approach with local context for named entity recognition in biomedical text. *Bioinformatics*, 34, 9, 1547–1554, May 1, 2018.
22. Hill, J., Horton, M., Kling, R., Krishnamurthy, L., The platforms enabling wireless sensor networks. *Commun. ACM*, 41–46, 2004.
23. Wang, J. and Nahrstedt, K., *Design and Implement Differentiated Service Routers in OPNET*, Technical Report. UMI Order Number: UIUCDCS-R-2000-2177., University of Illinois at Urbana-Champaign, New York, United States, 2000.
24. Mordvintsev, A., Olah, C., Tyka, M., Inceptionism: Going deeper into neural networks, 2015.

6

Detection of Phishing URLs Using Machine Learning and Deep Learning Models Implementing a URL Feature Extractor

Abishek Mahesh, Prithvi Seshadri, Shruti Mishra*
and Sandeep Kumar Satapathy

School of Computer Science and Engineering, Vellore Institute of Technology, Chennai, Chennai, Tamil Nadu, India

Abstract

Phishing is a deceitful process by which an attacker tries to steal sensitive information from a naïve user. These types of attacks are generally carried out through emails, text messages, etc. Phishing URLs are a significant threat to cybersecurity professionals and practitioners. A lot of research has been done to tackle the problem of Phishing. Several Machine Learning practitioners have developed ML models which can detect Phishing URLs. However, using Machine Learning and Deep Learning also has its challenges and obstacles. The proposed approach detects Phishing URLs by analyzing URL properties, URL metrics, and other certain URL external services. URL Feature Extractor was created in python to extract features from any URL. A dataset of 88,647 phishing and legitimate URLs is used in this study. Several Machine Learning algorithms such as Support Vector Machines (SVM), Logistic Regression (LR), K-Nearest Neighbors (KNN), Naïve-Bayes, Random Forests (RF), Ada-Boost, Gradient- Boosting and Artificial Neural Networks were used to predict Phishing URLs. The results obtained indicate a reasonable accuracy rate. The Gradient Boosting model produced the best Accuracy, Precision, Recall, F1-SCORE of 97% each compared to the other models.

Keywords: Phishing, support vector machines, logistics regression, K-nearest neighbors, random forest

Corresponding author: shrutim2129@gmail.com

Sachi Nandan Mohanty, Rajanikanth Aluvalu and Sarita Mohanty (eds.) *Evolution and Applications of Quantum Computing*, (93–110) © 2023 Scrivener Publishing LLC

6.1   Introduction

The Internet is an expanded network that connects computers all over the world. It has grown to a network with more than 2 billion end-users [1]. Getting expanded day by day, it has modernized the way individuals contact and reach out each other and provide services. However, there isn't any central control or authority, which generally leads to threats and suspicious activities [1].

Fraud is one of the major problems in the Internet world. Internet frauds generally include spam, spyware, Phishing, scams, or internet banking fraud. Phishing is a part of fraud in which the attacker attempts to gather personal information that the attacker can use to intrude a system or account using deceptive emails and websites. The phishers spoof their email address, set up fake websites. That said, various techniques fall under the umbrella of Phishing ranging from spear phishing to whaling. In General, the phishing prevention camp tries to get the victim to do hand over sensitive information or Download Malware. A company named Ironscales has documented the most popular brands that the attackers use in their phishing attack attempts [2]. Out of the fifty thousand plus fake login spoofing pages the company calculated, the top brand' s attackers used were: PayPal: 22%, eBay: 6%, Amazon: 3%, Microsoft: 19%, Facebook: 15%.

Therefore, these issues have raised the requirement for cybersecurity efforts to secure the websites and enhance the security of the end-user [3]. To develop a secured system and keep the devices safer, Google created an online service called Google's Safe Browsing. It helps protect over four billion devices daily by warning users to navigate dangerous sites or download harmful files. This works in a way such that when it recognizes unsafe and malicious URLs using a ML approach, it displays warnings in web browsers [4]. As explained above, Google Safe Browsing uses ML algorithms to classify malicious and suspicious URL addresses. In this work, several machine and deep learning approaches are study and compared, the model with high accuracy is selected and used to classify and detect phishing URLs.

6.2   Related Work

After various deep research and studies, there were several related techniques that were used in classifying and detecting suspicious URLs. There are several challenges and problems remain open questions. In the first place, the main problem is the massive volume of URLs in the world.

Over 1.7 billion websites exist, but this number fluctuates every day as websites are being launched or lost. Handling many URLs is challenging on a more extensive run [5]. In the second place, extracting appropriate URLs features is also a principal task to perform. Vrbančič *et al.* [6] in their study classified the importance of Lexical features such as URL address, domain properties, file properties, and the count of special characters such as percentage, star, etc. are widely used to identify malicious URLs. The researchers have developed an algorithm which segregates the URLs based on the lexical features. Deshpande *et al.* [7] in their work have worked on a focused literature survey and have developed several supervised machine learning methods for four different attack scenarios: Spam, Defacement, Malware, Phishing. However, the detection rate for phishing attack is moderate compared to optimistic deep learning methods. Saxe *et al.* [8] have described a focused literature study from a security perspective for phishing on developing a CNN with several lexical embeddings websites detection. Choosing the appropriate lexical features is very important to improve the detection performance of the constructed ML classifiers. Sven *et al.* [9] have presented a Gradient Boosting model which has been adapted to include prediction cost penalties. The main feature of the model created is its ability to construct deeps trees which can be evaluated with cheap cost.

6.3   Proposed Model

Figure 6.1 depicts the block diagram of the presented model involving its subprocesses. Initially, the URLs are passed through the URL Feature Extractor in order to extra the features and create a dataset which has been explained in Section 6.1; 111 features are extracted through the URL Feature Extractor and the dataset created is then passed to one of the seven classifier models developed elaborated in Sections 6.2 and 6.3 respectively. The results of the models are then compared to obtain the best model. On comparison it was found that the Gradient Boosting Classifier or the Random Forest Classifier can be used to classify the URL with high accuracy.

6.3.1   URL Feature Extractor

Every URL has substrings, which contains the characteristics of the URL as mentioned in Figure 6.2. Therefore, the URL strings need to be encoded into numerical vectors.

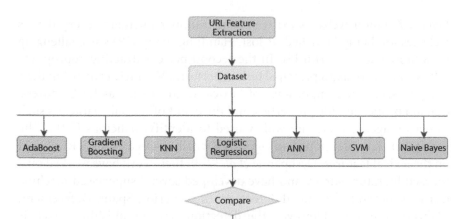

Figure 6.1 Proposed methodology.

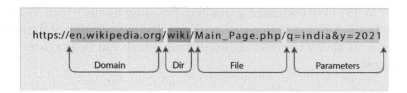

Figure 6.2 URL substrings visualization.

To automate the feature extraction process, a model was developed using a python script. The generated feature extraction model has been explained in Figure 6.3.

The attributes of the URLs are classified into six divisions based on substrings as the complete URL, Domain, Directory, URL properties, Parameter, and external services.

The first division is depended on the features on the complete URL explained in Table 6.1. The following divisions: Domain, Directory, File, parametric and external properties of the URLs have been elaborated in Tables 6.2, 6.3, 6.4, 6.5, 6.6, respectively.

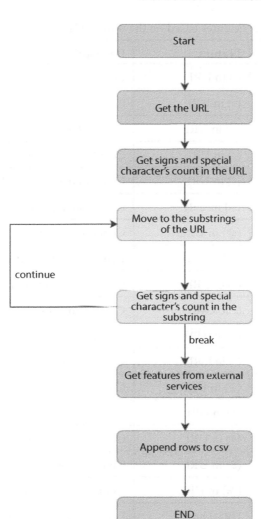

Figure 6.3 Flowchart of the extraction process.

Table 6.1 Features based on the whole URL.

S. no.	Feature	Description
1	(.) in URL	Count of dots
2	(-) in URL	Count of hyphens
3	(_) in URL	Count of underscores
4	(/) in URL	Count of backslashes
5	(?) in URL	Count of question marks
6	(=) in URL	Count of equal-to symbols
7	(@) in URL	Count of at-signs
8	(&) in URL	Count of ampersand signs
9	(!) in URL	Count of exclamation marks
10	() in URL	Count of blanks
11	(~) in URL	Count of tildes
12	(,) in URL	Count of commas
13	(+) in URL	Count of plus signs
14	(*) in URL	Count of asterisks
15	(#) in URL	Count of hashtag signs
16	($) in URL	Count of dollar signs
17	(%) in URL	Count of percent signs
18	URL Length	Length of the full URL
19	TLD Amount	Count of Top-Level Domains in URL

Table 6.2 Features based on domain properties.

S. no.	Feature	Description
1	(.) in Domain	Count of dots
2	(-) in Domain	Count of hyphens
3	(_) in Domain	Count of underscores
4	(/) in Domain	Count of backslashes
5	(?) in Domain	Count of question marks
6	(=) in Domain	Count of equal-to symbols
7	(@) in Domain	Count of at-signs
8	(&) in Domain	Count of ampersand signs
9	(!) in Domain	Count of exclamation marks
10	() in Domain	Count of blanks
11	(~) in Domain	Count of tildes
12	(,) in Domain	Count of commas
13	(+) in Domain	Count of plus signs
14	(*) in Domain	Count of asterisks
15	(#) in Domain	Count of hashtag signs
16	($) in Domain	Count of dollar signs
17	(%) in Domain	Count of percent signs
18	Domain Length	Length of the full Domain
19	Vowel in Domain	Count of Vowels
20	URL Domain in IP form	The IP address of URL
21	Domain client/ server	To check if the Domain has the server

Table 6.3 Features based on directory properties.

S. no.	Feature	Description
1	(.) in Directory	Count of dots
2	(-) in Directory	Count of hyphens
3	(_) in Directory	Count of underscores
4	(/) in Directory	Count of backslashes
5	(?) in Directory	Count of question marks
6	(=) in Directory	Count of equal-to symbols
7	(@) in Directory	Count of at-signs
8	(&) in Directory	Count of ampersand signs
9	(!) in Directory	Count of exclamation marks
10	() in Directory	Count of blanks
11	(~) in Directory	Count of tildes
12	(,) in Directory	Count of commas
13	(+) in Directory	Count of plus signs
14	(*) in Directory	Count of asterisks
15	(#) in Directory	Count of hashtag signs
16	($) in Directory	Count of dollar signs
17	(%) in Directory	Count of percent signs
18	Directory Length	Length of the full Directory

Table 6.4 File features based on file properties.

S. no.	Feature	Description
1	(.) in File	Count of dots in the File
2	(-) in File	Count of hyphens in the File
3	(_) in File	Count of underscores in File
4	(/) in File	Count of backslashes in File
5	(?) in File	Count of question marks in File
6	(=) in File	Count of equal-to symbols in File
7	(@) in File	Count of at-signs in File
8	(&) in File	Count of ampersand signs in File
9	(!) in File	Count of exclamation marks in File
10	() in File	Count of blanks in the File
11	(~) in File	Count of tildes in the File
12	(,) in File	Count of commas in the File
13	(+) in File	Count of plus signs in the File
14	(*) in File	Count of asterisks in the File
15	(#) in File	Count of hashtag signs in the File
16	($) in File	Count of dollar signs in the File
17	(%) in File	Count of percent signs in the File
18	File Length	Length of the full File

Table 6.5 Parameter features based on parameter properties.

S. no.	Feature	Description
1	(.) in Parameter	Count of dots in the Parameter
2	(-) in Parameter	Count of hyphens in the Parameter
3	(_) in Parameter	Count of underscores in Parameter
4	(/) in Parameter	Count of backslashes in Parameter
5	(?) in Parameter	Count of question marks in Parameter
6	(=) in Parameter	Count of equal-to symbols in Parameter
7	(@) in Parameter	Count of at-signs in Parameter
8	(&) in Parameter	Count of ampersand signs in Parameter
9	(!) in Parameter	Count of exclamation marks in Parameter
10	() in Parameter	Count of blanks in the Parameter
11	(~) in Parameter	Count of tildes in the Parameter
12	(,) in Parameter	Count of commas in the Parameter
13	(+) in Parameter	Count of plus signs in the Parameter
14	(*) in Parameter	Count of asterisks in the Parameter
15	(#) in Parameter	Count of hashtag signs in the Parameter
16	($) in Parameter	Count of dollar signs in the Parameter
17	(%) in Parameter	Count of percent signs in the Parameter
18	Parameter Length	Length of the full Parameter
19	TLD Presence in Args	To check the presence of Top-Level Domain in the arguments
20	Count Parameters	Counting the number of parameters
21	Email Presence in URL	Checking for presence of email in URL
22	File Extension	Checking for File Extensions in URL

Table 6.6 Attributes based on external services.

S. no.	Feature	Description
1	Response Time	Domain lookup time response
2	SPF Domain	Domain has SPF
3	ASN IP	ASN
4	Time domain activation	Activation time of the Domain
5	Time domain expiration	Expiration time of the Domain
6	Resolved IPs	Count of resolved IPs
7	Name servers	Count of resolved NS
8	MX servers	Count of MX servers
9	TTL Hostname	Time-To-Live (TTL)
10	TTL SSL Certificate	Has valid TLS/SSL certificate
11	Redirects	Number of redirects
12	Google Index	Is URL indexed on Google
13	Domain Google Index	Is Domain indexed on Google
14	URL Shortened	Is URL shortened
15	Phishing	Is phishing website

Visually for the Figure 6.4. We can see that benign URLs have higher entropy and are generally lengthier than the malicious URLs. Also, we can see that benign have at least one periods in them, whereas the malicious URLs have two periods.

6.3.2 Dataset

The dataset consists of 88647 URLs, out of which 58000 are legitimate URLs while 30647 are Phishing URLs. The dataset consists of 111 columns based on the extraction done by URL Feature Extractor. The visualizations of the count of Phishing and legitimate URLs are shown in Figure 6.5, where 0 indicates the count of legitimate URLs and 1 shows the count of Phishing URLs. The URLs are extracted from PhishTank Website [10].

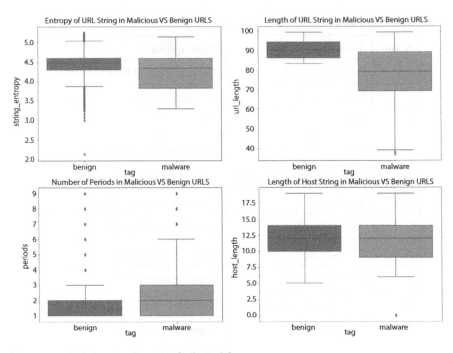

Figure 6.4 Boxplot visualizations for lexical features.

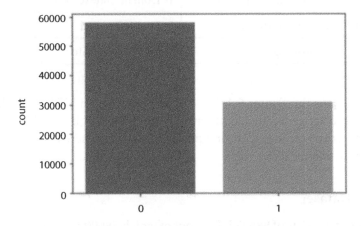

Figure 6.5 Visualization for the count of URLs.

6.3.3   Methodologies

The Machine Learning algorithms used here are Supervised Learning algorithms. Classification Algorithms are the main highlights of our research.

The phishing problem can be described as a classification problem if we create or use a dataset containing both Phishing as well as Legitimate URLs to train the classification model. A classification algorithm is a function that analyses (weighs) the input features to separate the output into different classes. In our scenario, we have to determine whether the given URL is malicious or legitimate. This is a binary classification problem. The classification algorithm divides the output into two classes, one positive class (i.e.: Indicates Phishing) and one negative class (i.e.: Indicates Legitimacy).

In the following subsections, we have briefly explained regarding the machine and deep learning algorithms used in the research.

6.3.3.1   AdaBoost Classifier

The AdaBoost Classifier is an ensemble boosting technique that behaves as an iterative ensemble method. It was developed by Robert Shapire to generate a strong classifier from a set of weak classifiers [11]. These classifiers combine several poorly performing classifiers to build a strong classifier that produces a good accuracy. AdaBoost sets the weights of classifiers and the training data sample in each iteration to ensure the prediction of extreme observations. AdaBoost however, is extremely sensitive to noisy data and hence the dataset used must be cleaned and pre-processed thoroughly to ensure proper working of the model.

6.3.3.2   Gradient Boosting Classifier

The Gradient Boosting Classifier [12] is a powerful ensemble technique that uses Decision Trees. This classifier combines several weak learners to create a strong learner which produces good accuracy. This model is very popular among large and complex classification datasets. XGBoost and LightBoost are versions of this classifier. Gradient Boosting is a generalization of AdaBoost. Gradient Boosting models are basically AdaBoost models with weighted minimization.

Gradient Boosting can cause overfitting by overemphasizing outliers. These models are expensive computationally and require more than 1000 decision trees which can utilize a lot of memory and time.

6.3.3.3   K-Nearest Neighbors

The KNN algorithm [13] is a very simple classification algorithm based on Supervised Learning. These algorithms assume the similarities between the new input data and the previously trained data and put the new data into a very similar category to the trained categories available. The algorithm trains on the available data and classifies the new input based on its similarity to the trained data. This algorithm does not make any assumptions based on underlying data and hence is non-parametric in nature.

The KNN algorithm is often called a lazy learner as it stores the training data rather than learning from it, and hence at the time of classification, it performs the action on the training dataset. The accuracy of the KNN algorithm is completely dependent on the quality of data, and if the dataset is large, the prediction of new data will be slow.

6.3.3.4   *Logistic Regression*

The Logistic Regression algorithm is one of the most widely used algorithms for predicting binary data (0/1). It has its odds in a two-level outcome of interest [14]. This model performs well if the relationship in data is linear. The Logistics Regression algorithm studies the relationship of input data and tries to learn a linear relationship between the dependent and independent variables. Non-Linearity is introduced through the form of a sigmoid activation function.

This model finds it difficult to learn complex relationships in data. Only features that are linearly related are used in this model to achieve a decent accuracy. This algorithm and datasets cannot solve Non-linear problems with high dimensionality may lead to over-fitting on the training dataset. The theory behind logistic regression algorithm limits the cost function between 0 and 1 as shown in Equation 6.1.

$$0 \leq h_\theta (x) \leq 1 \tag{6.1}$$

6.3.3.5   *Artificial Neural Networks*

Neural Networks are biologically inspired computational networks that use several processing elements to receive inputs and produce the output depending on the activation functions used by the processing elements. These networks consist of several linked units known as neurons. These linkages send signals between neurons. These signals are weighted data signals, and the weights are determined based on the training dataset. These weights keep getting updates as the Neural Network is trained. Artificial Neural Networks [15] have been generalized as mathematical models of the human nervous system.

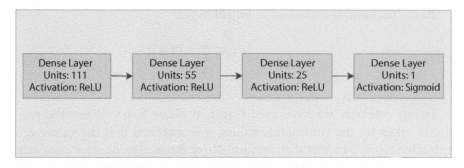

Figure 6.6 Proposed artificial neural network model.

The neural network given in Figure 6.6 contains an input layer, 2 hidden layers, and an output layer. The linkages in the shared neural network do not loopback, and hence the network is called a feed-forward network. The sigmoid activation function is used to introduce non-linearity in the network for it to understand complex mappings.

Neural Networks require high processing power and hence require processors with parallel processing capability. The main disadvantage of using Neural Networks is that there is no explanation for the output produced by the network.

6.3.3.6   Support Vector Machines (SVM)

SVM are the classifiers that are used for two-group classification problems. This algorithm tries to find a desirable hyperplane which separates the two classes. The desirable hyperplane is achieved by maximizing the margin between support vectors (i.e., closest point of each class to the hyperplane). Support Vector Machines have shown more incredible speeds and better performance with limited samples compared to other algorithms. Libraries like LIBSVM [16] tend to help users use the SVM in their applications. The main disadvantage of SVM is that it is not suitable for large datasets. It does not perform well when there is a large amount of noise in the dataset.

6.3.3.7   Naïve Bayes Classifier

The Naïve Bayes is a probabilistic classifier that uses Bayes theorem to classify data. Bayes theorem is applied based on strong independent assumptions between the features.

Bayes Theorem is explained in Equation 6.2:

$$P(A \mid B) = \frac{(P(A \mid B) * P(A))}{P(B)} \tag{6.2}$$

In our research, we have used Gaussian Naïve Bayes. When the predictor takes up the continuous values, it is assumed that the values are extracted from Gaussian distribution. Naïve Bayes algorithms are majorly used for projects involving Sentiment Analysis and Recommendation systems. Naïve Bayes [17–19] models may classify the label correctly even if the probabilistic estimates are inaccurate.

Though the Naïve Bayes model can be used for various classification problems, its main limitation is that it produces a 0 probability to a test input if its category is different from the categories present while training the model.

Table 6.7 Comparative result analysis.

Methods	Accuracy	Precision	Recall	F1 score
Proposed Methods				
AdaBoost	95	95	95	95
Gradient Boosting	97	97	97	97
KNN	95	95	95	95
Logistic Regression	93	93	93	93
ANN	96	96	96	96
Random Forest	97	97	97	97
SVM	94	94	94	94
Naïve Bayes	78	80	78	75
Existing Methods				
QDA [5]	78	77	84	76
GNB [5]	77	77	83	76
Random Forest [6]	96	-	-	-

6.4   Results

Table 6.7 implies the analysis of the comparative results of the proposed method with previous approaches through various metrics. The experimental outcome means that the proposed model Gradient Boosting and Random forest has shown a testing Accuracy, Precision, Recall, F1-score of 97 each which significantly outperformed other existing models.

6.5   Conclusions

In this study, we explored several Machine learning models and one deep learning model to predict whether a URL is Phishing or legitimate. The Machine Learning models investigated were AdaBoost Classifier, Gradient Boosting Classifier, K-Nearest Neighbors Classifier, Logistic Regression, SVM, Random Forests, and Naïve Bayes Classifier. An Artificial Neural Network was also created to classify the URLs from the dataset. We created a URL feature extractor to extract the features which determined the legitimacy of a URL. In the future, we would like to develop a fully scalable phishing detection service that can detect phishing URLs based on previous learning with high accuracy.

References

1. Hahn, H. and Stout, R., *The Internet Complete Reference*, McGraw-Hill, Inc., USA, 1994.
2. Roddas, B., 50,000–plus fake login pages spoofing over 200 brands worldwide, August 24, 2020. IronScales(blog)/fake-login-pages-spoof-prominent- brands-phishing-attacks/.
3. Alqurashi, R.K., AlZain, M.A., Soh, B., Masud, M., Al-Amri, J., Cyber attacks and impacts: A case study in Saudi Arabia. *IJATCSE*, 9, 1, 217–224, 2020.
4. Source Wikipedia, *Google Services: Google Chrome, Youtube, Google Maps, Gmail, Google Books, Google Street View, List of Google Products, Orkut, Chromium, Gmail Interface*, General Books, Canada, 2013.
5. Moghimi, M. and Varjani, A.Y., New rule-based phishing detection method. *Expert Syst. Appl.*, 53, 231–242, 2016. https://doi.org/10.1016/j.eswa.2016.01.028.
6. Vrbančič, G., Fister, I., Podgorelec, V., Datasets for phishing websites detection. *Data Brief*, 33, 106438, 2020. https://doi.org/10.1016/j.dib.2020.106438.

7. Deshpande, A., Pedamkar, O., Chaudhary, N., Borde, S., Detection of phishing websites using machine learning. *Int. J. Eng. Res. Technol. (IJERT)*, 10, 05, May 2021.

8. Saxe, J. and Berlin, K., eXpose: A character-level convolutional neural network with embeddings for detecting malicious URLs, file paths and registry keys, 2017, *arXiv*. https://doi.org/10.48550/arXiv.1702.08568.

9. Peter, S. *et al.*, Cost efficient gradient boosting, in: *Advances in Neural Information Processing Systems*, vol. 30, 2017.

10. PhishTank.org, Join the fight against phishing. http://www.phishtank.org/.

11. Rojas, R., *AdaBoost and the Super Bowl of Classifiers A Tutorial Introduction to Adaptive Boosting*, Technical Report, Freie University, Berlin, 2009.

12. Mishra, S., Mishra, D., Satapathy, S.K., Fuzzy frequent pattern mining from gene expression data using dynamic multi-swarm particle swarm optimization. 2nd International Conference on Computer, Communication, Control and Information Technology (C3IT 2012), *Proc. Technol.*, 4, 797–801, 2012.

13. Satapathy, S.K., Dehuri, S., Jagadev, A.K., Mishra, S., *EEG Brain Signal Classification for Epileptic Seizure Disorder Detection*, 1st Ed., Elsevier, USA, Feb. 2019.

14. Alshira'H, M. and Al-Fawa'reh, M., Detecting phishing URLs using machine learning & lexical feature-based analysis. *IJATCSE*, 9, 5828–5837, 2020.

15. Abraham, A., Artificial neural networks, in: *Handbook of Measuring System Design*, vol. 2, 2005.

16. Chang, C.C. and Lin, C.J., LIBSVM: A library for support vector machines. *ACM Trans. Intell. Syst. Technol.*, 2, 3, 1–27, 2011.

17. Rish, I., An empirical study of the naive Bayes classifier. *IJCAI 2001 Workshop on Empirical Methods in Artificial Intelligence*, vol. 3, 2001.

18. Satapathy, S.K., Dehuri, S., Jagadev, A.K., An empirical analysis of different machine learning techniques for classification of EEG signal to detect epileptic seizure. *Int. J. Appl. Eng. Res.*, 11, 1, 120–129, 2016.

19. Satapathy, S.K., Jagadev, A.K., Dehuri, S., An empirical analysis of training algorithms of neural networks: A case study of EEG signal classification using java framework, in: *Advances in Intelligent Systems and Computing*, vol. 309, L.C. Jain (Eds.), pp. 151–160, Springer, USA, 2015.

7

Detection of Malicious Emails and URLs Using Text Mining

Heetakshi Fating, Aditya Narawade, Sandeep Kumar Satapathy
and Shruti Mishra*

*School of Computer Science and Engineering, Vellore Institute of Technology,
Chennai, Chennai, Tamil Nadu, India*

Abstract

This work aims to create a combined model of two models, to first process whether an email is malicious or not, after which, a non-malicious email is further analyzed to check whether it contains a malicious URL. Features are created for one of the models after which the information gain feature selection technique is used, while the method of tokenization is used for the email model. For the combined model, a new dataset containing only non-malicious emails which contained a mix of good and bad URLs was created and features were created in a similar manner to the URL dataset's model to determine whether the flagged non-malicious emails were entirely non-malicious or whether they did contain a malicious URL of any sort. For the malicious URL detection alone, the best accuracy of 80.7% was achieved by the Random Forest algorithm while an accuracy of 98.9% was achieved for the email dataset using the Random Forest algorithm as well. For the final combined model, the Support Vector Machine and Logistic Regression algorithms gave the better accuracies among others of 81.88% and 81.49% respectively.

Keywords: Malicious emails, malicious URLs, machine learning, feature creation, feature selection

Corresponding author: shrutim2129@gmail.com

Sachi Nandan Mohanty, Rajanikanth Aluvalu and Sarita Mohanty (eds.) Evolution and Applications of Quantum Computing, (111–124) © 2023 Scrivener Publishing LLC

7.1   Introduction

A major and growing threat in the recent years is phishing. 2021 Tessian research found that workers did receive close to 14 malicious emails every year. CISCO's 2021 Cybersecurity threat trends report also suggested that at least one person would click on a phishing link in approximately 86% of organizations. Phishing is said to account for close to 90% of data breaches that occur in companies according to their data of which a significant 96% arrive by email, while nearly 3% are executed with the use of malicious websites and just 1% via phone [1]. All the mentioned statistics make a very strong case for the development of a system which is successfully able to detect the presence of such emails and URLs before they reach people within an organization, as it is quite difficult for humans to accurately differentiate between genuine and fake emails accurately each time. Hence, we have tried to create such a model which is not only effective against emails and URLs independently, but also against a combination of both.

The goal is to create a combined model consisting of models used for detection of malicious emails and URLs to be used on a dataset in which URLs are a part of the message body of the email. This would minimize, if not prevent the execution of these types of phishing attacks. This model can also serve as a basis for the detection of drive-by download URLs, which are generally sent to the target through an email.

7.2   Related Works

Typically, malicious URLs are identified by comparing them against blacklists. However, blacklists are never exhaustive and hence, this chapter discusses a machine learning ensemble-based approach with NLP and data mining, which makes use of lexical features extracted from the URL string. An NLP package is used to obtain lexical features, after which algorithms such as Random Forest, Decision Tree, Support Vector Machine, Naive Bayes, and Logistic Regression were used. Classifiers such as Adaboost and Gradient Boost were also used [1]. This chapter used a dataset that contained close to 2.4 million URLs and the approach of a binary classification problem was used. The algorithms used in this chapter are Naive

Bayes, Support Vector Machine, Multi-Layer Perceptron, Decision Tree, Random Forest, and K-Nearest Neighbors. Feature selection techniques were not used, and the Random Forest and Multi-Layer Perceptron gave the highest accuracies [2]. In this chapter, detection of malicious URLs is done by using the Adaboost algorithm together with Decision Trees [3]. This chapter also discusses the use of machine learning techniques for the detection of malicious URLs. It uses a balanced dataset and the Support Vector Machine, Confidence Weighted Algorithm, Perceptron, Logistic Regression and the Passive Aggressive algorithm [4]. This chapter discusses detecting malicious URLs inside an email. It uses a method of reduced feature set. Analysis of URLs can be based on both lexical and host based features. Lexical features focus on analysis of the format of the URL while the host-based features mainly analyses the owner and identifies the location. The count of sensitive words present in the URL was also taken into consideration.

The Bayes Classifier was used [5]. In this chapter, classification methods to detect new malicious emails were discussed. The classification methods identified unusual disruptive behaviors in the data set and used the same for detection of new malicious email viruses. Improvisation of the detection accuracy was attempted by using the prototype of the bagged classifier in the implementation of the system [6]. In this chapter, machine learning models were to be trained to analyze the common file format of the email attachments. A dataset of over 5 million malicious MS office documents was created and classifiers were used on it after feature extraction. Deep neural networks and gradient boosted decision trees were also used [7]. This chapter targeted at improvisation of detection of malicious with the use of feature selection. Accuracy and training time were improved with the use of feature selection. Comparison of the various classifiers used was also depicted [8]. In this chapter, the system proposed has a new set of URLs features and behaviors, a machine learning algorithm, and big data technology. Results made it evident that the UEL attributes that had been proposed could boost detection by a significant amount [9]. In this chapter, the various features of a URL are looked into and a detection model is trained on an existing dataset. A model making use of three supervised machine learning classifiers, namely support vector machine, logistic regression and Naive Bayes was proposed for effective and accurate detection purposes [10].

In this chapter the main objective of the authors is to classify phishing emails. Also the lexical analysis has been performed on the URLs which are present in the body of the email [11]. This chapter focuses on the detection of malicious URLs on the web through the use of machine learning classification techniques, which is achieved by the analysis of lexical and host based features of the URL [12]. In this chapter, the use of machine learning was proposed to identify whether or not the users are malicious based on data about URLs. A Logistic Regression model was implemented for the detection of malicious URLs. The dataset used was a collection from well-known sources such as PhishTank, Kaggle.com, and Github.com [13]. The goal of this research paper is to obtain a list of significant features which potentially play a part in detection of malicious URLs. The more significant lexical features from the various datasets were selected with the help of feature selection techniques such as the Chi-Square and ANOVA F-value. Along with which the authors also use a voting classifier which is a combination of multiple machine learning algorithms on the previously selected features [14–17].

7.3   Dataset Description

a. **URL Dataset**
   The URL dataset consists of 420464 URLs and labels indicating whether they are good or bad. Of the 420464 URLs, 344821 were good URLs and 75643 URLs were bad.

b. **Email Dataset**
   The email dataset consists of 2893 subjects, messages, and labels 1 and 0 indicate whether they are spam mail or not. Of the 2893 emails, 2412 are not spam mails and 481 are spam mails.

c. **Combined Dataset**
   A new dataset was formed of only the non-malicious emails to check whether they contained a malicious URL. There were a total of 3364 entries.

7.4   Proposed Architecture

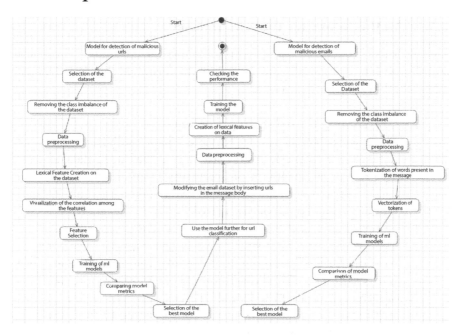

Two models started being trained simultaneously which were the models used for detection of malicious emails as well as the detection of malicious URLs. For the detection of malicious emails, vectorization was used. For the detection of malicious URLs, features analyzing the URL were created and new columns were created for the same, after which the information gain feature selection technique was used to calculate and reveal which features played a more signification role in the accuracy of results. To achieve the final goal, which was to first detect whether an email was malicious or not, and if it was found to be non-malicious, it was to be checked for whether it contained a malicious URL. For this, a modified dataset containing only non-malicious emails [18] was used, and the email message column was concatenated with the URL dataset and the labels from the URL dataset were used to indicate whether the email contained a malicious URL or not. Features were then created in a similar manner to those that were created for the URL model alone and machine learning algorithms were then applied on the same.

7.5   Methodology

7.5.1   Methodology for the URL Dataset

The URLs were tokenized using text mining methods to analyze the lexical features, which is essentially the analysis of the format of the URL to determine whether it is malicious or not.

i. Overcoming the overfitting problem
There were 344821 good URLs and 75643 bad URLs in the dataset, which made it an extremely unbalanced dataset. To prevent the problem of overfitting from arising in the future, a fraction of the good URLs were taken into consideration instead of all of them. To do so, first, the labels were encoded as 1 and 0 for good and bad URLs respectively. Then, the URLs were split into two separate data frames, to allow for a fraction of 0.23 to be taken of the total good URLs samples. This allowed for a fairer 79309 good URLs and the unchanged 75643 bad URLs as shown in Figure 7.1 and these two data frames were concatenated to form the final dataset of 154952 entries.

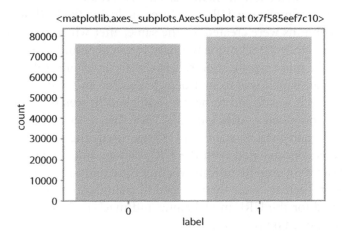

Figure 7.1 Balanced URL dataset.

ii. Creation of features

A total of 12 new features were created by analyzing the URLs, which included the following features as shown below in Figure 7.2.

```
RangeIndex: 154952 entries, 0 to 154951
Data columns (total 14 columns):
 #   Column           Non-Null Count    Dtype
---  ------           --------------    -----
 0   url              154952 non-null   object
 1   label            154952 non-null   object
 2   url_length       154952 non-null   int64
 3   no_of_digit      154952 non-null   int64
 4   params           154952 non-null   object
 5   param_count      154952 non-null   int64
 6   hostname_length  154952 non-null   int64
 7   path_length      154952 non-null   int64
 8   count-           154952 non-null   int64
 9   count@           154952 non-null   int64
 10  count?           154952 non-null   int64
 11  count.           154952 non-null   int64
 12  count=           154952 non-null   int64
 13  count/           154952 non-null   int64
dtypes: int64(11), object(3)
```

Figure 7.2 Final columns of URL dataset.

As seen in Figure 7.2, the features 'count' indicates the number of '-','@' and all the following special characters.

iii. Applying Feature Selection Techniques

The feature selection technique used was Information Gain. This feature selection technique was applied in an attempt to enhance the results by selecting the more relevant features that had a significant effect on the results. In information gain, the reduction in entropy is measured by splitting the dataset according to a given value of a random variable. A larger information gain suggests lower entropy which suggests less surprise.

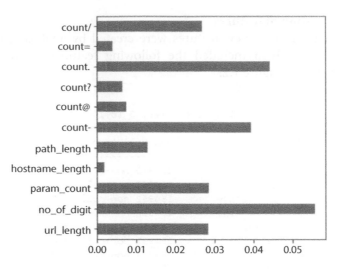

Figure 7.3 Information gain.

Based on the calculation of information gain, a graph was generated as shown in Figure 7.3 and it was observed that the 'count=', 'count?', 'count@' and 'hostname_length' features had a comparatively lower information gain and were hence not taken into consideration.

iv. **Applying Machine Learning Algorithms**
The machine learning modes used included Naive Bayes, Random Forest Classifier [17–20], Multi-Layer Perceptron and Logistic Regression, and the results for the same have been discussed in the next section.

7.5.2   Methodology for the Email Dataset

The email messages were tokenized using stopwords, after which the CountVectorizer was used to transform the tokenized text into vector form on the basis of the frequency of words occurring throughout the message.

7.5.2.1   *Overcoming the Overfitting Problem*

Of the 2893 emails, 2412 are not spam mails and 481 are spam mails which were also unbalanced. Hence, only a fraction of the 'not spam' emails were taken into consideration. The emails were split into two separate dataframes, to allow for a fraction of 0.2 to be taken of the larger sample set. This resulted in the existing 481 spam mails and newly selected 482 'not spam' emails as visible in Figure 7.4 which were then concatenated.

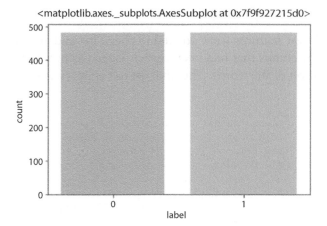

Figure 7.4 Balanced email dataset.

7.5.2.2   Tokenization

Firstly, the Natural Language Toolkit package was installed and 'stopwords' were downloaded from it. After which, a function was created for the purpose of tokenizing and cleaning the data. This resulted in printing of the tokens in an array format, separated by commas. The CountVectorizer was then used to transform the tokenized text into vector form on the basis of the frequency of words occurring throughout the message which was then used for the training of models.

7.5.2.3   Applying Machine Learning Algorithms

The machine learning algorithms applied included Naive Bayes, K-Nearest Neighbors, Decision Tree, and Random Forest.

7.5.3   Detecting Presence of Malicious URLs in Otherwise Non-Malicious Emails

A dataset containing 3364 entries was used which contained non-malicious emails and the aim was to detect whether these emails contained any malicious URLs in them.

7.5.3.1   Preparation of Dataset

The labels of the URL dataset were used and encoded into 1 and 0 for good and bad URLs respectively.

7.5.3.2   Creation of Features

A total of 7 new features were created to check for and analyze the URLs present in the emails that had been earlier flagged as non-malicious based on tokenization of the words. The final dataset appears as shown in Figure 7.5.

```
<class 'pandas.core.frame.DataFrame'>
RangeIndex: 3364 entries, 0 to 3363
Data columns (total 10 columns):
 #   Column       Non-Null Count  Dtype
---  ------       --------------  -----
 0   subject      2363 non-null   object
 1   label        3364 non-null   object
 2   final_email  3364 non-null   object
 3   count-       3364 non-null   int64
 4   count@       3364 non-null   int64
 5   count?       3364 non-null   int64
 6   count.       3364 non-null   int64
 7   count=       3364 non-null   int64
 8   count/       3364 non-null   int64
 9   param_count  3364 non-null   int64
dtypes: int64(7), object(3)
memory usage: 262.9+ KB
```

Figure 7.5 Final columns of dataset.

7.5.3.3   Applying Machine Learning Algorithms

The machine learning algorithms applied were Random Forest, Naive Bayes, Multi-Layer Perceptron, Logistic Regression, and Support Vector Machine.

7.6   Results

7.6.1   URL Dataset

It is evident that when paired with the information gain feature selection technique as shown in Table 7.1, the Random Forest Classifier gave the highest accuracy of 80.7% as compared to the other algorithms used.

Table 7.1 Accuracy obtained with information gain feature selection.

No.	Feature selection technique	Algorithm	Accuracy
1	Information Gain	Naive Bayes	62.7%
2		Random Forest Classifier	80.7%
3		Multi-Layer Perceptron	79.0%
4		Logistic Regression	64.6%

7.6.2   Email Dataset

For the email dataset alone, the Random Forest algorithm (as shown in Table 7.2) continued to give higher accuracy as compared to the other models.

Table 7.2 Accuracy obtained for the email dataset.

No.	Algorithm	Accuracy
1	Naive Bayes	97.4%
2	K-Nearest Neighbors	91.6%
3	Decision Tree	93.2%
4	Random Forest	98.9%

7.6.3   Final Dataset

It can be observed that the Support Vector Machine (as shown in Table 7.3) gave a higher accuracy of 81.88% for the final dataset.

Table 7.3 Accuracy obtained with final dataset.

No.	Algorithm	Accuracy
1	Random Forest	81.09%
2	Naive Bayes	78.81%
3	Multi-Layer Perceptron	81.00%
4	Logistic Regression	81.49%
5	Support Vector Machine	81.88%

7.7   Conclusion

Hence, it can be concluded that for the final dataset, the Support Vector Machine, and the Logistic Regression model both fared better among the other models with accuracies of 81.88% and 81.49% respectively. Meanwhile, the URL dataset and email dataset had a highest accuracy of 80.7% and 98.9% respectively, and both were achieved with the use of the Random Forest algorithm.

References

1. Joshi, A., Lloyd, L., Westin, P., Seethapathy, S., *Using Lexical Features For Malicious URL Detection–A Machine Learning Approach*, 2019, arXiv preprint arXiv:1910.06277.
2. Vanhoenshoven, F., Nápoles, G., Falcon, R., Vanhoof, K., Köppen, M., Detecting malicious URLs using machine learning techniques, in: *2016 IEEE Symposium Series on Computational Intelligence (SSCI)*, IEEE, pp. 1–8, December 2016.
3. Khan, F., Ahamed, J., Kadry, S., Ramasamy, L.K., Detecting malicious URLs using binary classification through AdaBoost algorithm. *Int. J. Electr. Comput. Eng.*, 10, 1, 2088–8708, 2020.
4. Ma, J., Saul, L.K., Savage, S., Voelker, G.M., Learning to detect malicious URLs. *ACM Trans. Intell. Syst. Technol.*, 2, 3, 1–24, 2011.
5. Ranganayakulu, D. and Chellappan, C., Detecting malicious URLs in e-mail– An implementation. *AASRI Proc.*, 4, 125–131, 2013.
6. Shih, D.-H., Chiang, H.-S., Yen, C.D., Classification methods in the detection of new malicious emails. *Inf. Sci.*, 172, 1–2, 241–261, 2005.
7. Rudd, E.M., Harang, R., Saxe, J., MEADE: Towards a malicious email attachment detection engine. *2018 IEEE International Symposium on Technologies for Homeland Security (HST)*, pp. 1–7, 2018.
8. Sah, U.K. and Parmar, N., An approach for malicious spam detection in email with comparison of different classifiers. *Int. Res. J. Eng. Technol. (IRJET)*, 4, 8, 2238–2242, Aug-2017.
9. Xuan, C.D. and Nguyen, H.D., Malicious URL detection based on machine learning, *Int J Adv Comput Sci Appl.*, 11, 1, 2020.
10. Wejinya, G. and Bhatia, S., Machine learning for malicious URL detection, in: *ICT Systems and Sustainability, Advances in Intelligent Systems and Computing*, vol. 1270, M. Tuba, S. Akashe, A. Joshi (Eds.), Springer, Singapore, 2021.
11. Khonji, M., Iraqi, Y., Jones, A., Lexical URL analysis for discriminating phishing and legitimate e-mail messages. *2011 International Conference for Internet Technology and Secured Transactions*, pp. 422–427, 2011.

12. Rupa, C., Srivastava, G., Bhattacharya, S., Reddy, P., Gadekallu, T.R., A machine learning driven threat intelligence system for malicious URL detection, in: *The 16th International Conference on Availability, Reliability and Security (ARES 2021)*, Association for Computing Machinery, New York, NY, USA, Article 154, pp. 1–7, 2021.

13. Chiramdasu, R., Srivastava, G., Bhattacharya, S., Reddy, P.K., Gadekallu, T.R., Malicious URL detection using logistic regression. *2021 IEEE International Conference on Omni-Layer Intelligent Systems (COINS)*, pp. 1–6, 2021.

14. Khan, H.M.J., Niyaz, Q., Devabhaktuni, V.K., Guo, S., Shaikh, U., Identifying generic features for malicious URL detection system. *2019 IEEE 10th Annual Ubiquitous Computing, Electronics & Mobile Communication Conference (UEMCON)*, pp. 0347–0352, 2019.

15. https://www.tessian.com/blog/phishing-statistics-2020/#:~:text=In%20 2021%20Tessian%20research%20found,receiving%20an%20average%20 of%2049.

16. Satapathy, S.K., Mishra, S., Mishra, D., Search technique using wildcards or truncation: A tolerance rough set clustering approach. *Int. J. Adv. Comput. Sci. Appl.*, 1, 4, 73–77, October 2010.

17. Satapathy, S.K., Dehuri, S., Jagadev, A.K., Mishra, S., *EEG Brain Signal Classification for Epileptic Seizure Disorder Detection*, 1st Eds., Elsevier Publication, Feb. 2019.

18. Satapathy, S.K., Dehuri, S., Jagadev, A.K., Weighted majority voting based ensemble of classifiers using different machine learning techniques for classification of EEG signal to detect epileptic seizure. *Informatica*, 41, 99–110, 2017.

19. Satapathy, S.K., Jagadev, A.K., Dehuri, S., An empirical analysis of training algorithms of neural networks: A case study of EEG signal classification using java framework, in: *Advances in Intelligent Systems and Computing*, vol. 309, L.C. Jain (Eds.), pp. 151–160, Springer, 2015.

20. Mishra, S., Mishra, D., Satapathy, S.K., Fuzzy frequent pattern mining from gene expression data using dynamic multi-swarm particle swarm optimization. *2nd International Conference on Computer, Communication, Control and Information Technology (C3IT 2012), Proc. Technol.*, 4, 797–801, Feb. 2012.

8

Quantum Data Traffic Analysis for Intrusion Detection System

Anshul Harish Khatri, Vaibhav Gadag, Simrat Singh,
Sandeep Kumar Satapathy and Shruti Mishra*

Vellore Institute of Technology, Chennai, Chennai, Tamil Nadu, India

Abstract

An IDS (Intrusion Detection System) is a device or software that inspects all network traffic and notifies the user or administrator if unauthorized attempts or access have occurred. Many assaults, on the other hand, make it censorious for security of networks since they permit you to observe and act against malicious traffic. These attacks primarily are dependent on various techniques pertaining to social engineering which the attackers can exploit to get user's data credentials and get access to target's network and active assets. Despite its potential and the fact that it is the focus of many academics, its applicability to real-world applications has been impeded by system complexity, since these systems require extensive testing, assessment, and tuning before deployment. The most idealistic way for testing and assessment is to run these systems on actually labeled network traces with a full and large set of intrusions and anomalous behaviors. The proposed approach detects such attacks by analyzing the transmitted packet properties, evaluating the models, and visualizing the output. A dataset of 1048575 rows and over 80 columns is used in this study. Several machine learning algorithms such as Random Forest (RF), Decision Tree (DT), Ada Boost Classifier (ADA), Ridge Classifier (Ridge), Logistic Regression (LR), SVM-Linear Kernel (SVM), Naive Bayes (NB), and Quadratic Discriminant Analysis (QDA), with the help of Auto ML were used in the model creation and testing. The results obtained indicate a reasonable accuracy rate. For each data file, when applied autoML generated the best-fit algorithm with unique metrics with accuracies as high as 99%. These saves were then used for the prediction and generation of an output CSV which was mapped onto various plots using the AutoViz library.

Corresponding author: shrutim2129@gmail.com

Sachi Nandan Mohanty, Rajanikanth Aluvalu and Sarita Mohanty (eds.) Evolution and Applications of Quantum Computing, (125–144) © 2023 Scrivener Publishing LLC

Keywords: AutoML, AutoViz, classification, IDS, visualization, business intelligence, supervised learning

8.1   Introduction

Businesses of all sizes have profited tremendously from the usage of the Internet and technological resources as a result of the broad use of technology. Virtual security risks, on the other hand, are becoming more prevalent, and an intrusion detection system (IDS) may assist guard against external attacks while also providing network security. An intrusion detection system monitors network traffic and notifies the network administrator if anything out of the ordinary occurs. For example, if a hacker tries to break into your computer or network, the intrusion detection system will quickly inform the network administrator of the attempted security breach. Once the suspicious activities have been detected, the manager can locate the specific area and follow the required safety procedures.

As corporations move to dispersed settings, the security landscape becomes more complex, and hackers are increasingly targeting employee's computers. In this scenario, the need for an intrusion detection system, or IDS, in securing endpoint devices and business networks against high-end assaults becomes more vital than ever since it can protect against all types of malware and internet viruses in addition to hackers. It is designed to monitor network traffic and send out automated alerts when abnormal activity is detected. To identify threats, most IDS systems use a combination of a signature-based and an anomaly based approach. The former one takes the traffic packets and compare it to a known database of assaults or attack techniques, while the later one, just assess the suspicious action or activity that is either unexpected or not following the basic protocols. In comparison to host-based intrusion detection system (HIDS), its counterpart, Network Intrusion Detection System (NIDS) analyzes data transmitting between various systems on a single network. It also looks over and gives a brief insight into incoming as well as outgoing organization's network packets. When suspicious behavior or recognized dangers are found, the network IDS analyses network traffic and sends out notifications.

As network characteristic and patterns modify and intrusions continue to develop, it has become increasingly important to shred from constant, one-time datasets and toward more real-time dynamic generated datasets that not only reflect the traffic intrusions at the current time, but are also alterable, expandable, and repeatable. This study is not only based on creating models on one such group of datasets and applying several

ML algorithms to get the best fit, but also on visualizing the correlation between different features sets and comparing them with the actual one.

8.2   Literature Overview

This part of our chapter pertains to the contemporary developments, work, and assessments done in the past few years, in the domain of network traffic analysis and intrusion detection systems. Our chapter stands apart from these in a way that we not only investigate the correlation between the two, and generate a model whose predictions can be visualized in a simple and interpretable approach. There are quite a many commendable works done in the recent past which we would light to highlight. The work presented in [1] by Thirimanne et al. focused on building an RT-IDS which can detect intrusions in real-time by monitoring inbound and outgoing network traffic. A deep neural network, (DNN) trained on the NSL-KDD dataset and an ML pipeline were used which can then be accessed via Rest API. In [2], Shahraki A et al. provides comprehensive evaluation regarding applications of Deep Learning (DL) in evaluating and monitoring of network's traffic (NTMA). These include giving some relevant background information for the analysis. They then discussed the similarities and differences between deep learning and NTMA, as well as some of the DL methods that have been proposed for NTMA implementations. Finally, they looked into some of the most pressing issues, hot themes, and promising research areas for deep learning applications in NTMA. The work in [3] presented by Qureshi AS et al. suggested an intrusion detection technique formed on the basis of deep SAE and self-taught learning. To extract critical features using this technique, unsupervised machine learning methods have already been proved out to be successful. The above talked about features from the NSL-KDD publicly available dataset were extracted by using a deep SAE model which had already been trained and tested on various tasks relating to regression aspect of ML. Although it is known that the data distribution of the source job differs from that of the target domain, the characteristic time-series nature of inputs and unexpected behavior connect the two domains. Finally, both the NSL-KDD publicly available dataset feature sets and the above extracted features were used to train the SAE. In an experiment performed earlier, they got the conclusions that an SAE model worked on with only original feature sets was more likely to cede to a SAE model which was trained on a mix of raw as well as extracted features and thus outperformed the former one. Sudeshna Chakraborty et al. in [4] provide a comprehensive assessment of several research papers that used single, hybrid, and ensemble classification techniques. The measurements, flaws, and datasets employed in the construction of IDS by the investigated publications were compared. There is also a suggestion for future study topics. Authors of [5], Muhammad Adnan Khan *et al.* presented an IDS, that initially develops the assessment of safety features that in turn lead to their upliftment before constructing an adaptive version of this, primarily concentrating only on the features relevant to it. This is based on a method named as deep extreme learning machine (DELM). The results of the experiments show that the proposed framework outperforms standard techniques. In reality, the proposed framework is useful not only for scientific study but also for practical use. Another work presented in [6] by Azidine Guezzaz *et al.* represented a viable NIDS using decision trees. For the enhancement of the quality of data and relevant training, network's data pretreatment and entropy decision feature extraction are performed; thereafter, a decision tree classifier is created for accurate intrusion detection. The suggested approach can produce reliable results, and in terms of accuracy (ACC), detection rate (DR), and false alarm rate (FAR), the unique technique outperforms existing models (FAR). Jiarui Man *et al.* In their paper [7] used deeper convolutional neural networks with residual blocks that are developed after the UNSW-NB15 data set is transformed into pictures to learn more key characteristics. Class imbalance issues in the training and to identify attacks in testing set are solved by, instead of incorporating cross-entropy loss functions, the modified focal loss function is employed. Also, to minimize overfitting chances and refine the model as a whole, batch normalization and global average pooling are utilized, giving a better set of metrics. In another work [8], Zeeshan Ahmad *et al.* categorized their article based on the prominent machine and deep learning approaches useful in developing network-based IDS (NIDS) systems. The benefits and drawbacks of the proposed solutions, output metrics, and dataset shortlisting as well as recent trends and breakthroughs in ML and DL based NIDS are also focused upon. They emphasized on multiple research difficulties and presented future enhancements in study of developing these NIDS by using the inadequacies of the existing approaches. Karin Eberhard in his paper [9] showed that there are many mixed impacts on various factors such as choice confidence but will increase the aptness of decision making in terms of quality as well as its fastness. The paper also offers in-depth insights and analysis on the basis of researches done, not only spanning to social disciplines but also information sciences, as well as suggestions for future management decision-making applications.

8.3   Methodology

Figure 8.1 depicts the block diagram of the presented model involving its subprocesses. Initially, the main dataset is splitted into different files and for each dataset AutoML is applied to figure out best performing ML [10–14] algorithm for each dataset. For each dataset, best performing ML algorithm is chosen and trained on it. The saved models are then uploaded to the drive. A new dataset (test) is then fed to these three models and each one generates an output classifying the attack. This approach of creating a custom algorithm would determine the class predicted by each trained machine learning model on test data and considers the majority predicted class as final predicted class. The unique approach eradicates the total dependency on a single model and in turn takes into account the predictions of all the three trained models, giving an edge by having higher performance metrics and precision in future attack predictions.

8.3.1   Autoviz

Autoviz in python language is an AutoviML maintained open-source toolkit. It takes data as input values and finds the basic structure and plots stunning visuals by determining the underlying structure and identifying impactful aspects. In our case, AutoViz seems to have an upper hand when it comes to visualizing outputs and feature sets than the traditional approach of using BI tools like Power BI, Tableau. In all these tools, the time to upload a CSV largely depends on its size. With our output file going as high as 300 MB, it's practically not viable to upload especially when you need the visualizations in a short time. Also in Tableau Public, there's a limit (1000000) on the number of rows a dataset should have. Given that, the number of rows in our case exceeds (104875), we can't use it unless we drop some of them. This makes us use the AutoViz library. It can find the most impactful columns and create meaningful visualizations ranging from scatter plot violin plots and heatmaps. You can also select particular variables to get the specific plots. Below are some of the plots. Figure 8.2 depicts the flowchart of how visualisations are made from the dataset using the Autoviz dataset. Figure 8.3 depicts the normed histogram distribution of the actual label vs. the predicted label distribution. The blue line represents the predicted distribution, while the other represents the actual class distribution for a specific set of data. Figure 8.4 depicts the percentage of distribution of classes, i.e., 1 [malicious] and 0 [benign], in a dataset.

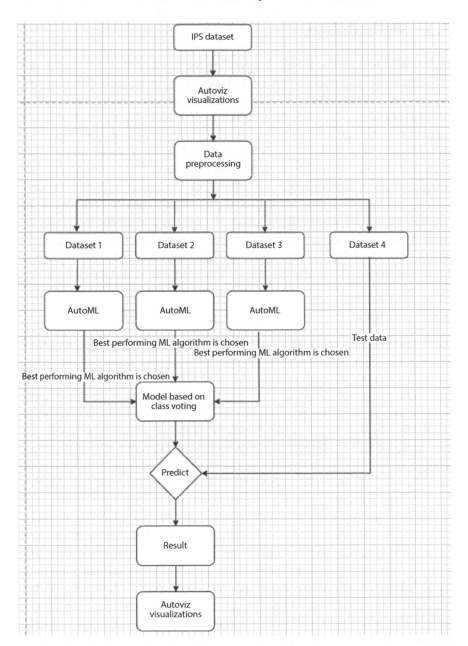

Figure 8.1 Proposed methodology.

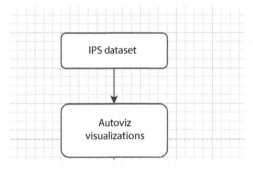

Figure 8.2 Flowchart for AutoViz.

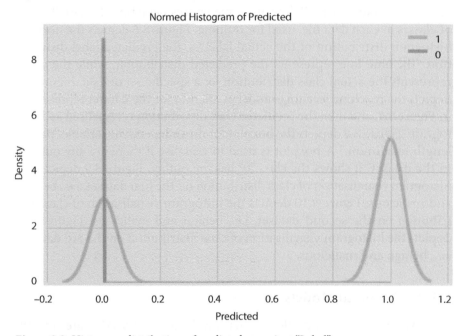

Figure 8.3 Histogram distribution of predicted as against "Label".

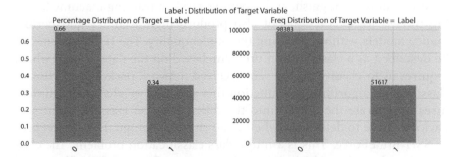

Figure 8.4 Percentage and frequency distribution of "Label".

8.3.2   Dataset

The dataset consists of 1048575 rows, out of which 667626 are Benign while 193360 are FTP-BruteForce type of attacks and the remaining 187589 are SSH-BruteForce. Briefly, there are eighty columns in total within this dataset, each of which pertains to an entry in the packet transmission. The most important columns within this dataset are Dst Port (i.e. Destination port), Protocol, Flow Duration, Tot Fwd Pkts (i.e. Total forward packets), Tot Bwd Pkts (i.e. Total backward packets) and Label (i.e. Label). The visualizations of the count of benign, FTP-BruteForce and SSH-BruteForce are shown in Figure 8.5, where the corresponding columns indicate the respective attack-types. Below are some figures depicting the distribution of classes in each data file, used for training. Figure 8.6 depicts the normed histogram distribution of the actual label vs. the predicted label distribution. The blue line represents the predicted distribution, while the other represents the actual class distribution for a specific set of data. Figure 8.7 depicts the machine learning model prediction for the dataset represented in Figure 8.4, and then the predicted class distribution is visualised as a histogram. Figure 8.8 depicts the boxplot for the independent variable "packet length maximum." A boxplot is used to visualise if there are any outliers in the dataset. It shows the class "0" has the outlier. Figure 8.9 depicts the histogram visualisation of class distribution on the first dataset, i.e., benign and malicious. Figure 8.10 depicts the histogram visualisation of class distribution on the second dataset, i.e., benign and malicious. Figure 8.11 depicts the histogram visualisation of class distribution on the 3rd dataset, i.e., benign and malicious.

8.3.3   Proposed Models

The Machine Learning algorithms involved in autoML are mostly Supervised Learning algorithms. By using autoML we not only reduce the time-consuming, sluggish, and repetitive tasks of training machine learning models for prediction but also produce high-accuracy and performance models without affecting the model quality. The IDS problem can be described as a classification problem, based on the dataset used which requires us to classify on the sent/received network packet properties. A classification algorithm is a function that analyses(weighs) the input features to separate the output into the different target classes. In our scenario, we have to determine whether an attack is Benign, FTP-BruteForce or SSH-BruteForce. This is a multi-class classification problem. The classification algorithm which the autoML suggests for each CSV file is used

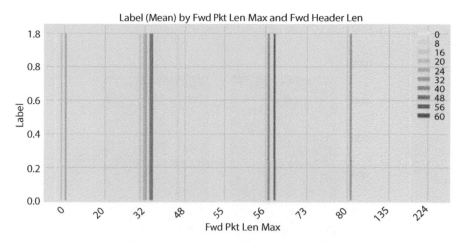

Figure 8.5 Pivot table by forward packet length and forward header length for "Label".

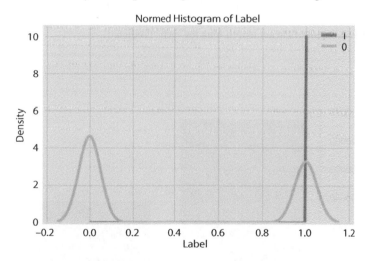

Figure 8.6 Histogram distribution of Label as against "Predicted".

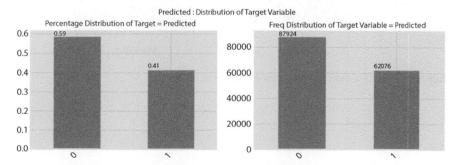

Figure 8.7 Percentage and frequency distribution of "Predicted".

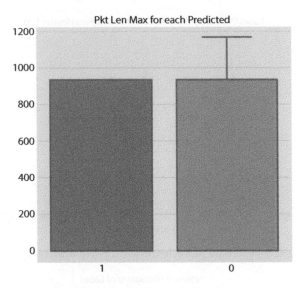

Figure 8.8 Box plot of Packet length max for each "Predicted".

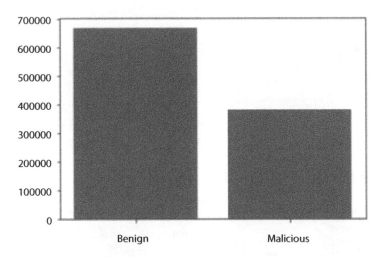

Figure 8.9 Visualization for the count of attacks in 1st dataset.

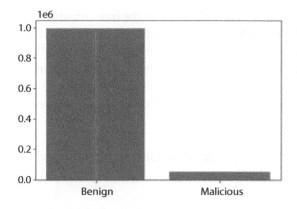

Figure 8.10 Visualization for the count of attacks in 2nd dataset.

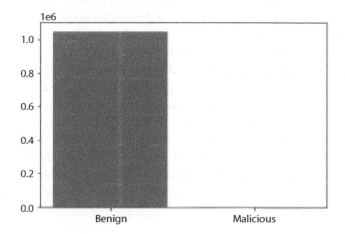

Figure 8.11 Visualization for the count of attacks in 3rd dataset.

to train the model and predict the output into three classes, Benign (safe), FTP-BruteForce (attack) and SSH-BruteForce (attack).

In the following subsections, we have briefly given an overview of all the algorithms that the autoML processes.

8.3.3.1 Decision Tree

The decision tree technique is employed to work out problems involving classification and regression. This model aims at developing a training model that can be utilized to anticipate multi-class values of the prescribed output variable, by analyzing and learning generic algorithm rules deduced from historical data. Internal nodes of the tree constitute of dataset feature sets, while the branches of tree describe the decision rules, and each leaf node illustrates the output. While computing, we usually begin at the top of the tree to identify the test class label. The figures of the root and the record's attribute are analyzed and compared and the same branch is followed corresponding to this and move on to the next node depending on the comparison.

Important Parameters: n_estimators, criterion, max_depth, max_features, n_jobs, random_state

8.3.3.2   Random Forest Classifier Algorithm

This algorithm is a widely used estimator which incorporates averaging to enhance accuracy for predicted values and monitor over-fitting by utilizing ample amount of decision trees on numerous breakdown samples obtained by dividing existing samples into further samples of the dataset. The size of the created sub-samples is regularized by the argument of the max samples if the bootstrap values equals True; regardless of which, the entire dataset is taken into account to create each tree. It forms decision trees from several samples created earlier, by using the majority output for mean of regression and classification. One of the foremost vital characteristic of this machine learning method is, it can be widely employed both in scenarios having data sets with continuous and categorical columns. For classification complications, it usually performs better with superior results than in other cases.

Important Parameters: n_estimators, criterion, max_depth, max_features, n_jobs, random_state

8.3.3.3   AdaBoost Classifier

The AdaBoost method, which is a short name given for Adaptive Boosting, is a boosting technique used in ML as an Ensemble Method. It's also a meta-estimator as random forest, that initiates by fitting itself to the raw dataset file, then gets fit into further copies to the similar data as earlier, but optimize the weights of imperfectly classified feature sets such that upcoming classifiers value on critical situations. Weights are recalculated and assigned to each data instance, with higher values applied to features that were vaguely categorized. In supervised learning which is based on the principle of successive learning, bias and inconsistencies are decreased by using boost. Each succeeding value, with the exception of the first in the list, is developed from earlier grown learners. It works on the same ideology as that of boosting with slight modifications.

Important Parameters: n_estimators, criterion, max_depth, max_features, n_jobs, random_state

8.3.3.4   Ridge Classifier

A Ridge Regressor is essentially a normalized variant of a Linear Regressor, in which we add a regularized term to the original cost function of the linear regressor to drive the learning process to match the data and maintain the weights as low as feasible. The parameter 'alpha' in the regularized term regulates the model's regularization, i.e., it helps to reduce the variance of the estimations. It uses the regression based approach to solve the problem by converting the target labeled data to [-1, 1] form. The final class with the highest prediction value is shortlisted. Similarly this approach is applied to multiclass data by using multi-output regression.

Important Parameters: alpha, fit_intercept, normalize, max_iter, solver, positive, random_state

$$J(\theta) = \frac{1}{m}(X\theta - Y)^2 + \alpha \frac{1}{2}(\theta)^2$$

Equation 8.1: Cost function for ridge regressor.

8.3.3.5   Logistic Regression

The method logistic regression based on supervised learning is used to formulate the probability of a target feature. Because the characteristic of the final output or dependent variables can take only two classifications, hence there are only binary(two) classifications possible. In easier terms, the variable being dependent is binary in nature, with dataset as 1 (indicating success/positive) or 0 (indicating failure/negative). A LR trained model predicts output as a function of X mathematically. It is one of the most simple and easier ML algorithm that may be put to use to a various categorizing tasks. The sigmoid function, having a non-negative derivative with only a single point inflection, transforms any real figure to its corresponding mapped value lying between 0 and , thus predicted values are converted to probabilities.

Important Parameters: penalty, dual, random_state, max_iter, n_jobs, l1_ratio, multi_class, verbose

$$0 \le h_\theta(x) \le 1$$

Equation 8.2: Cost function for logistic regression.

8.3.3.6　SVM-Linear Kernel

In large-dimensional spaces and when the value of number of dimensions exceeds the number of samples, support vector machines are effective. It is effective in memory usage because it employs a subset of support vectors in the decision making function. SVM helps to find the optimal hyperplane which separates the two classes and is found by maximizing the margin between the support vectors. SVC, NuSVC and LinearSVC are classes which are used for performing binary and multi-class classification.

If the number of features is substantially more than the number of samples, however, it is critical to prevent over-fitting when selecting Kernel functions and regularization terms. Other functions are slower than linear kernel functions.

Important Parameters: support_vectors, decision_function_shape

$$F(x, x_j) = sum(x. \, x_j)$$

Equation 8.3: Function for SVM-linear kernel.

8.3.3.7　Naive Bayes

The mentioned algorithm approaches, indicates as a subset of supervised learning ML methods and is primarily relied upon application of Bayes' theorem along with the naive assumption that every pair of feature sets in the data is conditionally independent to each other. The assumptions that various naïve Bayes classifiers make about the distribution of probability functions are what distinguishes them. To determine the required training parameters, they just need some quantity of training data. When contrasted to more high-end algorithms, these classifiers may be exceedingly fast with less processing time. This results in simplification of problems arising from the computational complexity. On the other hand, while

Naive Bayes is a good classifier, it is also a lousy estimator, therefore the probability output should be used with caution. (y is the class variable and x1..xn are the dependent features)

$$P(y \mid x_1, \ldots \ldots, x_n) = \frac{P(y)P(x_1, \ldots \ldots, x_n \mid y)}{P(x_1, \ldots \ldots, x_n)}$$

Equation 8.4: Naive Bayes formula.

8.3.3.8 Quadratic Discriminant Analysis

It is a boundary having quadratic decision classifier formed by incorporating Bayes' rule and optimization of densities of class to data. Gaussian Density is assigned to each class by the model, allowing the above classifier to evaluate non-linear correlations. Of course, its alternative, Linear Discriminant Analysis is incapable of accomplishing this. By assuming that each class has its own covariance matrix, quadratic discriminant analysis gives an alternate technique. As a result, the number of parameters increases significantly. This might be an issue if you have a lot of classes but not enough sample points. QDA is especially important if you are already aware that different classes have different measurement of direction between two variables. A major drawback is that it cannot be implemented as a technique used for dimensionality reduction.

Important Parameters: priors, reg_param, store_covariance, tol

Table 8.1 Algorithms used in AutoML.

AutoML abbreviations	Algorithm name
dt	Decision Tree
rf	Random Forest
ada	Ada Boost Classifier
ridge	Ridge Classifier
lr	Logistic Regression
svm	SVM - Linear Kernel
nb	Naive Bayes
qda	Quadratic Discriminant Analysis

8.4   Results

Table 8.1 shows the algorithms used in AutoML. Table 8.2 implies the analysis of the comparative results of the proposed method with previous approaches through various metrics. The experimental outcome means that the proposed model Gradient Boosting and Random forest has shown a testing accuracy of 97%, Precision of 97%, Recall of 97% and F1-score of 97%, which significantly outperformed other existing models. Figure 8.12 depicts the comparison of the performance of different machine learning models on the dataset represented in Figure 8.9. Figure 8.13 depicts the comparison of the performance of different machine learning models on the dataset represented in Figure 8.10. Figure 8.14 depicts the comparison of the performance of different machine learning models on the dataset represented in Figure 8.11.

Table 8.2 Comparative result analysis.

Models	Accuracy	Precision	Recall	F1 score
Proposed method				
First Model	92.24	97.25	98.11	97.65
Second Model	**99.90**	99.26	99.78	99.52
Third Model	99.97	99.98	64.81	72.85
Testing	97.08	96.87	97.95	97.40

	Model	Accuracy	AUC	Recall	Prec.	F1	Kappa	MCC	TT (Sec)
dt	Decision Tree Classifier	1.0000	1.0000	1.0000	1.0000	1.0000	1.0000	1.0000	2.648
rf	Random Forest Classifier	1.0000	1.0000	1.0000	1.0000	1.0000	1.0000	1.0000	59.718
ada	Ada Boost Classifier	1.0000	1.0000	1.0000	1.0000	1.0000	1.0000	1.0000	93.807
ridge	Ridge Classifier	0.9973	0.0000	1.0000	0.9925	0.9962	0.9941	0.9941	0.918
lr	Logistic Regression	0.9770	0.9958	0.9929	0.9467	0.9692	0.9509	0.9517	64.622
svm	SVM - Linear Kernel	0.8834	0.0000	0.7749	0.8905	0.8277	0.7403	0.7454	27.296
nb	Naive Bayes	0.6592	0.7638	1.0000	0.5172	0.6815	0.3874	0.4900	1.338
qda	Quadratic Discriminant Analysis	0.6363	0.5000	0.0000	0.0000	0.0000	0.0000	0.0000	6.910

Figure 8.12 Assessing algorithm performances on 1st created dataset.

	Model	Accuracy	AUC	Recall	Prec.	F1	Kappa	MCC	TT (Sec)
dt	Decision Tree Classifier	1.0000	1.0000	0.9999	0.9999	0.9999	0.9999	0.9999	5.117
rt	Random Forest Classifier	1.0000	1.0000	0.9997	0.9999	0.9998	0.9998	0.9998	87.985
ada	Ada Boost Classifier	1.0000	1.0000	1.0000	1.0000	1.0000	1.0000	1.0000	99.291
knn	K Neighbors Classifier	0.9989	0.9990	0.9940	0.9837	0.9998	0.9882	0.9882	80.884
ridge	Ridge Classifier	0.9956	0.0000	0.9548	0.9572	0.9560	0.9537	0.9637	0.926
lr	Logistic Regression	0.9729	0.7729	0.5319	0.8785	0.6626	0.6494	0.6716	139.531
qda	Quadratic Discriminant Analysis	0.9501	0.5013	0.0026	0.8000	0.0050	0.0048	0.0304	7.943
svm	SVM - Linear Kernel	0.9161	0.0000	0.5032	0.3120	0.3759	0.3350	0.3507	36.420
nb	Naive Bayes	0.8608	0.8651	0.2443	0.1076	0.1493	0.0858	0.0945	0.863

Figure 8.13 Assessing algorithm performances on 2nd created dataset.

	Model	Accuracy	AUC	Recall	Prec.	F1	Kappa	MCC	TT (Sec)
dt	Decision Tree Classifier	1.0000	0.9783	0.9566	0.9614	0.9584	0.9584	0.9587	14.175
rf	Random Forest Classifier	1.0000	1.0000	0.9329	1.0000	0.9650	0.9649	0.9657	119.420
knn	K Neighbors Classifier	0.9998	0.9548	0.7245	0.8258	0.7689	0.7689	0.7719	383.263
ridge	Ridge Classifier	0.9996	0.0000	0.0000	0.0000	0.0000	-0.0000	-0.0000	1.188
qda	Quadratic Discriminant Analysis	0.9993	0.9740	0.9491	0.3372	0.4928	0.4925	0.5622	9.057
lr	Logistic Regression	0.9915	0.5537	0.1545	0.3077	0.1508	0.1504	0.1800	39.696
svm	SVM - Linear Kernel	0.7371	0.0000	0.1254	0.0001	0.0003	-0.0003	-0.0057	7.280
nb	Naive Bayes	0.2309	0.6171	1.0000	0.0004	0.0009	0.0002	0.0102	0.848

Figure 8.14 Assessing algorithm performances on 3rd created dataset.

8.5   Conclusion

In this chapter, we explored the usage of AutoML and how it can be beneficial when you work with large datasets. It involved analysis of eight such algorithms. Out of the three trained models, two were trained on logistic regression and one was with K-nearest neighbors. All the three models gave accuracy as high as 99%. These were then used to predict a test dataset and the output file was visualized using AutoViz Library. This helps in analyzing the distribution of feature sets across the dataset in lesser time, thus better decision making. This chapter also justifies the use of AutoViz over BI tools, which may vary from case to case. In future, we would try to incorporate the findings in real-time cases as an integrated platform. We would also like to extend our sincere thanks to all those who stood by us and helped in completing the project.

References

1. Thirimanne, S.P., Jayawardana, L., Yasakethu, L., Liyanaarachchi, P., Hewage, C., Deep neural network based real-time intrusion detection system. *SN Comput. Sci.*, 3, 2, 1–12, 2022.
2. Abbasi, M., Shahraki, A., Taherkordi, A., Deep learning for network traffic monitoring and analysis (NTMA): A survey. *Comput. Commun.*, 170, 19–41, 2021.
3. Qureshi, A.S., Khan, A., Shamim, N., Durad, M.H., Intrusion detection using deep sparse auto-encoder and self-taught learning. *Neural Comput. Appl.*, 32, 8, 3135–3147, 2020.
4. Musa, U.S., Chakraborty, S., Abdullahi, M.M., Maini, T., A review on intrusion detection system using machine learning techniques, in: *2021 International Conference on Computing, Communication, and Intelligent Systems (ICCCIS)*, IEEE, pp. 541–549, February 2021.
5. Khan, M.A., Rehman, A., Khan, K.M., Al Ghamdi, M.A., Almotiri, S.H., Enhance intrusion detection in computer networks based on deep extreme learning machine, *Comput., Mater. Continua*, 66, 1, 467–480, 2021.
6. Guezzaz, A., Benkirane, S., Azrour, M., Khurram, S., A reliable network intrusion detection approach using decision tree with enhanced data quality. *Secur. Commun. Netw.*, vol. 2021, Article ID 1230593, 8 pages, 2021.
7. Man, J. and Sun, G., A residual learning-based network intrusion detection system. *Secur. Commun. Netw.*, 2021, 1–9, 2021.
8. Ahmad, Z., Khan, A.S., Shiang, C.W., Abdullah, J., Ahmad, F., Network intrusion detection system: A systematic study of machine learning and deep learning approaches. *Trans. Emerg. Telecommun. Technol.*, 32, 1, e4150, 2021.
9. Eberhard, K., The effects of visualization on judgment and decision-making: A systematic literature review. *Manage. Rev. Q.*, 1–48, 2021.
10. Satapathy, S.K., Dehuri, S., Jagadev, A.K., Mishra, S., *EEG Brain Signal Classification for Epileptic Seizure Disorder Detection*, 1st Eds., Elsevier Publication, San Diego, United States, Feb. 2019.
11. Satapathy, S.K., Dehuri, S., Jagadev, A.K., Weighted majority voting based ensemble of classifiers using different machine learning techniques for classification of EEG signal to detect epileptic seizure. *Informatica*, 41, 99–110, 2017.

12. Satapathy, S.K., Jagadev, A.K., Dehuri, S., An empirical analysis of training algorithms of neural networks: A case study of EEG signal classification using java framework, in: *Advances in Intelligent Systems and Computing*, vol. 309, L.C. Jain (Ed.), pp. 151–160, Springer, New Delhi, India, 2015.

13. Mishra, S., Mishra, D., Satapathy, S.K., Fuzzy frequent pattern mining from gene expression data using dynamic multi-swarm particle swarm optimization. *2nd International Conference on Computer, Communication, Control and Information Technology (C3IT 2012), Proc. Technol.*, 4, 797–801, Feb. 2012.

14. Satapathy, S.K., Mishra, S., Mishra, D., Search technique using wildcards or truncation: A tolerance rough set clustering approach. *Int. J. Adv. Comput. Sci. Appl.*, 1, 4, 73–77, October 2010.

9

Quantum Computing in Netnomy: A Networking Paradigm in e-Pharmaceutical Setting

Sarthak Dash[1], Sugyanta Priyadarshini[1]*, Sachi Nandan Mohanty[2], Sukanya Priyadarshini[3] and Nisrutha Dulla[1]

[1]*School of Humanities, KIIT Deemed to be University, Bhubaneshwar, India*
[2]*School of Computer Science & Engineering, VIT-AP University, Amaravati, Andhra Pradesh, India*
[3]*Department of Zoology, Berhampur University, Odisha, India*

Abstract

The epoch of the twenty-first marks a renaissance in the organizational context of pharmaceutical marketing by setting up a new-fangled market space via quantum computing of innovative services and technical applications that have dynamically changed the ecosystem of pharma marketing. The revolutionary changes in the quantum telecommunication infrastructure have given birth to the concept of Netnomics, which is considered a new paradigm in the economic system. Consequently, the new frontiers in multilayer networking have reshaped markets with comprehensive support of a wide data bank of skilled and functional departments controlling funding, licensing, marketing, and research and development via advanced quantum technology convergence and electronic commerce such as artificial Intelligence, blockchain, Augmented Reality, Virtual Reality, 3D Printing and the Internet of Things, paving the way for digitalized pharma market economy. The radical implication of Quantum Netnomy in the traditional medico landscape is the shift from tectonic shifts in culture to a deluge of data in medical space via quantum entanglement and quantum superposition in experimental marketing transitioning hierarchical strategic modeling to appointing skilled silos, from reviving outdated services to redesigning self-monitoring and self-controlling systems and from altering face to face transaction to human-computer interaction, making it convenient for unserved, and unreached masses deprived of potent

Corresponding author: sugyanta.priyadarshini@kiit.ac.in

Sachi Nandan Mohanty, Rajanikanth Aluvalu and Sarita Mohanty (eds.) Evolution and Applications of Quantum Computing, (145–162) © 2023 Scrivener Publishing LLC

health care services. The paper confronts the typical view about the mechanism of network economy by shedding light on the functioning of the pharmaceutical market in the Network Economy and usability of IoT in its development.

Keywords: Networking, IoT, interface, e-pharmacy, digitalization, quantum technology

9.1   Introduction

The dawn of the twenty-first century stands on a knowledge-driven economy in which knowledge is considered the basic economic resource, not land, labor, or capital. The network is highly capable of processing information which makes it acclimatize the knowledge-rich environment superiorly [1, 2]. Even though this Networking in the economy is intolerant towards traditional tools and authoritative control but has brought in a new set of managerial ethos without conducting any structural upheaval. As a result, quantum networking in the economy dampens down the commotion by stirring the information proficiently within the system and enabling organizations to adapt to the changes continuously [3]. The era of quantum marketing is how the marketers approach the digital marketing which is eventually going grab the market through Artificial Intelligence, Blockchain, Augmented Reality, Virtual Reality, 3D Printing and the Internet of Things. The contemporary economic system lays its foundation over a potent mobile network infrastructure, which has proved to be a solid ground for enriching economic development [4, 5]. Quantum technology in netnomy is the reinvention of the market that makes use of a class of technologies that comes into action by using certain principles of quantum mechanics in digital market such as quantum entanglement and quantum superposition in experimental marketing. The continuous and rapid development in telecommunication infrastructure has escalated the growth of business application services, resulting in a new paradigm in an economic system called "Netnomics." The concept of Netnomics relates to the network effect in the business economy.

Nevertheless, in a short span of quasi a century, the market scenario has transformed significantly from playing a pivotal role in shaping marketing policies to shaping firm's output, from transitioning technology to modeling strategic direction and from exploring innovative services to redesigning the market via technical convergence and e-commerce. A network organization is an interdependent coalition of task or skill-specialized economic entities that operate without hierarchical control but is embedded by dense lateral connections, mutuality, and reciprocity in a shared value system where membership roles and responsibilities are predetermined and defined [6, 7]. The implications of several marketing structures are likely to be radical and pervasive. To analyze this, it is essential to distinguish diverse market structures. The traditional hierarchal structure of the market exhibited dominance over the managerial part of the company, and production was provided comparatively greater prominence than its supply. However, this custom continued till the evolution of the network marketing structure, where a dynamic transition was observed from the hierarchal market form to the knowledge-rich environment. To enhance innovation flexibility, the companies are focusing on their main competency. For all other activities, they prefer outsourcing which will sooner or later make the firm more competent in the economy. This close relationship via outsourcing among the firms has pushed the economy into a new era of the networking economy. There is a voluminous research work on traditional market economy [8–11], but the evolving market scenario called for a growing literature on Network theory in marketing [12–18].

The emergence of quantum netnomics has set up a new-fangled market space via innovative services and applications that have dynamically changed the economy's ecosystem [19], especially and importantly in health care settings in the form of e-pharmacy. E-pharmacy or internet pharmacy provides healthcare services or medicines (operated through the internet) through shipping companies, further cutting the cost of long-chain distributors and directly getting delivered to the end customer [20]. Internet of things has massively transformed and renovated the healthcare system significantly, ranging from optimally structuring the healthcare system to procuring health care services for people from different corners and tracing data for audit information. By introducing e-pharmacy, consumers can now demand better services through a transparent system while accessing drugs without any third party (mediators). They can compare the drugs as per the required quality and price in an online platform without traveling but spotting across the world. Internet is an ocean of information, and once a consumer gets logged in, they can seek enough knowledge to come up with a more informed decision about the status of health condition, treatment options as well as counseling for managing the current health status irrespective of the existing location and financial status [21]. The present study explores the e pharma market functioning in quantum Netnomy and makes efforts to analyze the usability of Netnomics in attending its development.

9.2   Discussion

9.2.1   Exploring Market Functioning via Quantum Network Economy

The quantum network phenomenon developed in the market scenario is the future of marketing and has evolved substantially during the past three decades [22, 23]. The traditional market scenario focused on interpersonal ties within the organization or between the organizations in an informal way rather than formal ties. Nevertheless, it became challenging to coordinate among the organization in a hierarchal setup due to the growing expenses in maintaining a pace with rapid technological evolution. Focusing on the pharmaceutical industry, it is marked that the introduction of Networking has eased the task of drug distribution and its accessibility. However, the factors driving the escalating demand for e-pharmacy in India can be listed as the unmet health care needs of consumers staying at a remote location for retail pharmacy whose demand can be fulfilled at the click of a button due to increased penetration of the internet in both rural areas at competitive prices, greater efficacy, reliability, and transparency which is depicted in Figure 9.1. However, urban areas are transitioning from a family-size point of view. The joint families are replaced by nuclear families, isolating the elderly and reducing their access to medicines by traveling to retail pharmacies. Consequently, introducing e-pharmacy in the market can successfully overcome the barriers of accessibility and emergency. Further, due to the rapid change in consumer behavior, especially towards internet-friendly medical sources, in no time, e-pharmacy will undoubtedly accomplish the demand of underserved population by enhancing adherence and access to medicines.

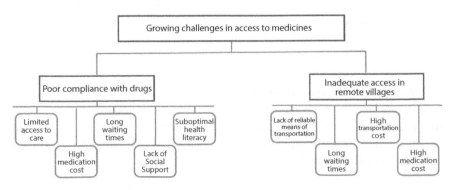

Figure 9.1 Challenges in accessing medicines from retail pharmaceutical stores.

To analyze the pharma market functioning in network phenomenon, the three levels of aggregation: Internal, Layered, and Vertical Networking is, taken into consideration.

9.2.1.1   Internal Networking Marketing

Internal Networking relates to reaching out or connecting internally within the organization, reducing hierarchy, improving cohesiveness, and boosting commercial ingenuity. An internal market network refers to a firm systematically structured into several internal enterprise units acting as a seller-buyer or investor for other internal and external units. These firms operate as semi-autonomous profit hubs, best serving their needs by remaining in the radius of the market terms conditions and conducting trade policies. However, there are a couple of internal monopolies in such firms. As these internal markets are profit hubs thus, they enjoy the freedom of buying or/and selling their product and services to any internal or external sources keeping in mind their competence of vending their products in the internal and external sources in the markets. For instance, one of the renowned pharma firms, such as X, which is considered one of Y's best component manufacturing firms, is currently an internal market. This manufacturing division also sells its components to Z in A and B nations.

The classical hierarchal organization of the 20th century focuses primarily on the technology of production, which is designed to economize the bounded rationality of top management and minimize the governance cost of sequential adaption to contingencies [24]. But after introducing networking culture inside the organization, a comparatively limited hierarchal approach, dense lateral connections, low departmental walls, and openness to the environment are observed. It is found that professional firms such as pharmaceutical companies, biotechnology industries, innovative firms, and research universities are on experiment for replacing the hierarchal system with two primary forms of internal networking structure: the team-based and the internal market organizations.

9.2.1.2   Layered Marketing

The focus of leading companies is shifting from brand management towards reviving team structure, evolving product management, and team, category management, and customer satisfaction management. The poor adaptive capability of firms put them in utter danger, which calls for hybrid team-based organizational silos referred to as layered network" [25, 26]. In other words, a layered network refers to a firm that comprises several functional

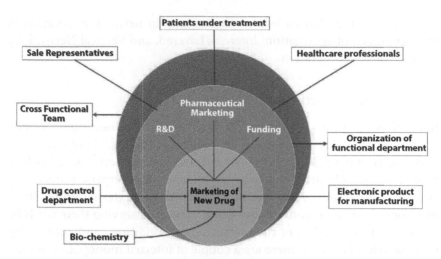

Figure 9.2 Layered networking in management.

layers of cross-operational teams backed by a layer of skilled silos that are interlinked internally and externally via a data bank of knowledge and crystal precise data flows. Figure 9.2 represents the layered network structuring in an organization. The crest layer of the organization comprises a team carrying the responsibility of drug output delivery and development as well as customer interaction and relations. However, the crest layer can function with comprehensive support of a wide data bank of skilled and functional departments controlling funding, production, marketing, and research and development. To maintain transparency in such a multi-layered networking structured organization, the data bank is accessible to every employee irrespective of their rank and department. The lowermost but core layer is the organization of knowledge that controls the company's database. This layer includes conventional science and technology or/and management science or/and biological sciences or/and behavioral sciences. However, the members operating in the core layer of skilled silos often rotate inside and outside their areas for reorientation and absorption. The structure is formed not based on hierarchical order but instead on the direction of information flow. Nevertheless, the sole idea of layered Networking is to develop a system of self-monitoring and self-controlling pharma firms established on the foundation of shared responsibilities and transparency of data.

9.2.1.3   Role of Marketing in Pharma Network Organizations

The most critical question in the twenty-first century remains the existence of the marketing department as a unique functional area or has to be merged in general management. Nevertheless, nobody will be answerable or blamed for marketing failures because if everyone is responsible for marketing, no one is also responsible for marketing. This requires a separate, defined, robust marketing department with a dynamic role. Consequently, the pharma marketing department in every organization will be solely responsible for being the architect and repository of marketing skills and operator of information systems and databases. In the case of pharma network organizations, marketing ranges from conducting real-time marketing to acting as an internal infomediary to being a creator of marketing knowledge and skills, organizational educator, stakeholder of connectivity, coordinator, and conflict manager, which is portrayed in Figure 9.3. The role of marketing in conducting real-time marketing by bringing the information which is very close to the real-time by associating R&D team to operating team comprising of storage keeper, packaging superintendent, advertiser, and transport head. The real-time data can analyze data efficiently and present the decision scenarios in a "battlefield view" to the management. However, consumer cooperation supports real-time marketing, which is possible by extracting consumer information. The marketing department can act as an internal infomediary, collect consumer information, and entrust them by providing security to their privacy. At the same time, the marketing management also acts as a creator of market knowledge by developing a strategic understanding regarding customer needs, competitor's tactics, innovative product technology, and market trend and competition.

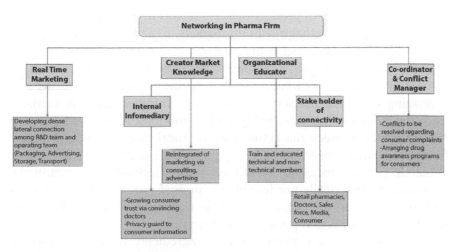

Figure 9.3 Role of marketing in internal networking firms.

Further, as an organizational educator, the marketing department organizes training programs for technical and non-technical staff to keep them updated about the latest drug market practices, decision models, and data banks. Additionally, the marketing department also acts as a stakeholder of connectivity for the organization by making critical strategic decisions regarding establishing partnerships and alliances, analyzing the firm's core competencies, and deciding that doctors be associated with promotion and sales upliftment. Last but not least, the pharma marketing department also intervenes in the matter of internal network relations for dealing with conflicts and disagreements among different units of the firm, thereby playing the role of coordinator and conflict manager.

9.2.1.4   Role of Marketing in Vertical Networking Organizations

It is observed that the functional specialists in vertical synergies focus more on production-oriented philosophy rather than marked-based inspired philosophy. For instance, the mechanical department will prefer to invest and explore to increase quality and reduce the cost of production by employing mechanical organization structure and thereby channelizing lesser funds for R&D and marketing. However, by revitalizing production-oriented thinking, production can be revived. The marketing department shades the foremost priority towards excelling in innovative ideas in product design. The marketing department looks into collaborative tasks among research scientists for better drug orientation, resource allocation, and developing organizational structure.

Further, overemphasizing product and product orientation and ignoring other approaches of product delivery results in market myopia which can be proved to be lethal in vibrant markets. In a vertical network structure, the integrator firm needs to be a marketing-oriented firm to adapt to the continuously changing consumer preferences, allocation structure, and rivalry. In such cases, marketing plays a significant role in organizing and managing vertical synergies for renovating customer research, demand and supply forecasting, advertising, and promotions. Additionally, to gasp the difference between marketing and technical independence, the marketing department needs to be highly proactive and less adaptive towards research performances to scrutinize future technology investments. However, it's practically not feasible to conduct radical, innovative ideas tests on consumers directly, which calls for rigorous research on alternative technology for forecasting and risk management.

Consequently, active pharmaceutical ingredients (API) are collected from several API suppliers used for manufacturing medicines. Drug

Figure 9.4 Role of marketing in vertical synergy.

manufacturers will look into drug engineering footprints which will be further provided to warehousing and distribution for disposal to pharmacy stores. Ultimately, based on the opinion of health care professionals, pharmaceutical stores will be bringing the product to market. However, the managerial strategy integrates long-term strategic plans, medium-term sourcing, and short-term operational plans. The given below Figure 9.4 serves as a flowchart for a quick understanding of the ground-level role of marketing in vertical synergies.

9.2.1.5 Generic e-Commerce Entity Model in Pharmaceutical Industry

From inventory to market-based model of e-commerce in the drug industry, it is observed that the invention of any drug after certification is introduced in e-commerce entity (website/mobile platform), thereby making it convenient for the consumers to access it directly without the intervention of the third party. However, consumers can seek the drugs directly from the licensed agency with an authenticated digital signature in the electronic record of prescription. Further, consumers can seek drugs from n number of pharmacies via digital and electronic networks that act as a facilitator

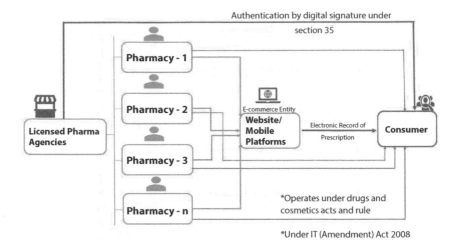

Figure 9.5 e-commerce entity model.

between seller and buyer. After the recipient of the order, it is verified by a group of registered pharmacists who take it forward to the pharmacy store for dispensing the drugs. Figure 9.5 portrays a generic e-Commerce marketplace in pharmacy via a technology-driven electronic platform under the IT act 2008. Drugs/medicines that are under violation or experimentation by Drugs and Cosmetics Act and Rules are strictly prohibited from being advertised in the e-commerce model.

Although e-pharmacy is considered a threat to retail pharmacy, newer e model have only led to the creation of new markets leading to the co-existence of both online and offline modes of pharmacy. The dilemma has taken place due to the perception of threat, which is barely any real threat as e-pharmacy is a shift in business, not the only way of business.

9.2.2   Analyzing the Usability of Quantum Netnomics in Attending Economic Development

In this evolving globe, the inveterate form of the market is rapidly transforming into a digitalized economy which is solely controlled by quantum technologies that has paved the way for e-commerce. As predicted in a prior research paper, one-third of the $60 trillion world economy has already entered into a digitalized form of marketing. It already has an adverse impact on the companies or firms who fail to switch to this digitalized form of marketing [27]. The digitalized version of the economic renaissance has pushed the market structure into a challenging state, creating confusion about the interaction between technology and humans operating in the market sphere. This interaction of humans and technology is not new. Still, the whole operation of the market depends upon the user interface, which is responsible for determining the firm's functioning.

E-commerce is dependent upon one thing that is the user interface which is majorly replacing many traditional shopping modes. For instance, face to face buying of drugs is replaced by virtual platforms where online search features before buying medicines such as doctor's prescription or buy medicine by selecting free doctor consultation at check out, medicine of different brand but same composition, price range, product descriptions, easy return are available and now smoothly adaptable by the general public. However, the entire shopping experience depends on the interface's creative design, quality of the interface, and usability of the interface. The success of e-pharmaceuticals has always been dependent upon the approach of the public towards computers and usability. The usability majorly depends upon five elements: learnability, efficiency, memorability, errors, and satisfaction. Besides these five elements, the core of usability is its user interface, navigation in the web page, simplified search element. All other domains of this digitalized market, such as branding of the product pricing policy, delivery and return service, a showcase of product, maintaining customer privacy, needs holistic study and understanding to make the human and computer interaction smooth and maximize customer satisfaction.

9.2.2.1   Theory of 4Ps in Pharma Marketing Mix

Marketing revolves around the concept of the four Ps: Promotion, Price, Product, and Place (distribution & logistics). In a physical pharma market, firms rarely compete for price, but in the case of online marketing, there is a fear of price sensitiveness between the pharma firms. The cause of the price war in the case of the online market can be the low cost of product information [28, 29]. There are many options available to choose from the online market with a minimal cost spent which brings in a death spiral price war in online marketing. According to [27], it is a dog and pony show of a product that significantly influences its price. As per research work by [30], performance/quality dramatically impacts the product's price. Keeping in mind the type of customer, the interface needs to be designed. If the consumers have a high-speed broadband connection, then making high size imagery and web design makes sense; otherwise, the company may lose the customer.

In e-commerce, brand differentiation comprises the usage of dialog and interactions. The longer a website could manage the customer to stay on the web page, the higher the target rating point will earn greater profits to the website. To engage the customers for a more extended period in the particular website, several services such as contact email, chatbox, feedback/consultation, focus discussions with previous customers are provided, which instigates a consumer to more likely buy the product. Further, services provided by the companies up to a satisfaction level can bind the consumer for a long time. Proper information about the product delivery and return status, in time response to the query of consumer and complaint redressal, can be a crucial factor to make the customer satisfied and come back again.

E-pharma firms need to focus on tracking information and delivery details to improve consumer satisfaction. One observation has shed light on an online drug site that failed to fulfill the customer's query. It could not address and keep track of its customer's repeated emails and phone calls regarding product tracking and delivery details in Covid times. Dissatisfied by the slow response to customer's query, these online shopping sites lost thousands of customers by the year-end. This instance calls for better *Human-computer interaction (HCI)* design, which can escalate global satisfaction by sending an email or message to the customers regarding the shipment status, probable delivery dates, courier brand, and additional handling charges, whether included or excluded from the price. This revised optimal interface has made it possible to click an item on the web and have it delivered to the doorstep from any possible corner of the world.

9.2.2.2   Buying Behavior of the e-Consumers

It was observed that unserved and unreached masses deprived of potent health care services are primarily dependent on online shopping of medicines which will save them during any emergency [31]. Further, it can be concluded that a buyer who prefers convenience in buying medicine online will spend less time on the internet to purchase. Keeping this in mind, the company should design the web page systematically to suggest the consumer choose according to their need in a while.

Online buyers buying behavior may be influenced by the experience they had. Sometimes bad experiences during the medicine purchase can cause dropouts, and it would be a difficult task to convince them again. Hitch during buying like lack of inappropriate product information, delivery problems, unsuitable pricing, billing error, unsatisfied responses to the consumer inquiry can cause consumer dropouts which need to be taken care of. The loopholes in online shopping mode have slowed down the online spending rate. Even if the overall online expenditure per person is escalating for most online buyers, the upsurge rate is slowing down, which is further a risk towards adopting the online mode of drug sale. Hence, customer service quality is essential for converting them to persistent online buyers of the products.

9.2.2.3   Maintaining of Privacy and Security via Quantum Technology in e-Structure

In the quantum marketing era, probabilistic thinking of quantum mechanics has resulted in profound implications for cyber security. Every surfing of data by the customer on the internet gets auto-recorded and saved in the web server log files. The recorded data can identify the consumer preferences of products and behavior. This can help the companies to provide suitable brand suggestions for the consumer. But different countries have different regulations that can prevent the use of the companies' collected data. [31] surveyed to gain a fair knowledge about the global privacy policy and its implications, and he found that many countries are concerned about the privacy and security norms of the data shared online. In general, people don't want to share their data related to health concerns which can be further misused. From this, it can be deduced that the privacy of data can be an influencing factor for the consumer's online buying behavior. The best possible way to entrust masses is to maintain customer privacy by not selling their data to other companies and by keeping it safe away from the reach of hackers [32]. By providing approval seals like VeriSign, TRUSTe, SLL Lock, customers can feel safe while surfing the web. Further, companies can operate things smoothly and profitably by ensuring that their data is sheltered.

9.2.2.4   Interface Influencing Sales

To increase the traffic and sales of an online drug store, it needs to utilize its resources to develop a user-friendly, attractive interface. To examine the role of the interface in sales, the relationship between the interface's design and the count of sales is analyzed. From the study, it was concluded that creative interface design has a positive impact on sales. The store's traffic and sales increment majorly depend upon the product information provided by the store. So it is important to design an effective information catalog for the accretion of sales and traffic [33]. The navigation feature makes the customer easy to find the appropriate product, which is a determining factor for the success of the store. As per the analysis, improving navigation in the web page for searching products and providing hyperlinks can significantly improve the sales number. Other important information of the product such as price, thumbnail image, and an accurate description of the product can have an enormous impact on the traffic and sales.

Nevertheless, the process of checkout is more complicated. Sometimes this process takes a long time, which negatively impacts the customer. The online store can bind its customer by making the checkout process smooth and hassle-free.

9.3   Results

In the era of the 21st century, the industrial revolution is converting into the information revolution. The organization that has played a vital role in the Industrial Revolution is morphing into internal and external quantum networks. These quantum networks make them responsible for the information processing, knowledge development, and adaptive towards convention firms. As the evolution in the quantum network economy is new, it is pretty challenging to find out the appropriate network structure to fit in the pharma market. But from some experiences, we can conclude some structures which fit appropriately. For instance, the internal market quantum network suits the pharma firms better than the Layered network and vertical network. However, a limitation that has been pointed out is the marketing department's close-knit and reciprocal relations between firms leading to biased advice in the financial decision and underrated strategies.

In a competitive e pharma market, customers have numerous choices, but a company has to invest in its quality improvement, attracting each consumer. Customer satisfaction depends upon the usability of a website. It may be usability that will ensure the company's profit in a digitalized market form. But the survival hack for a company is its qualitative interface. The company's responsibility is to take care of its customer by providing specific good experiences such as a quick responding webpage even in peak time, smooth and fast checkout process, and in-time complaint redressal during the shopping.

Nevertheless, usability is not the only thing that can influence the company's profitability. There are other factors such as branding, promotion, pricing, customer service, product display, consumer loyalty, privacy, and trust. A combined effort of human-computer interaction and these underlying issues can assure an effective design that can maximize the consumer experience, leading to establishing a profitable digitalized market.

9.4   Conclusion

Evolutions in the functioning of the market to the evolution of usability of the new quantum marketing habits are interlinked. The emergence of the new form of market functioning leads to the emanation of new marketing practices in quantum netnomy. By summarizing the implications of this new form, we can deduce that marketing liveliness has been stimulated by the new type of organized coordination between the networks where the whole market converted into a chain of internal units, suppliers, allies, and distributors. The advent of e-Pharmacy has clear, tangible benefits for its consumers and the growing industry. The growth of e-pharmacy is not substituting the retail; instead, are complementary in reinforcing each other. Leveraging the quantum technology towards internet-based transactions in pharmaceutical settings addresses the current retail issues by tracing authenticity and tracking the drug package, preventing the provision of drugs without prescription, averting abuse, and adding value-added services for consumer empowerment in healthcare.

Further, adopting e-prescription in e-pharmacy has also reduced the errors in drug provision by pharma retailers, which mainly occurred due to the misreading of doctors' handwriting, which will also rectify the data related to public health planning. By such modification, the market makes the customers more capable and organized, making the market more customer-oriented rather than only goods and services specific. Such a market condition where the consumer has more power can lead to latent conflict between the consumer and producer. But, it is the prime duty of the market agents to mediate the conflicts and ensure the smooth functioning of the market. Balanced coordination between the networks and between the market elements can lead to the formation of a sustainable futuristic market.

References

1. Kanter, R.M., *Evolve: Succeeding in the Digital Culture of Tomorrow*, Harvard Business School Press, Boston, 2001.
2. Porter, M.E., Strategy and the internet. *Harv. Bus. Rev.*, 79, 63–78, March 2001. https://hbr.org/2001/03/strategy-and-the-internet.

3. Brown, J.S. and Duguid, P., *The Social Life of Information*, Harvard Business School Press, Boston, 2000, https://hbswk.hbs.edu/archive/the-social-life-of-information.

4. Schmidt, E. and Cohen, J., The digital disruption: Connectivity and the diffusion of power. *Foreign Aff.*, 89, 6, 75–85, 2010.

5. Tapscott, D., *The Digital Economy: Promise and Peril in the Age of Networked Intelligence*, McGraw-Hill Company, USA, 1996.

6. Burt, R.S., Models of network structure. *Ann. Rev. Sociol.*, 6, 79–141, 1980.

7. Granovetter, M., The strength of weak ties. *Am. J. Sociol.*, 78, 1360–80, 1973.

8. Barrett, R.S., Employee selection with the performance priority survey. *Pers. Psychol.*, 48, 3, 653–662, 1995. https://doi.org/10.1111/j.1744-6570.1995.tb01776.x.

9. Kolesnikova, M. and Malovichko, S., New directions in regional history studies: History of the frontier areas of the North Caucasus. Science Innovations Technology (STI), 39, 48–58, 2004.

10. Durmaz, Y. and Efendioglu, I.H., Travel from traditional marketing to digital marketing, *Global Journal of Management and Business Research (GJMBR)*, 16, 34–40, 2016.

11. Tsui, A.S. and O'reilly, C.A., Beyond simple demographic effects: The importance of relational demography in superior-subordinate dyads. *Acad. Manage. J.*, 32, 2, 402–423, 1989. https://doi.org/10.5465/256368.

12. Achrol, R.S., Evolution of the marketing organization: New forms for turbulent environments. *J. Mark.*, 55, 4, 77, 1991. https://doi.org/10.2307/1251958.

13. Achrol, R.S., Reve, T., Stern, L.W., The environment of marketing channel dyads: A framework for comparative analysis. *J. Mark.*, 47, 4, 55, 1983. https://doi.org/10.2307/1251399.

14. Anderson, J.C., Hakansson, H., Johanson, J., Dyadix business relationships within a business network context. *J. Mark.*, 58, 4, 1, 1994. https://doi.org/10.2307/1251912.

15. Gadde, L.-E. and Mattsson, L.-G., Stability and change in network relationships. *Int. J. Res. Mark.*, 4, 1, 29–41, 1987. https://doi.org/10.1016/0167-8116(87)90012-7.

16. Snehota, I., *Developing Relationships in Business Networks*, Routledge, New York, 1995.

17. Iacobucci, D. and Hopkins, N., Modeling dyadic interactions and networks in marketing. *J. Mark. Res.*, 29, 1, 5, 1992. https://doi.org/10.2307/3172489.

18. Webster, F.E., The changing role of marketing in the corporation. *J. Mark.*, 56, 4, 1, 1992.

19. Achrol, R.S. and Kotler, P., Marketing in the network economy. *J. Mark.*, 63, 46–163, 1999.

20. Chaturvedi, A., Singh, U., Kumar, A., Online Pharmacy: An e-strategy for medication. *Int. J. Pharm. Front. Res.*, 1, 146–158, 2011.

21. Vp, P. and Bk, A., E-pharmacies regulation in India: Bringing new dimensions to pharma sector. *Pharm. Regul. Affairs*, 05, 02, 1–7, 2016.

22. Galaskiewigz, J., The "new network analysis" and its application to organizational theory and behavior, in: *Networks in Marketing*, pp. 19–31, SAGE Publications, Inc., India, 1996, https://doi.org/10.4135/9781483327723.
23. Nohria, N., Is a network perspective a useful way of studying organizations?, in: *Networks and Organizations: Structure, Form and Action*, N. Nohria, and R.G. Eccles, (Eds.), pp. 1–22, Harvard Business School Press, Boston, MA, 1992.
24. Williamson, O.E., Markets and hierarchies: Analysis and antitrust implications: A study in the economics of internal organization (SSRN Scholarly Paper ID 1496220). *Soc. Sci. Res. Net.*, 1–279, 1975. https://papers.ssrn.com/abstract=1496220.
25. Huber, G.P., The nature and design of post-industrial organizations. *Manage. Sci.*, 30, 8, 928–951, 1984.
26. Nonaka, I. and Takeuchi, H., *The Knowledge Creating Company*, Oxford University Press, New York, 1995.
27. Lohse, G.J.L., Usability and profits in the digital economy, in: *People and Computers XIV—Usability or Else!*, pp. 3–15, Springer, London, 2000, https://doi.org/10.1007/978-1-4471-0515-2_1.
28. Alba, J., Lynch, J., Weitz, B., Janiszewski, C., Lutz, R., Sawyer, A., Wood, S., Interactive home shopping: Consumer, retailer, and manufacturer incentives to participate in electronic marketplaces. *J. Mark.*, 61, 3, 38, 1997. https://doi.org/10.2307/1251788.
29. Bakos, Y., The emerging role of electronic marketplaces on the internet. *Commun. ACM*, 41, 35–42, 2000. doi: 10.1145/280324.280330.
30. Bellman, S., Johnson, E., Lohse, G., Mandel, N., Designing marketplaces of the artificial: Four approaches to understanding consumer behavior in electronic environments, *J. Interact. Mark.*, 20, 1, 21-23, 2006. https://doi.org/10.1002/dir.20053.
31. Bellman, S., Johnson, E.J., Kobrin, S., Lohse, G.L., *An International Survey of Concerns about Internet Security and Privacy, Working Paper Wharton Forum on Electronic Commerce*, 2000.
32. Hoffman, D.L., Novak, T.P., Peralta, M., Building consumer trust online. *Commun. ACM*, 42, 4, 80–85, 1999. https://doi.org/10.1145/299157.299175.
33. Lohse, G.L. and Spiller, P., Electronic shopping: The effect of customer interfaces on traffic and sales. *Commun. ACM*, 41, 81–87, 1998.

10

Machine Learning Approach in the Indian Service Industry: A Case Study on Indian Banks

Pragati Priyadarshinee

Chaitanya Bharathi Institute of Technology, Hyderabad, India

Abstract

Banks or any other organizations find it more profitable to have long term customers rather than short term customers. Banking sector is one of the most reputed Service Industry in India. In banks, long term customers profit them by depositing their money for a longer period of time, and hence increasing the bank's revenue through interests. Hunting for new customers and putting efforts towards them to make them stay, is more expensive than convincing an existing customer to opt for term deposits. With the introduction of machine learning algorithms for data processing, the efforts put towards campaigning can be pin pointed towards customers who show more probability of success in the sales. Such ease towards successful campaigns will also leave the bank with more resources and time for the development of other aspects of their business.

Keywords: Machine learning, banks, data processing, service industry

10.1 Introduction

Requirement specification is highly technical which explains about the software that has been used in the development process. This needs to be specified very accurately. A beginning step of requirement analysis is the requirement specification part. It provides a listing of software systems that are required for the proper functioning of the project. It includes

Email: pragatipriyadarshinee_it@cbit.ac.in

Sachi Nandan Mohanty, Rajanikanth Aluvalu and Sarita Mohanty (eds.) Evolution and Applications of Quantum Computing, (163–174) © 2023 Scrivener Publishing LLC

functional aspects, performance and security aspects of the project. The requirements also generate perspectives from the users or a test group or an admin point of view. The goal of software requirement specification is to enlighten groups of individuals about the working of the software system, its arguments and its purposes. It provides an idea to the user about the software and hardware that is required to run the project successfully. It also provides an idea about the extent of the project's functionalities.

A Portuguese Banking institution came to notice a decline in their revenue, and they urged their analytics team to investigate into the problem and to come up with actions that can be taken to tackle this problem. After thorough research, the team learned that the main issue arose because most of their clients were not choosing long term plans to deposit their money. The investment sect of the bank had taken a hit. People were investing their money less frequently and for lesser periods. Banks utilize the deposits from their customers to attain trades with more profitable businesses. Knowing all this, the Portuguese banking institution would like to identify existing customers who have a higher probability of subscribing for a term deposit. Being able to achieve this makes the bank to put more focus and effort towards marketing on such clients.

10.2   Literature Survey

In this chapter, the authors researched about a Portuguese bank's problem which was to make a prediction if a customer will opt for term deposits. They introduced a comparison between the classical Artificial Intelligence algorithms to find the most suitable algorithm that achieved the highest accuracy and took the least time in the process of training and prediction. The authors of this chapter suggested using Data Mining (DM) algorithms to analyses and guess the success of telemarketing for making the customers choose long term deposits. A Portuguese retail bank was chosen, with data collected through 5 years. That period also included the impacts of a financial crisis in Portugal. The authors made an analysis of a data set with more than a hundred features. This data set provided the information related to the bank's customers. A feature selection, which was not entirely automatic was chosen in the modeling phase, executed with the data prior to July 2012 which allowed them to make a selection of around 20 features from the total number of features. The authors also made a comparison of the 4 Data Mining models, *viz.*, Logistic Regression (LR), Decision Trees (DT), Neural Network (NN) and Support Vector Machines (SVM). The two metrics used were: Area Under the Curve (AUC) and Area of the

LIFT cumulative curve (ALIFT). Using these two metrics, the four chosen models were put to test on a deducing set, using the most recent data and a rolling window schematic. The Neural Network resulted in the best accuracy (AUC = 0.8 and ALIFT = 0.7), allowing to reach 79 percent. Two knowledge extraction methods, a sensitivity analysis and a Decision Tree, were passed to the Neural Network model which gave out many important attributes (e.g., Euribor rate, Outcome of the previous call and experience of the agent). Such knowledge extraction confirmed the obtained model as credible and valuable for telemarketing campaign managers [1, 2].

A set of data gathered by collecting information from various campaigns run by a bank was explored. It was observed that the aim of the bank was to improve the subscription rates towards a lengthier term deposit. A bunch of ML techniques/algorithms were applied to get a realistic solution to the problem. The problem being the question, 'In what way can institutions advertise their products such that those products are sold in a profitable manner?'. The goal was to acquire an efficient, accurate and best solution to the problem. Social media has increased the growth in case of communication and sharing of knowledge. It is really simple and easy to gather information. And hence, people are easily approachable. With the information gathered from a past campaign, the attributes of the client, the campaign, and economic conditions were examined. Depending on the data, Artificial Intelligence predictors will come up with the list of clients who are more probable of taking a chance on various subscriptions, thereby answering the question, 'what can banks do to improve the subscription rate?'. A lot of data structures like, arrays, vectors, dictionaries, are utilized according to the need. The beginning steps include, loading the data frame with a dataset for ease of data pre-processing using the distinct and various python libraries and packages. One of the attributes was excluded because there was a risk of leakage. The attribute which was dropped was the duration of the previous campaigning call made to the customer. This attribute was noticed to be too random which makes our data set very sparse. A dense data set is seemed to provide the best results. Such sparse data set would require more than one model to train the data. The further steps were to apply data cleaning methodologies to convert all the values into numeric type, so that it is easy to get a better accuracy from the predictive model. Graphs from each predictive model were generated and the most accurate model was chosen [3, 4].

The interesting thing about this chapter is the research done about the role of internet and social media in Relationship Marketing (RM). Their research was done particularly in the banking agenda. The purpose of the authors was to get an idea as to why a few banks don't feel interests in the social media trend. Another purpose was to learn about the methodologies used by such banks for improving relations with the customers. The authors focused upon the innovative ideas of banking institutions in quickly developing countries and regions, particularly in Europe [11, 12]. A good approach towards case-studies was used for this research. On the whole 3 case-studies were built, which explained the methods and ideologies of Relationship Marketing of retail banks in Europe. The data set utilized for building the case studies are collected via in-detail examinations of the top management, research and websites of the banks. Major reasons for abstaining from social media were: The form of approach was really famous among the customers; security issues about the internet and social media for banking; and lack of alignment with latest RM strategies. Social media seemed to be more relatable to younger generation banks, whereas these days social media is very dependable for gathering information about innovative ideas for campaigning activities. The chapter identifies significant requirements for the adaption of social media in Banking Industry and provides information on possibilities for alternative Relationship Marketing techniques which merges electronic sources with a more intimidate approach to banking. Case studies provide insights on marketing strategies of banks in the European region. The chapter presents challenges banks come across in their Relationship Marketing efforts and future vision of Relationship Marketing in a contemporary online setting [5, 6].

The convolution network is a well-known profound neural organization and it utilizes learned highlights and info information for include extraction which thusly extricated in an orderly fashion from the picture. The CNN is similar to correctly sort the article since it learns the highlights while the organization accumulates the pictures instead of pre-preparing. The powerful worldly expectation is utilized to decide the traffic stream in various conditions. As far as brief length, for example, 7 days and long term, for example, 30 days the forecast interaction is done. Profound learning has been utilized to do the powerfully through online. Hep-2 picture cells are arranged utilizing DSRN. The exactness of Traffic Net to order blocked and uncongested street states is improved [4]. FGFA and Deep Feature stream are proposed together to accomplish Image Net VID 2017. Work of fiction section assessment model is gotten from long momentary memory (LSTM). The broad tests are led to survey the activities of few Benchmark agent techniques like TC-128.

The proposed framework in this chapter chips away at the standard of IoT and related calculations. Ultrasonic sensors and arduinos have a significant influence in this framework. In this framework, the ultrasonic sensors will be set on street sides, which will check the quantity of vehicles, as they converge its reach. This check will be sent through arduino to another arduino. Another arduino will utilize this check to refresh the traffic signals as needs be, founded on constant information.

This chapter means to foster traffic light planning plans. Contextual investigation of Isfahan was required and by utilizing group examination season of-day was distinguished. Season of-day was dissected with the assistance of authentic information. Information mining methods are utilized like information assortment, information cleaning, information grouping and information change. Information assortment was finished with the assistance of sensors which are introduced in Isfahan at passage of street intersection. They kept up various tables for five traffic light intersections. Information cleaning was utilized as sensors used to go in a dormant state if vehicles were not at intersection and consequently, brought about zero as a worth in data set. Information was arranged based on work days and ends of the week as traffic variety is enormous. Change comprised of inquiries with the assistance of those diagrams and pic graphs are created. The time at various days is noted and bunch are made based on match in thickness of traffic [refer area IV]. Clementine information examination instrument was utilized. Microsoft dominate was utilized to draw diagrams for groups made by Clementine.

The intention of this exploration is to foster self-learning versatile and autonomous interstate control for repeating traffic designs. This chapter depends on man-made reasoning and AI calculations. Support learning, Q learning are utilized in this chapter for the improvement of self-learning autonomous model. Support learning is about how a specialist that faculties and acts in the climate can figure out how to pick ideal activities to accomplish its drawn out objectives. At whatever point the specialist plays out an activity in the climate, a mentor may give a prize or punishment to show the contrast between real state and accomplished state. Dynamic rerouting of traffic from the Expressway to an equal blood vessel/authority is executed in the field utilizing a solitary Variable Message Sign.

The intention of this exploration is to foster self-learning versatile and autonomous interstate control for repeating traffic designs. This chapter depends on man-made reasoning and AI calculations. Support learning, Q learning are utilized in this chapter for the improvement of self-learning autonomous model. Support learning is about how a specialist that faculties and acts in the climate can figure out how to pick ideal activities to accomplish its drawn out objectives. At whatever point the specialist plays out an activity in the climate, a mentor may give a prize or punishment to show the contrast between real state and accomplished state. Dynamic rerouting of traffic from the Expressway to an equal blood vessel/authority is executed in the field utilizing a solitary Variable Message Sign.

This chapter centers around lessening gridlock to diminish manual impedance in controlling rush hour gridlock. This chapter utilizes IoT based machines. This chapter depends on utilization of RFID (Radio Frequency Identification) and Raspberry Pi. In this proposed framework, RFID tag in set on vehicle, containing one of a kind number. The data from RFID tag is perused by RFID peruser and gave to Raspberry Pi by switch. The tally is kept up and traffic lights are coordinated likewise. It tends to be utilized to recognize taken vehicles too.

The primary point of this chapter is to decide the volume and thickness of the approaching traffic by utilizing picture handling method. Edge identification and ORB [Oriented FAST and Rotated BRIEF] calculations are utilized for handling the snapped pictures at fixed spans. Since the items are not followed in a video, the framework in this manner has a low computational expense. In the wake of snapping the pictures RGB tones are caught from the picture and shipped off the focal worker, where it is changed over into grayscale picture which then, at that point goes through edge detection. After edge identification, the picture is then changed into parallel image. The issues confronted while utilizing edge recognition calculation is overcome by utilizing Otsu's numerous thresholding over different pixel regions in the picture. Distance is recognized from the examined picture and after that this distance is increased with the width of street which gives the region covered by traffic. The framework then, at that point separates include focuses from the picture utilizing ORB algorithm, the street that is plain won't contribute towards highlights however the vehicles being versatile will do as such. Highlight coordinating is doing additionally utilizing savage power on two concurrent pictures to derive the traffic jam. Thus, a two-overlap cost saving methodology is embraced i.e. fuel and time cost reduction [refer segment IV].

The primary point of this chapter is to decide the volume and thickness of the approaching traffic by utilizing picture handling method. Edge identification and ORB [Oriented FAST and Rotated BRIEF] calculations are utilized for handling the snapped pictures at fixed spans. Since the items are not followed in a video, the framework in this manner has a low computational expense. In the wake of snapping the pictures RGB tones are caught from the picture and shipped off the focal worker, where it is changed over into grayscale picture which then, at that point goes through edge detection. After edge identification, the picture is then changed into parallel image. The issues confronted while utilizing edge recognition calculation is overcome by utilizing Otsu's numerous thresholding over different pixel regions in the picture. Distance is recognized from the examined picture and after that this distance is increased with the width of street which gives the region covered by traffic. The framework then, at that point separates include focuses from the picture utilizing ORB algorithm, the street that is plain won't contribute towards highlights however the vehicles being versatile will do as such. Highlight coordinating is doing additionally utilizing savage power on two concurrent pictures to derive the traffic jam. Thus, a two-overlap cost saving methodology is embraced i.e. fuel and time cost reduction [refer segment IV].

This chapter chiefly centers around executing a framework in which vehicle location and tallying is done from a video or camera sensor. In this chapter the framework utilizes camera as information sensor which gives continuous traffic information and is executed utilizing Beagle Board and AVR microcontroller. Video from camera is handled utilizing (PCA) Principal Component Analysis. PCA is utilized for examining and arranging the article on video outline for identifying vehicles. Dispersed Constraint Satisfaction Problem (DCSP) strategy is then utilized for deciding the span of each traffic signal, which depends on the vehicle tally from each lane. The consequence of DCSP is shipped off traffic light that is incorporated with traffic motor which gives signal likewise.

The Project proposes vehicle grouping and tallying execution conspire utilizing Scale Invariant Feature change (SIFT) algorithm.to improve the productivity and dependability of the vehicle checking and classification [9]. The strategy utilized in this framework is as follow 1. The video cut is perused by one capacity, then, at that point it is separated into number of casings. 2. The foundation deduction is finished continuously work. 3. Segmentation is acted in subsequent stage 4. Feature extraction is finished utilizing SIFT. 5. Features are coordinated to group vehicles as per class 6. Finally number of vehicles is checked. The classes of vehicles are characterized and by utilizing the calculation, highlight coordinating is done and check is expanded. Accordingly, SIFT gives picture includes that works over picture turn, scaling, interpretation, camera perspective giving the exact outcomes.

This chapter will in general improve current traffic the executives framework IoT based concepts [10]. The undertaking is executed in the accompanying manner. First the ultrasonic sensors are fixed on every path. They have utilized three sorts of sensors: High, Medium, Low. High is sent on first need Medium on second and Low on third need separately. Information is gathered from sensors and shipped off the framework. Traffic thickness is estimated and normal holding up time is determined. The model was constructed and correlation between time taken by existing framework and the proposed framework was done. Thus, holding up time was diminished effectively.

10.3   Experimental Results

Presently we will construct a graphical UI for our traffic conditions classifier with Tkinter. Tkinter is a GUI tool compartment in the standard python library. Make another record in the undertaking envelope and duplicate the underneath code. Save it as gui.py and you can show the code to composing python gui.py in the order line (Figures 10.1 and 10.2).

In this record, we have first stacked the prepared model 'traffic_classifier. h5' utilizing Keras. And afterward we assemble the GUI for transferring the picture and a catch is utilized to order which calls the characterize() work. The group() work is changing over the picture into the component of shape (1, 30, 30, 3). This is on the grounds that to foresee the traffic sign we need to give a similar measurement we have utilized when constructing the model. Then, at that point we foresee the class, the model.predict_classes (image) returns us a number between 0 and 42, which addresses the class it has a place with. We utilize the word reference to get the data about the class. Here's the code for the gui.py record.Code:

In this Python project with source code, we have effectively grouped the traffic conditions classifier with 95% precision and furthermore imagined how our exactness and misfortune changes with time, which is very acceptable from a basic CNN model.

The further steps include making a data frame with the outcome of every base-line model and make a graph of the results on a graph using the 'seaborn' library. We are going to make use of the AUC (Area Under

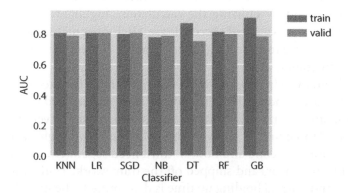

Figure 10.1 Classifiers.

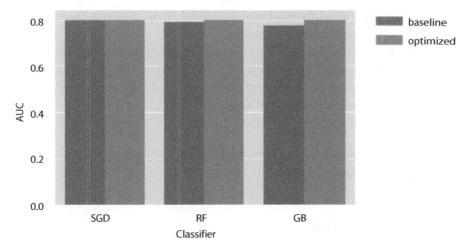

Figure 10.2 Comparing various classifiers.

the Curve) to calculate and select a finest model. AUC is one of the best metrics of data science performance-wise for picking the best model as it catches the trade-off among the actual positives and fake positives. We are not even required to set a threshold for this to function.

In this same way, the success rates and accuracies of the rest of the rest of the classifiers are compared and analyzed. These comparisons were plotted on a graph to get a clear picture (Figure 10.3).

Looking at the graph, we can make an observation that the Gradient Boosting Classifier with optimized hyperparameters has a higher AUC

```
In [115]:   1  # Load the model, columns, mean values, and scaler
            2  best_model = pickle.load(open('best_classifier.pkl','rb'))
            3  cols_input = pickle.load(open('cols_input.sav','rb'))
            4  df_mean_in = pd.read_csv('df_mean.csv', names =['col','mean_val'])
            5  scaler = pickle.load(open('scaler.sav','rb'))
            6

In [116]:   1  # Load the data
            2  df_train = pd.read_csv('df_train.csv')
            3  df_valid= pd.read_csv('df_valid.csv')
            4  df_test= pd.read_csv('df_test.csv')

In [117]:   1  # fill missing
            2  df_train = fill_my_missing(df_train, df_mean_in, cols_input)
            3  df_valid = fill_my_missing(df_valid, df_mean_in, cols_input)
            4  df_test = fill_my_missing(df_test, df_mean_in, cols_input)
            5
            6  # create X and y matrices
            7  X_train = df_train[cols_input].values
            8  X_valid = df_valid[cols_input].values
            9  X_test = df_test[cols_input].values
           10
           11  y_train = df_train['OUTPUT_LABEL'].values
           12  y_valid = df_valid['OUTPUT_LABEL'].values
           13  y_test = df_test['OUTPUT_LABEL'].values
           14
           15  # transform our data matrices
           16  X_train_tf = scaler.transform(X_train)
           17  X_valid_tf = scaler.transform(X_valid)
           18  X_test_tf = scaler.transform(X_test)
```

Figure 10.3 Evaluating the performance.

value when compared to the Baseline Model. It is obvious that the best model is 'Gradient Boosting Classifier'.

We have chosen the 'Gradient Boosting Classifier' as the best model for our project, because it had the best AUC values when implemented on the validation set. In order to make our prediction model reusable, we will save the classifier using the 'pickle' package.

At last, we will test the performance of our best classifier upon the test sample.

As a closing statement, let us preview the concluding evaluation of the performance on test sample.

10.4   Conclusion

In this chapter an Artificial Intelligence-based technique is used to predict if the customer is willing to opt for term deposits or not. We successfully created a predictive model based on Artificial Intelligence. After analyzing all the classifiers, through graphs and plots, we arrived at the conclusion that Gradient Boosting Classifier is the most accurate one. This is bases on the testing done with optimized hyperparameters [7, 8]. The test performance (AUC) is nearly 80%. The ratio of precision and prevalence is 1.6. This ratio indicates that the selected model is 1.6 times better at predicting the outcome compared to guesses made by the marketing agents [9, 10]. The selected model i.e., Gradient Boosting Classifier has correctly predicted that more than 60% of customers are going to subscribe for term deposits. During the development of this project, most of the focus was put on customers who had a significant con_price_idx (consumer price index) and euribor3m (3-month period for clearing the loans) because these features were deemed as important by the feature-importance algorithm. A lot of time, efforts, and resources can be saved by analyzing the data set in this manner.

References

1. Guyon, I. and Elisseeff, A., An introduction to variable and feature selection. *J. Artif. Intell. Res.*, 3, 1157–1182, 2003.
2. Martens, D. and Provost, F., Explaining data-driven document classifications. *MIS Q.*, 38, 1, 73–100, 2014.
3. Cortez, P. and Embrechts, M.J., Using sensitivity analysis and visualization techniques to open black box data mining models. *Inf. Sci.*, 225, 1–17, 2013.

4. Javaheri, S.H., Response modeling in direct marketing: A data mining based approach for target selection, 2008.
5. Phillips, R., Optimizing prices for consumer credit. *J. Revenue Pricing Manag.*, 12, 4, 360–377, 2013.
6. Moro, S., Cortez, P., Rita, P., A data-driven approach to predict the success of bank telemarketing. *Decis. Support Syst.*, 62, 22–31, 2014.
7. Mitic, M. and Kapoulas, A., Understanding the role of social media in banking industry. *Mark. Intell. Plan.*, 2012.
8. Priyadarshinee, P., Examining critical success factors of cloud computing adoption: Integrating AHP-structural mediation model. *Int. J. Decis. Support Syst. Technol.*, 12, 2, 80–96, 2020.
9. Gedam, V.V., Raut, R.D., Priyadarshinee, P., Chirra, S., Pathak, P.D., Analysing the adoption barriers for sustainability in the Indian power sector by DEMATEL approach. *Int. J. Sustain. Eng.*, 14, 3, 471–486, 2021.
10. Nayal, K., Raut, R.D., Narkhede, B.E., Priyadarshinee, P., Panchal, G.B., Gedam, V.V., Antecedents for blockchain technology-enabled sustainable agriculture supply chain. *Ann. Oper. Res.*, 1–45, 2021.
11. Nayal, K., Kumar, S., Raut, R.D., Queiroz, M M., Priyadarshinee, P., Narkhede, B.E., Supply chain firm performance in circular economy and digital era to achieve sustainable development goals. *Bus. Strategy Environ.*, 2021.
12. Raut, R.D., Mangla, S.K., Narwane, V.S., Gardas, B.B., Priyadarshinee, P., Narkhede, B.E., Linking big data analytics and operational sustainability practices for sustainable business management. *J. Clean. Prod.*, 224, 10–24, 2019.

11

Accelerating Drug Discovery with Quantum Computing

Mahesh V.* and Shimil Shijo

T. John college, Computer Application Department, Bengaluru, Karnataka, India

Abstract

The evolution of molecular formulations into medications to treat or remedy diseases is the foundation of the pharmaceutical business. Therefore, it is crucial that the pharmaceutical industry devotes a full 15% of its sales to research and development, which accounts for more than 20% of all R&D expenditures across all productions in the global economy. The trial-and-error method is typically used to create drugs, which is not only expensive but also risky and difficult to complete. Drug companies may potentially save a huge money and time by using quantum computing to better understand drugs and their effects on people. By enabling businesses to undertake more drug discoveries and develop break-through medical treatments, these computer advancements have the potential to significantly boost efficiency and lead to a more productive pharmaceutical industry. Pharmaceutical research and development has recently embraced artificial intelligence (AI). The succeeding digital frontier in drug detection is quantum computing (QC).

Keywords: Quantum computing, drug discovery, computer-aided drug design, artificial intelligence, quantum circuit, Qubit

11.1 Introduction

Computer science significant advancements in hardware and algorithms, quantum computing has developed quickly in recent years. The eventual

Corresponding author: mahesh92411@gmail.com

Sachi Nandan Mohanty, Rajanikanth Aluvalu and Sarita Mohanty (eds.) Evolution and Applications of Quantum Computing, (175–182) © 2023 Scrivener Publishing LLC

commercial utility of quantum computers is being brought closer by these developments. These innovative machines will find many applications in the exciting field of drug discovery. In contrast to current quantum chemistry techniques, quantum simulation will make it possible to characterize molecular systems more quickly and accurately.

Finding novel therapeutic medications is a time-consuming, challenging, and expensive procedure. It is a drawn-out procedure that involves steps including identifying the illness target, looking for new drug molecules, optimizing existing drug molecules, conducting clinical trials, and filing. From target discovery to market launch, it might take up to 12 to 15 years to develop new therapies. These days, quantum-inspired technologies are replacing the conventional clinical drug development process, reducing the time needed for drug discovery to a few weeks. In summary, quantum computing has the potential to speed up this process by enabling us to model molecules, perhaps one day doing away with the need for lab work altogether [3].

The world could alter as a result of the speed of quantum computers, which Google and NASA have previously shown can be at least a hundred million times faster than current computers.

11.2   Working Nature of Quantum Computers

The field of quantum information science has evolved in recent years to investigate if there is any potential benefit to encoding, storing, transferring, and processing data in systems with unusual quantum features. Today [4], it is acknowledged that the answer is indeed "yes," and numerous research organizations from all over the world are attempting to achieve the technologically extremely ambitious aim of building a quantum computer, which would significantly increase computational capability for specific assignments. For quantum computation, a diversity of physical systems that covers a large portion of contemporary physics, is being constructed. Quantum computers use the peculiar laws of the quantum realm while classical computers are built on mechanical structures that operate through the language of mathematics. They rely on two phenomena that occurred above the atomic scale: superposition and quantum entanglement. Bits used in traditional computers can either be zero or one. But a quantum bit, also known as a qubit, can simultaneously be zero and one.

(a) Quantum computing using the standard gate paradigm. Time moves from left to right in the circuit design, where each horizontal wire stands in for a qubit. Each qubit is measured in the final state of the quantum computation, which is produced by the quantum computer through a series of operations. A quantum circuit is the collection of quantum gates.

(b) Quantum computation with variation. There are gates with variable parameters in this quantum circuit (illustrated as x and y in the diagram). Every time the quantum circuit breaks down, the classical computer analyses the measurement results and suggests new values for the quantum circuit's parameters.

Bits serve as the foundational units for information processing in the majority of digital devices. The discrete, "classical" states of 0 or 1 are expressed by each bit. The term "classical computers" refers to devices that operate on bits to compute. For the purpose of computation, quantum computers alter the quantum states of matter. Combining qubits, which are two-level quantum systems, is a common method for creating those quantum states. Quantum computers can accomplish computing tasks in ways that are superior to those made feasible on their classical equivalents by modifying the qubit states and making use of peculiarly quantum mechanical occurrences like superposition and entanglement. A quantum algorithm is a predetermined method of modifying quantum states to address

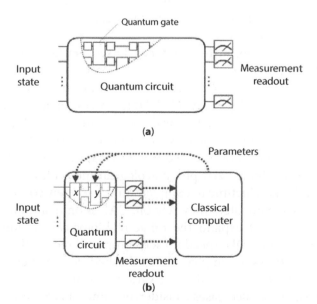

Figure 11.1 Schematic diagrams of two quantum computing paradigms [2].

a computational issue. It can often be demonstrated that quantum algorithms perform better than classical algorithms for particular tasks with less steps necessary by looking at how many steps they require. Quantum speedup is the term for this capacity (Figure 11.1) [2].

11.3   Use Cases of Quantum Computing in Drug Discovery

- **DNA Sequencing**
  Faster DNA sequencing, more thorough analysis, and the ability to more accurately anticipate disease prevention and diagnosis are all possible thanks to quantum computing.
- **Drug Design**
  Drug development would take advantage of quantum computing's inherent properties as well as its speed and processing capability. Because quantum computers used to simulate quantum phenomena use the same theory that governs how electrons in medication molecules interact with the human body. It will lead to considerably faster and more precise outcomes.
- **Clinical Trials**
  Quantum computing can enable *in silico* clinical trials, in which a medicine is tested without the use of humans or animals. Compared to *in-vivo* testing, it is a faster, cheaper, and safer alternative [1].
- **Quantum computing in Drug Discovery Research and Development**
  Currently, pharmaceutical companies use computer-assisted drug discovery (CADD) to process molecules using non-QC methods including dynamics simulation (MD) and finite-temperature density functional theory (DFT). The basic computations needed to reliably anticipate the behavior of medium-sized pharmacological molecules, however, could take a lifetime to complete on the severely constrained classical computers they rely on. CADD on quantum computers might expand the range of biological machineries willing to CADD, speed up screening, and reduce the number of times an empirically established development cycle must be run by eradicating various research-related "dead ends," which decreases considerable time and expense to the drug discovery segment [5].

11.4   Target Drug Identification and Validation

Quantum Computing (QC) can be used to accurately anticipate the 3-D structures of proteins during target identification. It takes a lot of time and frequently produces low-quality results to obtain high-quality structural data. Despite these attempts, many physiologically significant proteins have yet to be crystallized, whether as a result of their size, solubility, or inability to direct and cleanse in adequate quantities. Because the commercial justification for a particular drug may be so compelling, pharmaceutical corporations occasionally produce drugs without even understanding the arrangement of a protein, embracing the risk of a trial-and-error method in succeeding stages of drug development.

Although Google's DeepMind's AlphaFold was a milestone in AI-driven protein folding, it hasn't fully overcome the difficulties associated with traditional computing-based modeling. Pharma companies may only use CADD on small to medium-sized drug applicants with current technology, and primarily in a successive fashion. The bottleneck lies in the computing power. Pharma enterprises would be able to multiply all use cases to specific biologics, such as fusion proteins or semi-synthesized biologics, and undertake *in silico* search and validation studies in a more high-throughput manner with sufficient QC. Beyond just identifying the protein, this use case would eventually cover practically all of biological knowledge. This stage would already offer potential lead molecules that are more simpler and quicker to enhance with a robust enough hit-generation and validation approach.

11.5   Drug Discovery Using Quantum Computers is Expected to Start by 2030

Early commercial quantum computing initiatives are already under way as we exit the first horizon, which focused on quantum stimulated algorithms throughout the preceding 40 years, and approach the horizon of partially error-corrected QC. This stage, which is also known as "noisy intermediate-scale quantum" (NISQ), explains the non-fault-tolerant features of near-term devices that are constructed on an initially significant number of quantum bits (qubits) to address issues that classical computers can't yet resolve. It is hotly contested when QC technology will be developed, put into use, and adopted by various businesses. For a small number of application situations, NISQ, a class of probabilistic computers that nevertheless give error-prone outcomes, could be able to offer a quick fix. Businesses interested in QC's impending must consider this uncertainty into account [7].

After 2030, it's anticipated that quality control will be totally error-corrected and all of its benefits will be realized. In this future, QC is widely used, and well along adopters also use the technology. In other way, by the middle of the 2020s, chemical players might begin generating value using QC. Soon after, pharma corporations are anticipated to enter the market more firmly. Pharma researchers focus on larger, more complicated molecules than their counterparts in the chemical industry because neither high-performance computers nor the current generation of quantum computers are capable of simulating them.

Pharma invested in its digital transformation as early as everyone else, yet at every point they are faced with extremely difficult issues. Digital, in a sense, is about having extensive information and performing calculations on it. In pharma, it's quite challenging to accomplish this. In a trial with 100 patients, these are 100 unique people, not a homogeneous object. Furthermore, even though molecules are not individuals, the physics that regulates their interactions is complicated and difficult to calculate. So, in order to make calculations possible, pharma relies on simplifications, yet every simplification introduces errors and uncertainty. It does so occasionally. But when working with complicated substances like metals, which have hard to mimic atoms, simplifications make it difficult to interpret the findings of experiments. This is why a fully computerized pipeline for drug research and development is still a long way off. But with recent advances in computing, we might be able to move in that direction [6].

11.6   Conclusion

As we saw during the pandemic, diseases may spread exponentially over a short period of time. It is crucial to develop an alternate notion that can speed up the drug discovery process because it takes longer to find new drugs using standard approaches, especially when trying to treat terminal illnesses. But with the help of quantum computing technologies, drug discovery can be considerably improved in both speed and quality.

References

1. Keinan, S., Hatcher Frush, E., Shipman, W.J., Leveraging cloud computing for *in-silico* drug design using the quantum molecular design (QMD) framework. *Comput. Sci. Eng.*, 20, 4, 66–73, Jul./Aug. 2018.

2. Cao, Y., Romero, J., Aspuru-Guzik, A., Potential of quantum computing for drug discovery. *IBM J. Res. Dev.*, 62, 6, 6:1–6:20, 1 Nov.-Dec. 2018.

3. Li, J., Alam, M., Sha, C.M., Wang, J., Dokholyan, N.V., Ghosh, S., Invited: Drug discovery approaches using quantum machine learning. *2021 58th ACM/IEEE Design Automation Conference (DAC)*, pp. 1356–1359, 2021.

4. Bayerstadler, A., Becquin, G. *et al.*, Industry quantum computing applications. *EPJ Quantum Technol.*, 8, 25, 2021. Quantum Technology and Application Consortium – QUTAC, https://doi.org/10.1140/epjqt/s40507-021-00114-x.

5. https://www.mckinsey.com/industries/life-sciences/our-insights/pharmas-digital-rx-quantum-computing-in-drug-research-and-development, accessed on June 20, 2022.

6. https://www.labiotech.eu/interview/quantum-computing-drug-discovery, accessed on June 24, 2022.

7. Evers, M., Heid, A., Ostojic, I., Quantum computing in drug research and development, pp. 1–12, 2021, https://www.alcimed.com/en/alcim-articles/advanced-computing-in-pharma-3-reasons-why-quantum-computing-could-disrupt-the-pharma-rd/, accessed on June 18, 2021.

Problems and Demanding Situations in Traditional Cryptography: An Insistence for Quantum Computing to Secure Private Information

D. DShivaprasad[1]*, Mohamed Sirajudeen Yoosuf[2], P. Selvaramalakshmi[1], Manoj A. Patil[3] and Dasari Promod Kumar[4]

[1]Faculty of Science and Technology, International University of East Africa, Kampala, Uganda
[2]School of Computer Science and Engineering (SCOPE), VIT-AP University, Amaravathi, India
[3]Department of Information Technology, Vasavi College of Engineering, Hyderabad, India
[4]Department of Computer Science and Engineering, Lendi Institute of Engineering and Technology, Vizianagaram, Andhra Pradesh, India

Abstract

Most of the traditional cryptographic algorithms are based on mathematical models and try to perform encryption/decryption by factoring large numbers as their prime values. Both public and private key encryption uses mathematical operations to secure the information. However, these mathematical based cryptographic models are becoming vulnerable as the computation power is increasing. Also, the evolution in modern mathematics like factoring large integers are making it possible to crack traditional cryptography algorithms. In this chapter, we would like to elaborate the issues and the challenges with the traditional mathematical model based cryptographic algorithms. Also, we intend to elaborate the need of integrating quantum physics and cryptography to ensure the security of confidential data. Quantum cryptography is one of emerging technologies in the cyber world. The scope of this paper covers the weaknesses of modern digital cryptosystems, the fundamental concepts of quantum cryptography, the real-world implementation of this technology along with its limitations, and finally the future direction in which quantum cryptography is headed towards.

*Corresponding author: shivadulam@gmail.com

Sachi Nandan Mohanty, Rajanikanth Aluvalu and Sarita Mohanty (eds.) Evolution and Applications of Quantum Computing, (183–206) © 2023 Scrivener Publishing LLC

Keywords: Cryptography, quantum physics, quantum computing, quantum cryptography

12.1   Introduction to Cryptography

In usual practice the data from one computer will be transferred to another, while transferring it may come across various networks and different physical surroundings but we are not sure whether they are protected or not. Here the computer network part will assure only that the data reached the specified destination, along with this it needs an additional important concept called cryptography to ensure that the data delivered is safe and secure.

Cryptography is the art or science; it will convert the information into an insensible form for the unauthorized users by using encryption technique and make sense to the authorized end users after decrypting it with its appropriate process or key. This complete process will go through some serious mathematical procedures. That mathematical process will ensure how strong the algorithm is, depending on the strength of this algorithmic process it will apply to the applications where it is needed. If the applied crypto technique is weak or not strong enough for the application then there is a chance of data disclosure or data loss may happen. Most of today's applications, more specific to the computer-related or computer-dependent, were involved with the cryptographic techniques and these techniques must ensure that they are having the key which is not outdated.

The organization should have proper awareness about the compliance and guidance by the organizations like NIST, ISO, etc. for the recommendations to secure the digital business.

Cryptography contains two processes one is encryption and another one is decryption, in Encryption process the normal text (plain text) will be converted into an a cipher text (the text which is not understandable to the middlepersons) by using some encryption technique or method. When it reaches to the authorized destination then the recipient will decrypt the cipher text with the pre agreed key with the sender, then after decryption process the recipient are able to access the plain text [1]. This complete process is called Cryptography.

12.1.1   Confidentiality

This is one of the important principles of information security. Confidentiality promises that the sensitive data never be disclosed to the unauthorized user's .If the confidentiality fails the following challenges may occur [1].

a) If the confidentiality of the data or information from the company were not protected properly there will be a huge loss for the business/clients.
b) Unfortunately if the data or information has been in the wrong hands then there may be a chance of unethical activity.

In general confidentiality can be achieved by using encryption.

12.1.2   Authentication

This is one of the important principles of information security. In layman's view, authentication makes sure that the communication was initiated from the original sender. If the authentication fails the following challenges may occur [1].

a) There is a chance of logging in with invalid credentials.
b) If the authentication fails, then there is no validation process for the users, anyone can enter into the system.

For example the person who carries the keys will have a chance to get into the house (means he is the authorized one).

12.1.3   Integrity

This is one of the important principles of information security, Integrity will ensure that the information which is transferred between authorized users was tamper proof, the other meaning of this statement is when the data was transferred between the authorized parties this information may be transformed through the public networks when the data gone through the public networks there is a high chance of data disclosure, so data integrity make sure that these actions never exists [1].

If the Integrity fails the following actions may raise:

a) An unauthorized user in the network may change the information.
b) An unauthorized user may change the recipient address.
c) An unauthorized user may place a replay attack.

12.1.4   Non-Repudiation

Non-repudiation is achieved through cryptography, like digital signature, and includes other services for authentication, auditing, and logging. In online deals, a digital signature ensures that a party can't later deny transferring information or deny the authenticity of its hand. A digital hand is created using the private key of an asymmetric key pair, which is public-key cryptography and vindicated with a corresponding public key [1]. Only the private crucial holder can pierce this key and produce this hand, proving that a document was electronically linked by that holder. This ensures that a person cannot later deny that they furnished the hand, furnishing non-repudiation.

For example, if the customer debits the money from the bank and claims that he/she is not the one who made that transaction, in the same way the banker may claim that the transaction was not done even though the transaction was done in real life. Non-Repudiation will ensure these types of transactions and find who is guilty. One popular application digital signature will address in the banking systems.

12.2   Different Types of Cryptography

There are various types of cryptography techniques one is one way processing techniques and the other is two way processing techniques [2].

12.2.1   One-Way Processing

The one-way means that it's extremely delicate to turn the digest back into the original communication. It's also exceedingly rare that two different communication inputs can affect the same digest product. The best methods are hash algorithms.

12.2.1.1   Hash Function (One-Way Processing)

This mode doesn't need any key involvement, where as it uses a fixed length hashes value that's reckoned on the base of the plain textbook communication. Hash functions are used for the process to check the integrity of the communication to ensure that the communication has not been altered, affected or compromised by contagion. This mode is having many real-time application like to check the integrity of the software form the sources

Table 12.1 Various hash functions.

Type of hash function	The output hash length
MD2	128 bits
MD4	128 bits
MD5	128 bits
MD6	up to 512 bits
RPEMD	128 bits
RPEMD-128	128 bits
RPEMD-160	160 bits
RPEMD-320	320 bits
SHA-1	160 bits
SHA-224	224 bits
SHA-256	256 bits
SHA-384	384 bits
SHA-512	512 bits

while downloading generating the output of fixed size even though the input size varies.

Hash Algorithms

Encryption doesn't cover data from reworking by other parties. There should be a need to guarantee that data arrives at the recipient in its original form as it transferred from the original sender. The hash function will ensure that the data received is in the same original form as it is transferred from the original sender. There are various hash functions (Table 12.1) which are differentiated on the basis of its output length, the number of rounds and its strength [2].

12.2.2   Two-Way Processing

By using this method we can encrypt the given plain text into ciphertext and by using the decryption process we can get the plain text again from the ciphertext., but In one way processing we can encrypt the data and generate the ciphertext but it is really tough to get the plain text from the given cipher text.

12.2.2.1   Symmetric Cryptography

This type of encryption mode has a single key for both encryption and decryption so that's the reason this mode is also called as private key encryption/secret key encryption (Figure 12.1). The sender initiates the process by applying a secret key to the plain text to cipher a communication while the receiver applies the same key to decipher the communication and get the plain text [3]. Since only a single secret key is used on both sides so for encryption and decryption we say that this is a symmetric encryption.

In (Figure 12.2) we will find various private key algorithms, means both the receiver and sender will maintain same Key.

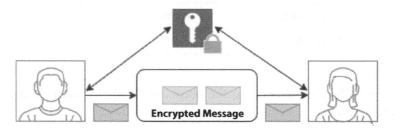

Figure 12.1 Symmetric key encryption.

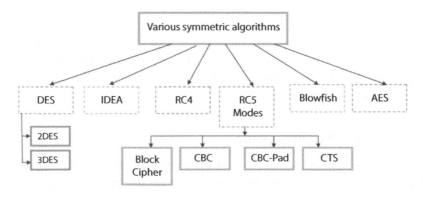

Figure 12.2 Various symmetric key algorithms.

All these algorithms are differentiated based on the size of the output, size of the input block, number of rounds to follow.

12.2.2.2   Asymmetric Cryptography

This type of encryption mode involves a pair of keys; the other name for this mode is public key encryption. In this approach each participant will have a pair of keys one is a public key and the other one is private key. The private key is secret and isn't revealed to any other participants, where the public key is shared with all those users whom you want to communicate with. However, also Alice will cipher it with Bob's public key and Bob can decipher the communication with its own private key, you can observe the differences from the (Figure 12.3) that both the participants have their own private keys, If Alice wants to shoot a message to Bob he has to encrypt the message with Bob's public key then Bob will decrypt the message with its own secret key.

This encryption is better than the symmetric encryption because there is no need to maintain a secure channel to transfer the secret key between the two parties [3]. Each participant will have a pair of keys (private key

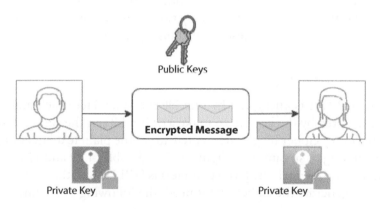

Figure 12.3 Asymmetric key cryptography.

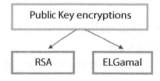

Figure 12.4 Various asymmetric key algorithms.

and public key) one is for encryption and the other for the decryption process. RSA public key encryption is one of the most used (Figure 12.4).

Comparison between symmetric key and asymmetric key encryption [1, 2]:

Symmetric key	Asymmetric key
i) It is a faster algorithm	i) It is slower compared to symmetric
ii) Usually the output size is less then are equal to the original size	ii) Usually the output size is more than the original size
iii) a Secret key is shared between two authorized parties for the encryption and decryption	iii) Different key is used for the encryption and decryption
iv) prior to encryption it should have an agreement for the key	iv) no need of prior agreement

12.2.3   Algorithms Types

We have been talking about the transformation of plaintext messages into cipher text messages, it's been done by two primary ways i) stream cipher ii) block cipher basing on these algorithms types was categorized.

12.2.3.1   Stream Cipher

The original text is encrypted by one bit at a time. Here each and every bit is encrypted by the key bit to make a cipher bit , in the similar fashion each and every cipher bit gets decrypted to get the plain text bit. For better understanding of stream refer Figure 12.5 and Tables 12.2 and 12.3.

Example problem: if the given plain text is HELLO and the private key is 101101 to generate the cipher text it needs the following procedure:

Step 1: According to given data PT = HELLO and the Key = 101101 to generate the cipher text it needs to perform Xor operation.
Step 2: Find the ASCII value of PT = HELLO, after generating the ASCII values are
Step 3: Perform Ex-or operation between key and the plain text is

PT	H	E	L	L	O
Ascii	72	68	76	76	79
BB	1001000	1000100	1001100	1001100	1001111
Key	1011011	0110110	1101101	1011011	0010110
CT	0010011	1110010	0100001	0010111	1011001
Ascii	DC3	r	!	ETB	Y

PT = plaintext, BB = Binary bits, CT = Cipher text

Figure 12.5 ASCII characters after applying key.

Table 12.2 Conversion from plain text to binary.

PT characters	ASCII	Binary equivalent
H	72	1001000
E	68	1000100
L	76	1001100
L	76	1001100
O	79	1001111

Table 12.3 Ex-or truth table for reference.

X	Y	Ex-or
0	0	0
0	1	1
1	0	1
1	1	0

Step 4: After applying the ex-or operation with the key, we got the Cipher text.

This is how we generate the cipher text for the given plain text.

12.2.3.2   Block Cipher

Here the plaintext will be considered in the fixed block sizes and perform the same procedure.

12.2.4   Modes of Algorithm

Primarily, there are four types of modes: i) Cipher feedback mode, ii) Electronic code book. iii) Cipher block chaining mode. iv) Output feedback mode (Figure 12.6).

12.2.4.1   Cipher Feedback Mode

This mode works on flow cipher, it needs to be transmitted without delay with the aid of an operator in a comfortable manner after typing the keystrokes at a terminal, to reap protection in such programs, The Cipher feedback mode will satisfy these desires [2].

12.2.4.2   Output Feedback Mode

This mode is extremely analogous to the CFB. The only difference is that in the case of CFB, the ciphertext is fed into the coming stage of the encryption process. But in the case of OFB the affair of the IV encryption process is fed into the coming stage of the encryption process [1, 2].

12.2.4.3   Cipher Block Chaining Mode

We saw that in the case of ECB, within a given communication, a plaintext block always produces the same cipher- textbook block. The CBC mode ensures that it generates different cipher blocks for the same text pattern [1, 2].

12.2.4.4   Electronic Code Book

Is the easiest mode of operation. Here, the incoming plain text communication is categorized into equal sized blocks of 64 bits length each. Each block is encrypted with the same key and generates the cipher text, because

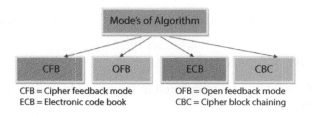

Figure 12.6 Modes of algorithm.

of this reason there may be a chance of getting the same cipher key for the same plain text block; this will be a drawback for this approach [2].

12.3   Common Attacks

The basically common attacks are further grouped up into two types they are:

1) Passive attacks
2) Active attacks.

12.3.1   Passive Attacks

In these types of attacks the attacker will continuously monitor the communication channel. The target point of the passive attackers is to capture the information from the communication channels and gain the knowledge from it [2]. Here passive means the attacker never intends to change or modify the existing data. Due to this reason it is tough task for the authorised user to check or detect the passive attack. That's the reason prevention is the best approach to handle passive attacks (Figure 12.7). Here we list few possible passive attacks. These attacks come under interception.

12.3.1.1   *Traffic Analysis*

In the usual practise the data which is transferred from sender to recipient will be in the encoded format, the passive attacker will check for the repeated patterns and start analysis on that data and try to capture the legitimate information (Figure 12.8). To perform these type of task's there

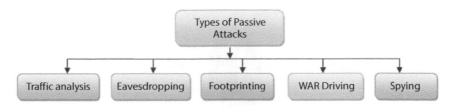

Various types of Passive Attacks

Figure 12.7 Various types of passive attacks.

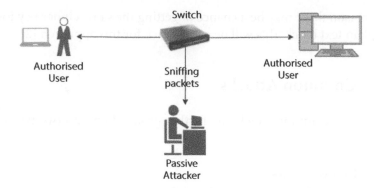

Figure 12.8 Traffic analysis.

are Packet Sniffer programs like Wireshark, network packet analyzer are used.

12.3.1.2　Eavesdropping

Listening to the sensitive information from the communication line, it sounds similar to the snooping, but in snooping approach if the attacker is able to gainaccess from the communication his work is done. But here the attacker may handle "Man in the middle" and "Replay attack" (Figure 12.9). Firstly the attacker will extract the legitimate information like (login credentials, passwords, Remote login sessions, Telnet, FTP) from

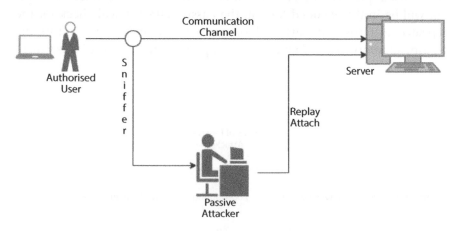

Figure 12.9 Eavesdropping.

the communication link by using sniffing. After extracting valid information the attacker will use Replay attack to the server claiming that he is an authorized user.

12.3.1.3   Foot Printing

This is a process of extracting all the information about the target system/organization like login credentials, organization's network, Class of IP addresses, Employee details, Networking passwords etc. This process is usually done before the penetrating testing.

12.3.1.4   War Driving

This attack is mainly concentrates for the open wifi networks or vulnerable network; there are already existing Software's and websites which allow hackers to get map for the open Access points. Nowadays this become a hobby for some individuals to access the unsecured network and try to find the legitimate information.

In the above (Figure 12.10) the dotted line covered area in the vulnerable zone because it has an open access point, so the person who is sitting in the car is performing the War driving to gain the access.

12.3.1.5   Spying

The Attacker can manage to enter into the network and claimed as an authorized user and observe the traffic of the network and learn the encoded

Figure 12.10 War driving.

method used for data traffic and gain the information. This information will be used for the future use.

12.3.2   Active Attacks

Here the attacker will modify the contents where as in passive attacks the attacker just view the legitimate information but never modifies like Active attackers (Figure 12.11). These attacks can be detected but hard to prevent.

12.3.2.1   Denial of Service

These Denial of Service attack and Distributed Denial of Service attack will concentrate on organization and tries to breach their services for the authorised users and most of times these attacks never performed on individuals (Figures 12.12). In Denial of Service attack the attackers flood the server with messages to make the server busy and make the resources fully occupied.

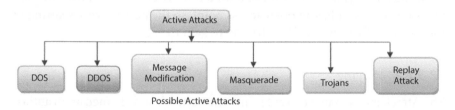

Figure 12.11 Various types of active attacks.

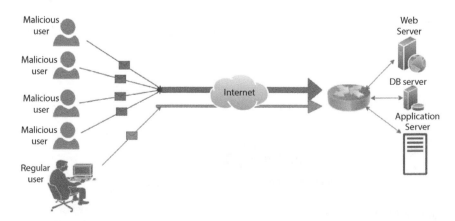

Figure 12.12 Distributed denial.

From Figure 12.12 we can find that the malicious users are occupying the most of the bandwidth so the services which are intended to serve for the legitimate user will not be served [4].

12.3.2.2   Distributed Denial of Service (DDOS)

Here the intention is similar to denial of service but the approach is different [4]. In this approach the malicious user will create a handlers these handlers will run theshow; here the question is what exactly the handlers will do? The malicious user (attacker) will train the handler to create infected systems and those systems will act according to the malicious user instructions, so finding the malicious user is a biggest challenge.

The general features to recognize DDOS (Figure 12.13) attack are:

1) Sudden increase in SPAM count
2) The performance will be degraded
3) It will be tough to access the websites.

12.3.2.3   Message Modification

Most of the times this message modification attacks occur at the Email, once they achieved the access the attacker will inject the malicious code or they will redirect to other mailing address [10].

12.3.2.4   Masquerade

In this attack the attacker will fool/bluff the authorized recipient and claims that he/she is a authorised user and make attempt's to get in Figure 12.14.

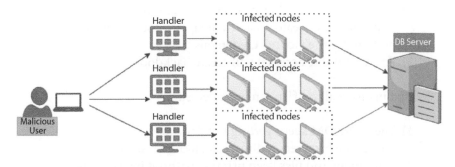

Figure 12.13 Distributed denial of service.

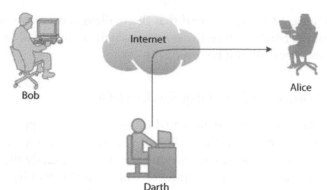

Darth
Darth is communicating with alice claiming Bob credentials (Masqurade)

Figure 12.14 Masquerade.

Once he gets into the network he will try to get the greater privileged services from the target organization [10].

12.3.2.5   Trojans

Trojans is a malicious program, which is managed to get into the victims system by email, file transfer, internet relay chat... etc. it won't harm any files in the victims system, it will wait for the attacker will and it will start acting according to it (Figure 12.15). Once the System is affected with the Trojan then various types of damages may be possible [5].

1) The victim system may be acted as an active bot for the Illegal distributed denial of service.
2) It may reveal the sensitive financial information to the attacker.
3) It may act as a FTP server for the Pirated software.
4) It may gain the higher privileged access from the organization and may create greater damage to the organization by pretending the victim's credentials.
5) For the remote access it will create backdoors.

Symptoms to analyze if Trojan was affected:

1) The CD/ROM keeps getting notified.
2) Sometime browsers redirects to unknown sites.
3) Document and files keep printing without instruction.

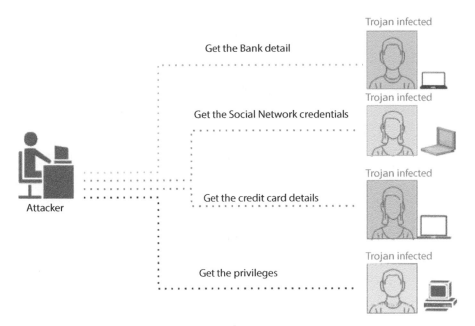

Figure 12.15 Trojan attack.

4) Your computer keeps IP scanning without victim concern, so that ISP provider will intimate you regarding this issue. These are few indication of Trojan horse attack.

12.3.2.6 *Replay Attacks*

This attack will be performed by copy and paste the conversation which is already made by the genuine user and the server [5, 10]. When this message which is received by the receiver, he/she feels this is generated by the genuine costumer soothe server will act accordingly, but it was a Replay attack by the attacker.

12.3.3 Programming Weapons for the Attackers

One of the weapons for the attackers is virus; it can perform huge damage to the victims system like deleting files, deleting programs, making copies of the files. Targeting victims contact addresses and Email contacts [11]. Virus can be programmed to activate in regular events like, for example if the attacker is intended to active the virus program at specific time (like

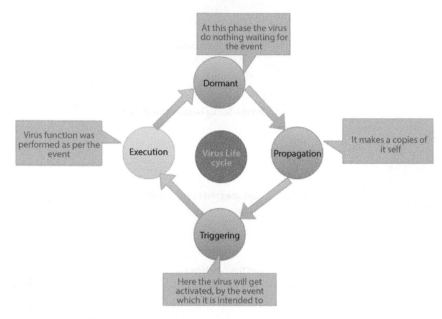

Figure 12.16 Different phases of the virus [12].

activate at 1:00AM) it can perform accordingly. Virus will gone through four phases (Figure 12.16).

12.3.3.1   Dormant Phase

At this phase the virus do nothing it simply wait for its action, the action or event will be locked up with the virus activation, so at this phase it simply wait for that event to occur.

12.3.3.2   Propagation Phase

At this phase the virus starts replicating by itself means it makes multiple copies on disk. Sometimes these copies will adopt new techniques that which can hide form detection programs.

12.3.3.3   Triggering Phase

At this phase the virus will get its instruction (from the event or action) it is waiting for to get activated. It will change from Dormant phase to Activate phase.

12.3.3.4   Execution Phase

At this phase the virus actual works start working means its load was released and start damage the contents, deleting files, making copies, creating too many dialogs, re-directing to unknown sites etc.

12.4   Recent Cyber Attacks

Some of the cyber-attacks listed in the (Table 12.4) that created a huge damage.

Table 12.4 Various types of attacks and its damage level.

Type of attack	Nature of attack	Targeted organization	Damage level
Ransomware attack [9]	It holds the legitimate data and ask for Ransom to release it	Big Organizations	❖ Organization infected with Ransomware n 2020 is 51% ❖ Organization paid back the ransom is 21% ❖ There are some organization even though the ransom was the data was not released is 1% Source (Sophus 2021, SonicWall 2020)

(Continued)

Table 12.4 Various types of attacks and its damage level. (*Continued*)

Type of attack	Nature of attack	Targeted organization	Damage level
Phishing [13]	These attacks will be handled through Emails or calls	Most of the time's Individuals	❖ Recently on a single day Threat analysis group has blocked 800 million Covid-19 th1;emed phishing. Source (Security Magazine 2020)
Business Email Compromise Attack [13]	They try to capture the corporate financial transaction and redirect to their own accounts.	Business Employees, and that too mainly high profiled corporate employees	❖ Nearly 200% increase in Business Email Compromise (BEC) attacks was held in 2020 Source (Proof point 2019)
Mobile Malware [14]	The computing power of the mobile device will be used for mining and Mobile Ransomware	Most of the time's Individuals	❖ Iran, Bangladesh, and Algeria are top 3 countries which is badly affected with Mobile malware's Source (Kaspersky 2020)
Crypto jacking [15]	This malware was designed to do mining from the victims system, and the mining rewards are forward to the attackers account. There are some crypto-currencies like "Manero" which can mine with mobile or computer computing power.	It includes individual, Small organizations, middle organization and large organizations.	❖ They can earn more with minimal effort. ❖ It was new cyber threat rising very faster. ❖ Crypto jacking is suddenly increased 450% in 2018 Source (Security intelligence 2018)

(*Continued*)

Table 12.4 Various types of attacks and its damage level. (*Continued*)

Type of attack	Nature of attack	Targeted organization	Damage level
Data breaches [16]	Due to lack of proper tight security measures Data breaches (Stealing the information from other organization) will occur	Targets mainly on Small scale business	❖ It was observed that 33% of data breach was occurred in 2019 when compared with 2018 ❖ Due to this data breach almost 25% of the small businesses was filed for bankrupt ❖ Due to this data breach almost 10% of the small business were completely closed. Source (National Cyber security alliance, Verizon 2020)

12.5   Drawbacks of Traditional Cryptography

The traditional cryptography suffers from few serious challenges which cannot be omitted [6].

12.5.1   Cost and Time Delay

This is one of the biggest challenges for traditional cryptography, because while applying the cryptographic techniques to the application it consumes more computing power, and it also needs time to execute these complex algorithms which leads to delay.

12.5.2   Disclosure of Mathematical Computation [7]

Most of the traditional cryptographic algorithms based on some complex mathematical computations, if this mathematical logic was disclosed then the whole algorithm will become weakened.

12.5.3   Unsalted Hashing

Only hashing technique without salt for storing passwords is prone to rainbow attacks, because nowadays simple hashes are too easy to break down.

12.5.4   Attacks

For the attacks like Distributed Denial of service (DDOS) or Denial of Service (DOS) attacks, these traditional cryptography techniques is seriously failed to address, handling the service level access to an organization/business domain is bit challenging.

12.6   Need of Quantum Cryptography

As we see that traditional cryptography is purely based on mathematical calculation. And with the latest available computing power these mathematical computations can be broken down in less time. Because of this reason the business models have to adopt a new technology which can address the problems which are faced by traditional computing.

Quantum cryptography is purely based on quantum mechanics [6].

12.6.1   Quantum Mechanics

Einstein has proposed the light theory; light travels in bunch of tiny particles (photons) with energy. The quantum cryptography is dependent on two major principles of quantum mechanics [8]:

  i)   Photon polarization principle.
  ii) Heisenberg uncertainty principle.

Quantum Computing equips the unique behaviour of quantum physics, which allows these photons to stay in any orientation. By using the features of quantum physics like Superposition and entanglement, this quantum computing will generate qubits. These qubits will be considered as basic bits in quantum computing. These qubits can be super positioned to generate all possible combinations of a qubits [8]. This will create complex multi-dimensional computational spaces. Whereas entanglement which will correlate the two qubits the correlation of qubits will be used to find the solution for the complex problems. It's really hard to guess the secret key, that's the reason adoption of quantum cryptography is seriously needed for modern cryptographic procedures.

12.7   Evolution of Quantum Cryptography

Quantum cryptography was the name first stemmed by Bennett, Bassard and Wiesner. In 1983 quantum coding was first introduced by Wiesner. Feynman introduced an earlier version of first quantum circuit. The first quantum cryptography algorithm was "BB84" this algorithm was used for the quantum key distribution [8].

12.8   Conclusion and Future Work

Traditional cryptography has numerous applications, even today most of the secure websites uses algorithms like RSA and ElGamal but to provide the more security these algorithms were increasing key length and also increases the number of rounds for the computations but here the biggest challenge is all the traditional cryptographic depends on the integer factorization. So these algorithms are prone to breakdown because of integer factorization. Quantum cryptography has changed the approach by using qubits which will generate the key (guessing the quantum generating key is real hard). Quantum cryptography can be maintained with less resource. Now the quantum cryptography is working for the limited distance (60 miles), if the distance is increased then the applications of quantum cryptography will also be increased.

References

1. Stallings, W. and Tahiliani, M.P., *Cryptography and network security: Principles and practice*, vol. 6, Pearson London, UK, 2014.
2. Kahate, A., *Cryptography and network security*, Tata McGraw-Hill Education, Uttar Pradesh, 2013.
3. Yegireddi, R. and Kumar, R.K., A survey on conventional encryption algorithms of cryptography. *2016 International Conference on ICT in Business Industry & Government (ICTBIG)*, pp. 1–4, 2016.

4. Farmer, M.E. and Arthur, W., Study of the phenomenology of DDOS network attacks in phase space. *Proceedings of the International Conference on Security and Cryptography*, pp. 78–89, 2011.

5. Zhao, X., Liu, H., Xue, G., Cao, W., Analysis of trojan horse events by query of vulnerability information in searching engines. *2014 Seventh International Symposium on Computational Intelligence and Design*, pp. 268–271, 2014.

6. Knight, P.L., Quantum communication and quantum computing. *Technical Digest. Summaries of Papers Presented at the Quantum Electronics and Laser Science Conference*, p. 32, 1999.

7. Arun, G. and Mishra, V., A review on quantum computing and communication. *2014 2nd International Conference on Emerging Technology Trends in Electronics, Communication and Networking*, pp. 1–5, 2014.

8. Zhang, H., Ji, Z., Wang, H., Wu, W., Survey on quantum information security. *China Commun.*, 16, 10, 1–36, Oct. 2019.

9. Ekta, and Bansal, U., A review on ransomware attack. *2021 2nd International Conference on Secure Cyber Computing and Communications (ICSCCC)*, pp. 221–226, 2021.

10. Harrald, J.R., Schmitt, S.A., Shrestha, S., The effect of computer virus occurrence and virus threat level on antivirus companies' financial performance. *2004 IEEE International Engineering Management Conference (IEEE Cat. No.04CH37574)*, vol. 2, pp. 780–784, 2004.

11. Ge, W. and Qin, X. -h., Research on virus spreading and protection on internet. *2012 Fourth International Conference on Computational and Information Sciences*, pp. 69–72, 2012.

12. Lee, J., Lee, Y., Lee, D., Kwon, H., Shin, D., Classification of attack types and analysis of attack methods for profiling phishing mail attack groups. *IEEE Access*, 9, 80866–80872, 2021.

13. Husainiamer, M.A., Mohd Saudi, M., Yusof, M., Securing mobile applications against mobile malware attacks: A case study. *2021 IEEE 19th Student Conference on Research and Development (SCOReD)*, pp. 433–438, 2021.

14. Tekiner, E., Acar, A., Uluagac, A.S., Kirda, E., Selcuk, A.A., SoK: Cryptojacking malware. *2021 IEEE European Symposium on Security and Privacy (EuroS&P)*, pp. 120–139, 2021.

15. Joseph, R.C., Data breaches: Public sector perspectives. *IT Prof.*, 20, 4, 57–64, Jul./Aug. 2018.

16. The-2020-Verizon-Data-Breach-Investigations-Report-DBIR. https://www.cisecurity.org/wp-content/uploads/2020/07/The-2020-Verizon-Data-Breach-Investigations-Report-DBIR.pdf

13

Identification of Bacterial Diseases in Plants Using Re-Trained Transfer Learning in Quantum Computing Environment

Sri Silpa Padmanabhuni[1], B. Srikanth Reddy[1], A. Mallikarjuna Reddy[2]* and K. Sudheer Reddy[3]

Department of Computer Science & Engineering, PSCMR College of Engineering & Technology, Vijayawada, India
Department of Artificial Intelligence, Anurag University, Hyderabad, India
Department of Information Technology, Anurag University, Hyderabad, India

Abstract

The digitization of any field has become prominent with the advancement of AI techniques. Rapid development has happened in the field of Agriculture to identify the diseases in the plants to protect the crop. Using traditional approaches, researchers performed disease identification for specific plants but in this proposed system usage of quantum computing techniques integrated with deep learning helps to identify any bacterial disease in different plants. This helps the farmers to use a single window application while the farmer changes the crop seasonally. The deep learning module needs a huge amount of data to train the system, so the model deploys quantum computing particles in the GPUs and uses ImageNET module as dataset. This dataset is popular for annotated images with more than 1000 class labels and 1.2 Million images. Since, the dataset contains high quality images, general CPU's and super computers consume more energy to perform any complex operation. Instead of, control unit bits, quantum computing uses "qubits" to reduce the energy consumption. Deep learning model uses the CNN architecture with pre-trained models like VGGNET, ALEXANET and others to train the weights of input features but the dataset

Corresponding author: mallikarjunreddycse@cvsr.ac.in

Sachi Nandan Mohanty, Rajanikanth Aluvalu and Sarita Mohanty (eds.) Evolution and Applications of Quantum Computing, (207–232) © 2023 Scrivener Publishing LLC

contains different patterns because of the different natured symptoms. So the model requires re-training of the model due to variation shift in the data. This retraining model helps the system to work with the continuous flow of image stream from the captured image of the sensors. The major advantage in this proposed system is utilization of re-training module helps in building the new dataset by combining the training images with captured image. This is in turn helps the neural network to obtain the best values and also the chances of building the balanced dataset improves. Transfer learning is the process of solving the complicated problems with the help of few training techniques for hidden layers without starting from scratch. The main focus of the pre-trained model is to identify the correct weights for every feature in both forward and backward propagations. It also generalizes the images available in existing dataset. The proposed system fine tunes the pre-trained model GoogleNet by removing the last layer and utilizes that as "Feature Extraction" model. It also changes the hidden layers partially by adding normalization layers by defining the customized activation function to fasten the process.

Keywords: Quantum computers, GPU's, pre-trained model, googlenet, frozen layers, customized activation, transfer learning

13.1   Introduction

Agriculture accounts for over 70% of the Indian economy. Diseases, on the other hand, have a tendency to reduce crop productivity. As a result, it's critical to employ new approaches to boost agricultural product productivity and farmers' financial income [7]. Pathogens, fungi, bacteria, and viruses are the most common causes of plant disease. Table 13.1 presents some examples for each classification.

Unfavorable environmental conditions are another factor that affects agriculture. Because environmental factors are beyond human control, approaches for detecting diseases that affect crop quality and quantity have attracted a lot of attention [8]. Traditionally, continuous onsite inspection of agricultural produce by framers or agricultural professionals has been used. However, this procedure necessitates a significant amount of time and money, as well as additional staff. As a result, research into advanced computer technology that can detect diseases on plants, fruits, and vegetable harvests earlier and thus boost quality productivity with fewer resources has gained relevance.

Table 13.1 Common pathological diseases in plants.

S. no.	Disease name	Image	Description	Common among
Virus diseases				
1	Mosaic Virus		The leaf contains different color spots representing that their growth rate is poor. Some plants have wrinkled leaves [10]	Tomatoes, cucumber, cauliflower, squashes
2	Barley Yellow Drawf		The tip of the leaf starts getting the discoloring phenomenon i.e., yellow to red color	Wheat, Oats, Barley

(Continued)

Table 13.1 Common pathological diseases in plants. (*Continued*)

S. no.	Disease name	Image	Description	Common among
3	Bud Blight		The edges, margins, or tips of the leaves are burnt or may have faded color	Tomatoes, Cannabis, Soya beans
Fungal Diseases				
1	White Rust		The dermis of the plants contains many white spores	Mustard, Beetroot, Cabbage, Lettuce

(*Continued*)

Table 13.1 Common pathological diseases in plants. (*Continued*)

S. no.	Disease name	Image	Description	Common among
2	Downy Mildew		These turn the green leaf veins to either yellow or brown	It is common in all the leafy vegetables
3	Powdery Mildew		The upper part of the leaf is covered with white spores or they will completely dry	Pumpkins, Eggplants, Tomatoes, Peppers

(*Continued*)

Table 13.1 Common pathological diseases in plants. (*Continued*)

S. no.	Disease name	Image	Description	Common among
4	Club Root		Leaves become wilt or swollen at bushes	Broccoli, sprouts, radish, cabbage
Bacterial Diseases				
1	Cankers		It creates yellow tan patches and veins become dark	Cherry, plum trees

(*Continued*)

Table 13.1 Common pathological diseases in plants. (*Continued*)

S. no.	Disease name	Image	Description	Common among
2	Bacterial Wilt		It forms tan whites and brown spots on leaves. The leaf becomes too sticky	Tomato, Common Bean
3	Blight		These are formed as either green or yellow spots	Tomato, Potato, Pepper Bell

(*Continued*)

Table 13.1 Common pathological diseases in plants. (*Continued*)

S. no.	Disease name	Image	Description	Common among
4	Brown Spot		It forms oval shapes with brown filled segments	Basil, Cucumber, Coconut
5	Leaf Spot		Irregular shapes are formed with brown margins	Tomato, Potato, Eggplants

The methodology used in this research is computer vision techniques on quantum computers using leaf images as input and pre-trained models to identify plant illnesses. This approach entails early detection of plant illnesses in order to boost production and save labor costs [9]. The issue that has arisen in the system is that it is extremely difficult to detect diseases in their early stages. As a result, researchers suggest an automatic detecting system for identifying plant diseases in this system. Experts used to use a method called naked eye observation to identify and detect plant illnesses back in the olden days [11]. This strategy necessitated a big team of experts as well as ongoing plant monitoring. Simultaneously, in certain countries, farmers lack adequate facilities or even knowledge of how to seek and contact experts, which is a time-consuming process. Table 13.2 illustrates the disadvantages of manual observation and advantages of automated systems using intelligent approaches.

The major goal of this system is to use computer vision techniques to identify healthy and diseased leaves from an open access data set known as "Plant Village" [12]. Figure 13.1 presents few commonly available diseases in different plants.

As a result, crop yields can be boosted by recognizing and treating illness at an early stage. The technology was enhanced to make this method fully functional within the organization.

Table 13.2 Illustration of traditional versus intelligent automation.

Limitations of the traditional approach	Advantages of the automation approaches
In traditional approaches, the images are not accessible directly, so they represent them in the vector form. This conversion process takes a lot of time and delays the prediction process	Automation approaches GPU's to access the images, which helps to fasten the process
Accessing of huge amount of data requires additional resources which increases the cost of equipment	All the GPUs are associated with cloud resources, which reduces the cost
The evaluation metrics are less performed	The evaluation metrics performs more accurate with good learning rate

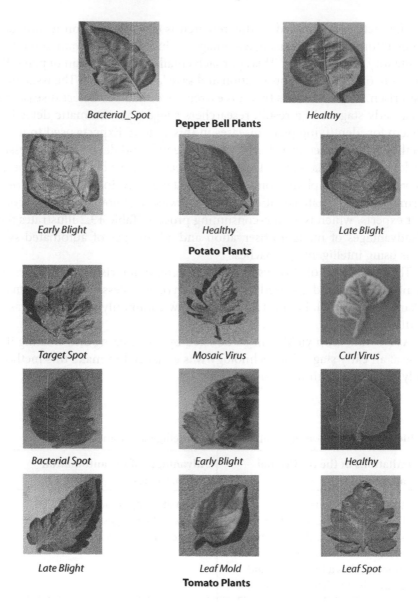

Bacterial_Spot   *Healthy*
Pepper Bell Plants

Early Blight   *Healthy*   *Late Blight*
Potato Plants

Target Spot   *Mosaic Virus*   *Curl Virus*

Bacterial Spot   *Early Blight*   *Healthy*

Late Blight   *Leaf Mold*   *Leaf Spot*
Tomato Plants

Figure 13.1 Common diseases and healthy plant images from dataset.

1. There is a need to design a rapid, automatic, efficient, and accurate method for detecting disease on diseased leaves, so instead of collecting real time data from the crops, the proposed system uses "ImageNet" dataset, which contains nearly 1.2 Millions of images with 1000 class labels [13]. Figure 13.2 shows the sample images available in the ImageNet dataset.

Figure 13.2 Sample images of different class labels in ImageNet dataset.

The model also uses a pre-trained model known as "AlexNet", because these model train the dataset with less efforts and the application need not develop the entire system from scratch [14]. Figure 13.3 shows the brief architecture of the pre-trained model.

2. The application should be able to recognize all types of pathological disease in all sorts of plants at a faster rate. In order achieve this, the model implemented "transfer learning" mechanism by freezing the training layers and customizing the last layers of dense network.

3. The model also uses tuning process to identify the configuration required for the customizing the estimators in dense layers.

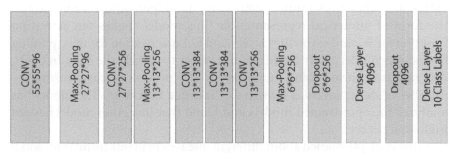

Figure 13.3 "AlexNet" pre-trained model architecture.

13.2   Literature Review

Ramesh *et al.* [1] proposed optimized DNN integrated with Jaya algorithm for classification of paddy leaves. The pre-processing of images started with resizing the images to 300*450. The background subtraction is performed using the HSV model and a fusion of images is created based on threshold values. The model implements olden "K-Means" approach to extract the disease part in the leaf image. From the extracted regions, it works on both color and text features. The text features are extracted using GLCM to identify the homogenous regions based on correlation, energy patterns. The color features are extracted using the statistical parameters. The weights of the neurons are optimized using the Jaya genetic approach. It found that only two hidden layers are sufficient and sigmoid activation function is efficient for customization of NN.

Jayasooriya *et al.* [2] implemented light GBM approach for classification of diseases in rice plants. The model initially validated the image for checking the integrity of the rice leaf. The validation of the image is done by performing the XOR operation on hue and RGB colors. The model extracts 13 attributes in the form of numerical values using open CV library. The model later analyzed these attributes and found that all are not necessary. The model applied feature ranking and found 9 attributes are important. Among the extracted values, the model smoothens the border pixels and removes the green color regions. So that it can identify the different colored regions. This doesn't mean the plant is diseased, so to classify the leaves it implemented light GBM. All the variants of gradient boosting are ensemble approaches, where the classification is based on the entropy and Gini index.

Ashiqul *et al.* [3] designed an automated CNN for performing multi classification on plant diseases using the pre-trained models. The Conv blocks with feed forward network are used for performing the feature extraction. This gives feature map vector as output, whose values are in the form of numerical representation. This model applies tan activation function for feature extraction layers and ReLu activation for max-pooling layers. Any model needs single column vector to classify the data. In CNN, this task is achieved using dense layers. The process of customizing the number of dense layers is known as "Transfer Learning". The model has analyzed four pre-trained models and found that Inception model has got highest accuracy.

Sethy *et al.* [4] studied about different diseases in plants using traditional image processing approach. This studied identified that Gaussian filter is

Table 13.3 Comparative analysis.

S. no.	Author name	Algorithm	Merits	Demerits
1	Ramesh	ODNN using Jaya	It calculates the number of neurons in each hidden layer dynamically	The false classification rate is high in this system. This can be solved by turning other parameters also
2	Jayasooriya	Light GBM	Ensemble mechanisms prunes most of the unwanted data and constructs an efficient tree	Machine learning approaches are not efficient in handling the image processing operations
3	Ashiqul	CNN using transfer learning	The model implements pre-trained models to reduce the cost of designing	Even though for Inspection, the model has analyzed good accuracy but the number of parameters and number of layers are high
5	Roy	Oriented Fast	Feature extraction is based on histogram. So only frequent patterns are utilized	The training needs more amount of data which crashes the model while working on CPUs

efficient for noise reduction. The segmentation is best evaluated using the K-Means clustering and Otsu method. The model presented that the mineral deficiency is analyzed by fuzzy C-means techniques. The model also justified that among text and color feature extractions, color gives more accuracy in finding the unhealthy regions. Most of the traditional classifiers have given an accuracy of nearly 90% but the combination of unsupervised with SVM classifier has reached 97.5%, which is inexpensive mechanism. The model gathered information on several paddy dysfunctions in relation to their growth rate. Other imaging techniques such as hyperspectral and thermal imaging are also briefly discussed.

Roy *et al.* [5] developed oriented Fast algorithm to store the key patterns associated with disease as a vector. The model stores the key points for both the training and testing images and combines them to generate a detector pattern. This technique helps the model to identify the essential features. The model combines PCA and random forest to identify the patterns, so that the dimensions of the similar clusters can be reduced.

Zhaoyi Chen *et al.* [6] proposed a CNN & improved YOLOv5 network model for the rubber tree disease detection. Initially, CNN is used for detecting powdery mildew and anthracnose diseases in rubber trees. Improved YOLOv5 is a combination of involutionBottleneck and SE modules. In pre-processing the image is resized to 640*640 pixels. YOLOv5 backbone is replaced with InvolutionBottleneck for reducing the number of calculations. SE is added to the last layer of the backbone for feature fusion. SE modules combine powdery mildew and anthracnose in a weighted manner to improve performance. Finally, the Loss Function uses the EIOU function to calculate the discrepancies in the target and anchor boxes' center point, width and height, and aspect ratio of a leaf. To evaluate performance precision, recall, average precision, and mean average precision was considered as the evaluation metrics. Therefore, Improved YOLOv5 results are 5.4% high efficient compared to YOLOv5. The analysis of the existing mechanisms are presented in Table 13.3.

13.3   Proposed Methodology

In traditional approaches, most of the researchers implemented Support Vector Machine (SVM) and Random Forest (RF) algorithms for classification of diseases. This section discusses about the working of SVM in brief [15]. In these models they first extract the features using HOG (Histogram Oriented Gradients). It performs edge detection for extracting the shapes by resizing the shape to 128*64 and their gradients are computed as shown in equation (13.1). The gradients are based on the magnitude and intensity and an ordered pair is formed.

Gradient(Input$_x$) = Intensitty(n, m + 1) - Instensity(n, m - 1)

Gradient(input$_y$) = Intensity(n - 1, m) - Intensity(n + 1, m)   (13.1)

The magnitude is computed as shown in the Equation (13.2)

$$Magnitude = \sqrt[2]{\left(Gradient\left(Input_x\right)\right)^2 + \left(Gradient\left(Input_y\right)\right)^2} \quad (13.2)$$

Then the features extracted from the created data sets undergo training process for classification [16]. Later, these trained sets are tested based on SVM classifier. Overall, using Machine Learning it is providing a clear way to detect the diseases of the plants at initial stages. The results of the feature extraction are presented in Figure 13.4.

Figure 13.4 Input of scanned image and output of the mask image using HOG.

13.3.1 SVM Classifier

It is a supervised machine learning approach for classification or regression issues, in which a dataset trains SVM about numerous classes in order to categorize the data [17]. The SVM is divided into two categories. They're as follows:

Linear SVM: The training data are separated by hyperplane based on the margins chosen, which considers maximum distance between the two class labels. The model applies the theory of optimization to identify the unknown vectors into probability distribution values with the goal to maximize the accuracy.

Non-Linear SVM: It is difficult to separate the training data using hyperplane. Its major focus is to reduce the dimensionality in the vector space. The geometric shapes in the hyper plane are solved using the regularization parameters [18]. During this process, the 3-D data is converted into 2-D data. The efficiency of the model depends on the kernel trick it applies.

The researchers employed linear SVM to process the data samples in this dataset. The dataset's training data is put to the test using several SVM classifier concepts. As a result of the preprocessed data, the output is either a healthy or infected leaf. The results of the SVM classifier are presented in the Figure 13.5.

Figure 13.5 Classification of image masked in Figure 13.4.

13.3.2   Random Forest to Classify the Rice Leaf

This section discusses about the applying random forest on the rice plant leaves.

Step 1: Load the dataset with trained images of rice leaf.
Step 2: Take the test image as input.
Step 3: After scanning the test image, the preprocessing of an image is performed.
Step 4: In the preprocessing the image can be converted into resized image and gray scale.
Step 5: After preprocessing, the feature will be extracted by considering mean, Standard deviation, and variance.
Step 6: Now classification of image is done by using random forest algorithm.

13.3.2.1   Image Pre-Processing

The model needs a gray scale image rather than RGB image for efficiently manipulating the image [19]. In order to achieve this task, the opencv library has resize(), pre-defined function, with height and width as its input parameter. It is easy for any numerical model to access a small range of values rather than working on the various intensity values. The model internally uses the equation (13.3)

$$Image\_Gray = 0.289 * R + 0.58 * G + 0.114 * B \qquad (13.3)$$

Figure 13.6 represents the resized image of rice leaf using the above equation.

13.3.2.2   Feature Extraction

Systems must extract features from a pre-processed image in this procedure. The statistical approaches like mean and standard deviations find the points at which the values are deviated from their original path. The region under which the points are evenly distributed then it is considered as "Essential Region" and is extracted [20, 21]. The measures of central tendency of data are mean, median, and mode (either grouped or ungrouped). The retrieved features of the test leaf are shown in Figure 13.7.

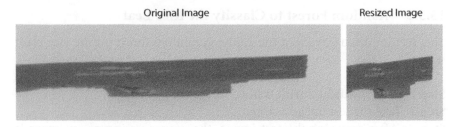

Figure 13.6 Original image transformed to resize image.

Figure 13.7 Numerical representation of feature extraction.

13.3.2.3   Classification

Random Forest is an ensemble algorithm that works on the concept of combining different models as into one. The model first creates various training sets using different samples of data and applies learning algorithm and predicts an output. Then it identifies the weaker parts and builds new model based on the majority voting [22, 23]. While performing generalization on weaker parts it applies row sampling techniques to aggregate the data. The output of this model is presented in Figure 13.8.

All these mechanisms have achieved nearly 90% accuracy. So the proposed model utilized a pre-trained model known as "AlexNet" to classify the diseases. The architecture of the proposed system is shown in Figure 13.9. From the invention of object oriented programming languages, it is well known fact in the IT industry that "Re-use" is the basic for developing any model with less effort and cost. The same concept is applied in the field of AI using the pre-trained models. The steps like feature extraction, hyper tuning, and designing the framework is available as API's. Every layer in the neural network performs different tasks starting from simple to complex as the system goes deeper into the network. The starting layers identify simple lines but last layers focuses on the analyzing the complex patterns. The proposed system takes "AlexNet" as pre-trained model because it's a simple eight-layered architecture with no "vanishing point" problem. It runs on GPU, so it 4 times faster than any other pre-trained model. The loss

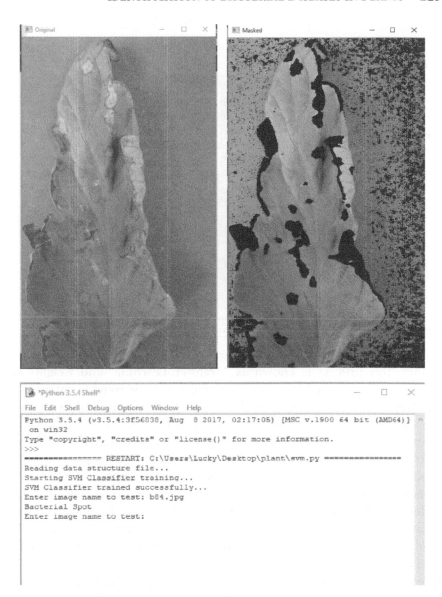

Figure 13.8 Classification using random forest algorithm.

rate gradually decreases in every iteration [24–26]. It also solves the color changing parameters with time very effectively.

The proposed model removes the final layers of model, because these layers are responsible for classifying the images. The model also adds few layers after the input layer by taking the weights from the pre-trained

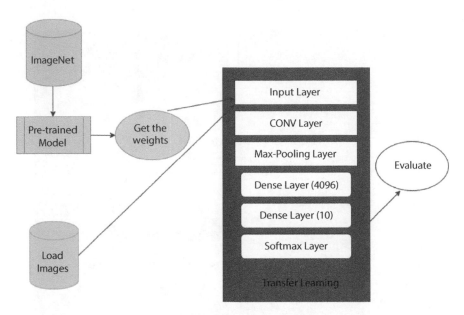

Figure 13.9 Proposed architecture for classing using AlexNet.

model. This process is known as "Transfer Learning" and weights are known as "Fine Tuned Weights". The model uses the weights obtained by learning the features 1000 class labels of ImageNet are utilized for predicting the class labels of plant diseases. For simplicity, the model has considered one Convolution layer and one max-pooling layer. The conv layer recognizes the patterns hidden in the images. It gets the information as dot product of neurons available in the input layer. The important features are detected using the filters and performs pooling operating through window slides. The filters generate the output as feature map. The model to have great dimensionality reduction in images, added the next layer as "Max-pooling". This helps in solving the over fitting problem, and computational load because the system only identifies the huge areas with good resolution thresholds. In every window slide, it picks the pixel with high intensity value and forms a kernel for next operation in the network [27, 28].

13.4   Experiment Results

The summary of the pre-trained model is shown in sub sections of Figure 13.10. The model contains five blocks with each block containing three Conv layers and 1 max-pooling layer. It also contains one flatten layer.

```
Model: "model"
```

Layer (type)	Output Shape	Param #
input_1 (InputLayer)	[(None, 150, 150, 3)]	0
block1_conv1 (Conv2D)	(None, 150, 150, 64)	1792
block1_conv2 (Conv2D)	(None, 150, 150, 64)	36928
block1_pool (MaxPooling2D)	(None, 75, 75, 64)	0
block2_conv1 (Conv2D)	(None, 75, 75, 128)	73856
block2_conv2 (Conv2D)	(None, 75, 75, 128)	147584
block2_pool (MaxPooling2D)	(None, 37, 37, 128)	0
block3_conv1 (Conv2D)	(None, 37, 37, 256)	295168
block3_conv2 (Conv2D)	(None, 37, 37, 256)	590080
block3_conv3 (Conv2D)	(None, 37, 37, 256)	590080
block3_pool (MaxPooling2D)	(None, 18, 18, 256)	0

(a)

block4_conv1 (Conv2D)	(None, 18, 18, 512)	1180160
block4_conv2 (Conv2D)	(None, 18, 18, 512)	2359808
block4_conv3 (Conv2D)	(None, 18, 18, 512)	2359808
block4_pool (MaxPooling2D)	(None, 9, 9, 512)	0
block5_conv1 (Conv2D)	(None, 9, 9, 512)	2359808
block5_conv2 (Conv2D)	(None, 9, 9, 512)	2359808
block5_conv3 (Conv2D)	(None, 9, 9, 512)	2359808
block5_pool (MaxPooling2D)	(None, 4, 4, 512)	0
flatten_1 (Flatten)	(None, 8192)	0
dense (Dense)	(None, 2)	16386

```
Total params: 14,731,074
Trainable params: 16,386
Non-trainable params: 14,714,688
```

(b)

Figure 13.10 (a) First section of summary model. (b) Second section of summary model.

Figure 13.11 represents the training accuracy, validation accuracy, training loss, and validation loss obtained in every epoch.

Table 13.4 demonstrated the comparison of the literature survey with the proposed system performance to validate its efficiency.

Figure 13.12 visualizes the table x in the form of graph by representing the x-axis as algorithm names and y-axis as measurement in terms of percentage.

Figure 13.13 presents the accuracy for training and test data along with their loss values. X-axis represents epochs and Y-axis represents the accuracy in percentage.

```
Epoch 1/10
WARNING:tensorflow:Can save best model only with val_acc available, skipping.
4/4 - 257s - loss: 0.6776 - accuracy: 0.8846 - val_loss: 0.7426 - val_accuracy: 0.8968 - 257s/epoch - 64s/step
Epoch 2/10
WARNING:tensorflow:Can save best model only with val_acc available, skipping.
4/4 - 257s - loss: 0.5000 - accuracy: 0.9135 - val_loss: 1.4131 - val_accuracy: 0.8185 - 257s/epoch - 64s/step
Epoch 3/10
WARNING:tensorflow:Can save best model only with val_acc available, skipping.
4/4 - 257s - loss: 0.3203 - accuracy: 0.9712 - val_loss: 2.4136 - val_accuracy: 0.7364 - 257s/epoch - 64s/step
Epoch 4/10
WARNING:tensorflow:Can save best model only with val_acc available, skipping.
4/4 - 285s - loss: 0.5540 - accuracy: 0.9423 - val_loss: 2.1053 - val_accuracy: 0.7641 - 285s/epoch - 71s/step
Epoch 5/10
WARNING:tensorflow:Can save best model only with val_acc available, skipping.
4/4 - 285s - loss: 0.2890 - accuracy: 0.9519 - val_loss: 0.8805 - val_accuracy: 0.8777 - 285s/epoch - 71s/step
Epoch 6/10
WARNING:tensorflow:Can save best model only with val_acc available, skipping.
4/4 - 285s - loss: 0.5221 - accuracy: 0.9038 - val_loss: 0.4123 - val_accuracy: 0.9322 - 285s/epoch - 71s/step
Epoch 7/10
WARNING:tensorflow:Can save best model only with val_acc available, skipping.
4/4 - 285s - loss: 0.4986 - accuracy: 0.9135 - val_loss: 1.0877 - val_accuracy: 0.8500 - 285s/epoch - 71s/step
Epoch 8/10
WARNING:tensorflow:Can save best model only with val_acc available, skipping.
4/4 - 255s - loss: 0.4191 - accuracy: 0.9519 - val_loss: 2.5109 - val_accuracy: 0.7650 - 255s/epoch - 64s/step
Epoch 9/10
WARNING:tensorflow:Can save best model only with val_acc available, skipping.
4/4 - 254s - loss: 0.5614 - accuracy: 0.9519 - val_loss: 2.8157 - val_accuracy: 0.7230 - 254s/epoch - 64s/step
Epoch 10/10
WARNING:tensorflow:Can save best model only with val_acc available, skipping.
4/4 - 285s - loss: 0.5550 - accuracy: 0.9231 - val_loss: 1.3823 - val_accuracy: 0.8348 - 285s/epoch - 71s/step
Training completed in time: 0:47:03.725329
```

Figure 13.11   A sample screenshot of Epochs using the proposed model.

Table 13.4   Evaluation metrics analysis.

S. no.	Algorithm	Accuracy	Recall	Precision
1	ODNN using Jaya	89.5	92	91
2	Light GBM	85	83	84
3	CNN using transfer learning	92	90	87
4	Oriented Fast	91	86	84
5	SVM	85	80	76
6	Random Forest	83.33	81	78
7	Proposed	92.31	87	88

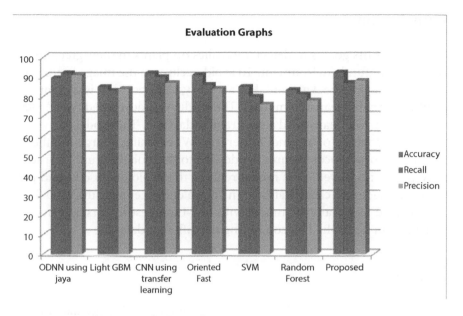

Figure 13.12 Evaluation graphs for analysis.

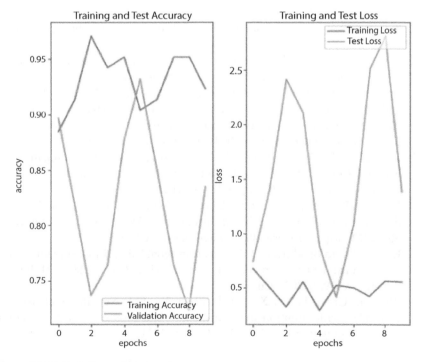

Figure 13.13 Training and test graphs.

Conclusion

This algorithm's goal is to detect anomalies on plants in their greenhouses or in their natural environment. To avoid occlusion, the image is normally taken with a plain background. For accuracy, the algorithm was compared to other machine learning models. The model was developed using 15000 images of various leaves and a pre-trained classifier. The model had a classification accuracy of around 99 percent. When using a large number of images and other local features in addition to the global features, the accuracy can be improved. This model reduces the deployment cost and produces the accurate classifications. In future enhancement, the model can be extended to retrain the model with fine-tuned estimators and transfer learning can be applied by combining the different datasets.

References

1. Shunmugam, R. and Dharmar, V., Recognition and classification of paddy leaf diseases using optimized deep neural network with jaya algorithm. *Inf. Process. Agric.*, 7, 249–260, 2019.
2. Jayasooriya, R.I.L., and Arachchi, S.M., Diagnosis of bacterial leaf blight, brown spots, and leaf smut rice plant diseases using light GBM. *Int. J. Comput. Appl.*, 183, 48, 53–58, January 2022.
3. Islam, Md, Shuvo, Md, Shamsojjaman, M., Hasan, S., Hossain, Md, Khatun, T., An automated convolutional neural network based approach for paddy leaf disease detection. *Int. J. Adv. Comput. Sci. Appl.*, 12, 280–288, 2021.
4. Sethy, P.K., Barpanda, N.K., Rath, A.K., Behera, S.K., Image processing techniques for diagnosing rice plant disease: A survey. *Proc. Comput. Sci.*, 167, 516–530, 2020, https://doi.org/10.1016/j.procs.2020.03.308.
5. Roy, S., Ray, R., Dash, S.R., Giri, M.K., Plant disease detection using machine learning tools with an overview on dimensionality reduction, in: *Data Analytics in Bioinformatics*, pp. 109–144, 2021.
6. Chen, Z., Wu, R., Lin, Y., Li, C., Chen, S., Yuan, Z., Chen, S., Zou, X., Plant disease recognition model based on improved YOLOv5. *Agronomy*, 12, 2, 365, 2022, https://doi.org/10.3390/agronomy12020365.
7. Roy, A.M. and Bhaduri, J., A deep learning enabled multi-class plant disease detection model based on computer vision. *AI*, 2, 3, 413–428, 2021, https://doi.org/10.3390/ai2030026.
8. Zhao, Y., Chen, J., Xu, X., Lei, J., Zhou, W., SEV-Net: Residual network embedded with attention mechanism for plant disease severity detection. *Concurr. Comput.: Pract. Exp.*, 33, 10, 1–18, 2021.

9. Divakar, S., Bhattacharjee, A., Priyadarshini, R., Smote-DL: A deep learning based plant disease detection method. *2021 6th International Conference for Convergence in Technology (I2CT)*, pp. 1–6, 2021.

10. Joshi, R.C., Kaushik, M., Dutta, M.K., Srivastava, A., Choudhary, N., VirLeafNet: Automatic analysis and viral disease diagnosis using deep-learning in Vigna mungo plant. *Ecol. Inf.*, 61, 101197, 2021, https://doi.org/10.1016/j.ecoinf.2020.101197.

11. Sujatha, R., Chatterjee, J.M., Jhanjhi, N.Z., Brohi, S.N., Performance of deep learning vs machine learning in plant leaf disease detection. *Microprocess. Microsyst.*, 80, 103615, 2021, https://doi.org/10.1016/j.micpro.2020.103615.

12. Mostafa, A.M., Kumar, S.A., Meraj, T., Rauf, H.T., Alnuaim, A.A., Alkhayyal, M.A., Guava disease detection using deep convolutional neural networks: A case study of guava plants. *Appl. Sci.*, 12, 1, 239, 2022, https://doi.org/10.3390/app12010239.

13. Chen, J., Zhang, D., Zeb, A., Nanehkaran, Y.A., Identification of rice plant diseases using lightweight attention networks. *Expert Syst. Appl.*, 169, 114514, 2021, https://doi.org/10.1016/j.eswa.2020.114514.

14. Kundu, N., Rani, G., Dhaka, V.S., Gupta, K., Nayak, S.C., Verma, S., Ijaz, M.F., Woźniak, M., IoT and interpretable machine learning based framework for disease prediction in pearl millet. *Sensors*, 21, 16, 5386, 2021, https://doi.org/10.3390/s21165386.

15. Gadekallu, T.R., Rajput, D.S., Reddy, M.P.K. *et al.*, A novel PCA–whale optimization-based deep neural network model for classification of tomato plant diseases using GPU. *J. Real-Time Image Process.*, 18, 1383–1396, 2021, https://doi.org/10.1007/s11554-020-00987-8.

16. Gahiware, A., Bawake, N., Dhage, B., Ahir, L., Abang, P.V., Potato plant disease detection using deep learning. *Int. J. Adv. Res. Sci. Commun. Technol.*, 2, 63–66, 2022.

17. Padmanabhuni, S.S., An extensive study on classification-based plant disease detection systems. *J. Mech. Continua Math. Sci.*, 15, 5, 20–36, 2020, https://doi.org/10.26782/jmcms.2020.05.00002.

18. Kavati, I., Mallikarjuna Reddy, A., Suresh Babu, E., Sudheer Reddy, K., Cheruku, R.S., Design of a fingerprint template protection scheme using elliptical structures. *ICT Express*, 7, 4, 497–500, 2021, https://doi.org/10.1016/j.icte.2021.04.001.

19. Grandhe, P., A novel method for content based 3D medical image retrieval system using dual tree M-band wavelets transform and multiclass support vector machine. *J. Adv. Res. Dyn. Control Syst.*, 12, 279–286, 2020.

20. Kumar, P., Pradeepini, G., Kamakshi, P., Feature selection effects on gradient descent logistic regression for medical data classification. *Int. J. Intell. Eng. Syst.*, 12, 5, 278–286, 2019.

21. Sudheer Reddy, K., Varma, G.P.S., Reddy, S.S.S., Understanding the scope of web usage mining & applications of web data usage patterns. *2012*

International Conference on Computing, Communication and Applications, pp. 1–5, 2012.

22. Santhosh Kumar, C.N., Pavan Kumar, V., Reddy, K.S., Similarity matching of pairs of text using CACT algorithm. *Int. J. Eng. Adv. Technol.*, 8, 6, 2296–2298, 2019.

23. Ayaluri MR, K.S.R., Konda, S.R., Chidirala, S.R., Efficient steganalysis using convolutional auto encoder network to ensure original image quality. *PeerJ Comput. Sci.*, 7, e356, 2021, https://doi.org/10.7717/peerj-cs.356.

24. Mallikarjuna Reddy, A., Krishna, V.V., Sumalatha, L., Obulesh, A., Age classification using motif and statistical features derived on gradient facial images. *Recent Adv. Comput. Sci. Commun.*, 13, 965, 2020, https://doi.org/10.2174/2 213275912666190417151247.

25. C.R.T., Sirisha, G., Reddy, A.M., Smart healthcare analysis and therapy for voice disorder using cloud and edge computing. *2018 4th International Conference on Applied and Theoretical Computing and Communication Technology (iCATccT)*, Mangalore, India, pp. 103–106, 2018.

26. Reddy, A.M., SubbaReddy, K., Krishna, V.V., Classification of child and adulthood using GLCM based on diagonal LBP. *2015 International Conference on Applied and Theoretical Computing and Communication Technology (iCATccT)*, Davangere, pp. 857–861, 2015.

27. Papineni, S.L.V., Yarlagadda, S., Akkineni, H., Mallikarjuna Reddy, A., Big data analytics applying the fusion approach of multicriteria decision making with deep learning algorithms. *Int. J. Eng. Trends Technol.*, 69, 1, 24–28, 2021.

28. Reddy, A.M., Krishna, V.V., Sumalatha, L., Niranjan, S.K., &orofacial recognition based on straight angle fuzzy texture unit matrix. *2017 International Conference on Big Data Analytics and Computational Intelligence (ICBDAC)*, Chirala, pp. 366–372, 2017.

14

Quantum Cryptography

Salma Fauzia

Electronics and Communication Engineering Department, Muffakham Jah College of Engineering and Technology, Hyderabad, India

Abstract

A cryptosystem is a collection of algorithms used to securely encrypt or decrypt messages by transforming plaintext to ciphertext. The abbreviation "cryptosystem" stands for "cryptographic system" and designates a computer system that employs cryptography, a technique for securing electronic information so only authorized users may read and process it. Prototype quantum cryptography devices are now securing Internet traffic in the nation's largest cities. The third and final major development in the evolution of cryptography in the 20th century might be regarded as quantum key distribution i.e. QKD or quantum cryptography. The level of security of the cryptographic scheme depends on the key employed.

A secure message, such as a credit card number or other sensitive information, is sent over the internet using cryptosystems. For instance, a platform for secured electronic mail might incorporate key management procedures, strong cryptographic functions, and digital signature systems. Another use of cryptography may be a secure electronic mail system that uses key management procedures, cryptographic hash functions, and digital signature mechanisms.

The following is a breakdown of the chapter's structure. The fundamentals of classical cryptography, symmetric and asymmetric encryption are described in Section 14.1. The principle of quantum cryptography is presented in Section 14.2. The Quantum Key Distribution Protocols are discussed in Section 14.3. The impact of the sifting and distillation steps on the key size is Section 14.4, cryptanalysis in Section 14.5, Quantum Key Distribution in the real world and conclusions are discussed in Section 14.6.

Keywords: Quantum, cryptography, encryption, decryption, asymmetric, key, filter, photon

Email: salmafauzia@mjcollege.ac.in

Sachi Nandan Mohanty, Rajanikanth Aluvalu and Sarita Mohanty (eds.) Evolution and Applications of Quantum Computing, (233–248) © 2023 Scrivener Publishing LLC

14.1   Fundamentals of Cryptography

In order to clarify the ideas pertaining to cryptography, we here use the traditional Alice and Bob scenario [1]. In order to avoid having their communications monitored, Alice and Bob desire to send information over a secure channel. In that context, an algorithm, or "cypher," uses some rule to scramble Alice's message, making it challenging, if not difficult, to recover the original information without the secret key. The "scrambled" communication is referred to as the ciphertext. Bob, on the other side, has the secret key and can quickly decrypt Alice's ciphertext and recover her original plaintext as shown in Figure 14.1.

Information can be encrypted and decrypted using one secret key in symmetric encryption. It is one of the most popular and extensively researched methods. In this system, a key can be any string of characters, a number, or a word. In plain text, it is a special form of message that is placed to change the content in a specified way. All the messages will be encrypted by a key and all messages must be known by both communicating parties. Blowfish, DES, AES, RC4, RC5, and RC6 are examples of symmetric encryption. Symmetric encryption's fundamental drawback is that all participants must first share the key used to encrypt data before decrypting it.

Asymmetric encryption Figure 14.2, in contrast to symmetric encryption, is also referred to as public key cryptography. It is a rather recent technique. Two keys are used in asymmetric encryption to encrypt plain text. Over a sizable network or the Internet, secret keys are traded. It prevents an attacking entity from using the keys. Asymmetric encryption uses two related keys to boost security since it is crucial to keep in mind that anyone

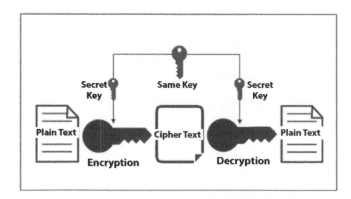

Figure 14.1 Symmetric encryption.

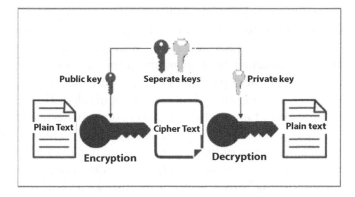

Figure 14.2 Asymmetric encryption.

with a secret key can decipher a message. The public key is accessible to anyone who wishes to message you. Only the intended receiver is aware of the second private key, which is kept secret. A message that has been encrypted using a public key can be decrypted using a private key, in contrary to the fact that a message that has been encrypted using a private key can be decrypted using a public key. Since it is public and it can be communicated via the internet, the public key does not have to be protected.

An asymmetric key has a much higher ability to guarantee the security of data sent during transmission. Especially on the Internet, asymmetric encryption is frequently utilized in daily communication. Popular asymmetric key encryption algorithms include EIGamal, RSA [3], DSA, elliptic curve methods, and PKCS.

The cryptography methods of the present technology relies on the difficulty of certain mathematical problems. Many conventional cryptosystems depend on the challenge of issues like the discrete logarithm or integer factoring to assure their security [2]. The cryptosystems may be insecure as these problems can be solved easily.

For example, if it was easy to factorize large integers, a very well and broadly used public-key cryptosystem i.e. RSA [3] could be easily broken. The difficulty of integer factoring, on the other hand, is a hypothesis rather than a proven fact. In passing, we mention that coding the RSA secret key from the corresponding public key takes polynomial time, which is the same as integer factoring [4]. Second, new techniques have been created using the quantum computation theory for solving these mathematic in a much more equitable way.

There are a number of challenges in the way of building a quantum computer with the desired power; a wonderful machine like this can easily break RSA type of cryptosystems. While quantum computation appears to pose a serious threat to cryptology in the not-too-distant future, it also opens up new possibilities for developing encryption standards that are secure even when attacked by a quantum computer. By encrypting the message using the physical principles of quantum mechanics, quantum cryptography increases the strength of cryptographic algorithms. A cryptosystem is the method of encryption and decryption, whereas a key is the qualitative data used for encrypting and decrypting in an individual communication. The insecurity of the communication is caused by the limited array of potential keys that can be used for encryption, not by the assertion that the cryptosystem is known publicly. Auguste Kerckhoffs stated in the 19th century that the security of a cryptosystem should be based strictly on the secrecy of the key.

As a result, when creating new cyphers, the algorithm should always be treated as if it has been known to the public. The amount of data that needed to be encrypted exploded over time, making simple and insecure procedures like the scytale obsolete [2].

Mechanical devices had been initially developed to speed up the encryption and (authorized) decryption processes while also adding to the complexity of the keys used to scramble the messages. The massive increase in the speed with which mathematical calculations could be performed necessitated the development of much more secure cryptosystems, such as symmetric block cyphers like the Data Encryption Standard (DES) and the Advanced Encryption Standard (AES) and public-key cryptosystems like RSA and others, which are now used in modern cryptographic applications. Singh [5] offers a nice and intuitive historical overview of cryptography. We appear to be at the start of some kind of epoch of cryptography, thanks to the recently developed theory of quantum computation.

Further cryptographic techniques can be classified into

1. Quantum breakable

   i.   RSA
   ii. Diffie-Hellman key exchange
   iii. Elliptic curve cryptography

2. Quantum secure

   i.   Lattice based
   ii. Code based
   iii. Multivariate cryptography

14.2   Principle of Quantum Cryptography

Alice and Bob want to communicate. Alice uses QKD to deliver Bob a string of polarized photons as shown in Figure 14.3 [6]. This connection does not require security since photons have a completely random quantum state. Eve, the eavesdropper, will have to analyze each photon to understand what is being said if she tries to hear in on the conversation. The photon she's possessing must then be given to Bob. As a result of Eve reading the photon, the photon's quantum state is changed, introducing errors into the quantum key. It serves as a warning to Alice and Bob that someone is listening in and that the key has been compromised, prompting them to throw away the key. A new key will be sent by Alice to Bob that has not been compromised. For decryption, Bob should use the new key. In the same way that a bit is the primary unit in a classical computer, a qubit is the primary unit of information in a quantum computer. It is referred to as a "quantum bit," which is the quantum computing equivalent of the binary digit or bit used in classical computing.

14.2.1   Quantum vs. Conventional Cryptography

After being transformed into ciphertext, the original message is sent through a channel controlled by a key in traditional cryptography. The receiver will only be able to acquire the original information and decode the original text

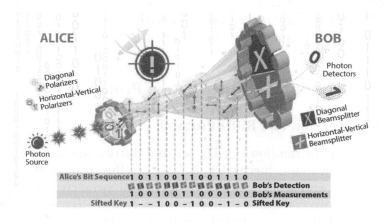

Figure 14.3 Quantum cryptography [6].

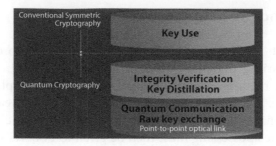

Figure 14.4 Illustration of convention cryptography and quantum cryptography [16].

with this key. In classical cryptography, there are two primary techniques: symmetric and asymmetric cryptography. On the other hand, quantum algorithms pose a threat to these cryptography techniques. The well-known Shor's algorithm [7] is capable of decrypting asymmetric cryptography techniques such as RSA and Elliptic Curve. The Grover's algorithm [8] is capable of breaking symmetric cryptography. On the other hand, quantum cryptography makes use of quantum mechanics to strengthen the safety of key exchanges. Furthermore, the security of traditional cryptography is threatened by weak random key generators, enhanced CPU power, new attack methodologies, and the advancement of quantum computers. In the case of quantum computers, however, an encryption of such type is rendered ineffective. Data that has been encrypted can be intercepted and saved for quantum computers to decrypt in the future. Security and detection of sniffing are two advantages of quantum cryptography. For the internet architecture and applications like the internet of things and smart cities, these characteristics may be helpful in tackling cyberspace security challenges. Quantum cryptography involves, verification, key distillation apart from involving raw key exchange. Figure 14.4 illustrates conventional symmetric cryptography and Quantum cryptography.

14.3 Quantum Key Distribution Protocols

14.3.1 Overview and BB84 Protocol

Quantum key distribution (QKD) is a key distribution algorithm that incorporates quantum mechanics. It facilitates the creation of a shared key between two parties that may be applied to symmetric encryption. The fact that two communicating parties can easily detect an eavesdropper attempting to obtain knowledge of the key is a key property of QKD. This is because, depending on the protocol, QKD uses superposition and/or entanglement and in order to obtain information on the key, the eaves-dropper must take measurements of the particles, which causes the par-ticles to lose their superposition or entanglement. Both parties will notice this, and communication will be terminated if a certain threshold of tam-pered particles is reached. Otherwise, because the eavesdropper lacks suf-ficient information, the key is guaranteed to be safe.

The disadvantages of QKD include the assumption that quantum mechanics apply and that neither party is being impersonated by a man in the middle. This is in addition to the fact that the key must currently be authenticated over a secure channel. This means that QKD isn't very useful right now, because in order to use QKD to create a secure channel, you must already have one.

Quantum Cryptography will transform the cryptography in 20th cen-tury like never before. Ciphers or the encryption algorithms should be as long as the message itself, at least, and should be never reused i.e. Vernam cipher which is impractical and not widely adopted [9]. The cryptographic techniques as proposed by RSA prime factor and Diffie Hellman key exchange algorithms were designed based on computation complexity. These techniques used public keys. Instead of being dependent on complex mathematical formulas, C.H. Bennet and G. Brassard preferred that these cryptographic approaches be reliant on the laws of physics [10].

It ensures that an eavesdropper "Eve" cannot obtain information about the key, therefore there is no means to decrypt the information exchange between Alice and Bob, which is sent over a public, presumed channel which is unsecure, without Alice's knowledge. Figure 14.5 depicts the BB84

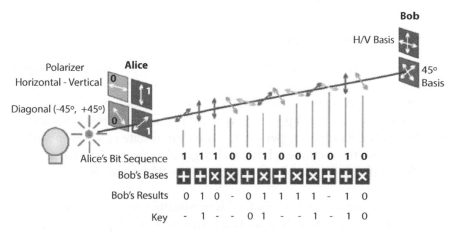

Figure 14.5 The BB84 protocol by Bennet and Brassard [10].

protocol developed by Bennet and Brassard (which can be used with vertical, horizontal, vertical, +45 degrees, and -45 degrees polarizations). To carry Alice's random key, four different non-orthogonal quantum states (e.g., different polarizations of a photon) are used that are transmitted through a quantum channel. In the preceding example, Alice assumes that the horizontal and +45 degree polarizations will be used to encode the "0," and that the vertical and -45 degree polarizations will be used for encoding the "1".

When a quantum bit is sent over, it is critical to record each and every polarization decision made by the sender, Alice. Nevertheless, if Bob employs a polarizer for diagonal polarizations or another polarizer that randomly operates in the horizontal or vertical direction (it is critical for Bob to remember each selection he makes and the state of polarization he measures), one can see that the probability of a random result is 50%, which is the probability of using the incorrect analyzer. After exchanging and transmitting photons with at least twice the number of bits in the final key, Bob discloses to Alice the series of analyzers he used via the public channel (however, without its results). Alice then compares sequence received from Bob and returns information about the mapping between the bits and photons Alice sent. Thus, the shared key contains only bits that are compatible. QKD's security is based on its ability to detect any intrusion into the QKD transmission. Due to photons' unique and fragile properties, any third party (or eavesdropper) attempting to read or copy them in any way will alter their state. The endpoints will detect the change and notify you that the key has been tampered with and must be discarded. Following that, a new key is transmitted. Additionally, because the generated keys are truly random, they are protected against future hacking attempts.

14.3.2   The B92 Protocol

B92 procedure was suggested by Charles Bennett. "Quantum cryptography using any two non-orthogonal states," published in 1992, which stands for "any two non-orthogonal states." This protocol is a slightly tweaked variation on the popular BB84 protocol, with the primary difference being that, the B92 protocol only uses two i.e. H-polarization state and +45° polarization state from the rectilinear basis and diagonal respectively whereas BB84 uses four states. It is possible to summarize the B92 protocol as follows:

1. A string of random photons is transmitted by Alice in either the H-state that is associated with 0 or +45° polarization state that is associated with bit '1'.

2. At random, Bob has to determine the polarization of the received photon and hence has to choose between rectilinear and diagonal basis. Bob can measure either in rectilinear or diagonal basis.

3. Two outcomes are possible when a rectilinear basis is employed. If 'H' polarization is used the outcome is 'H' with probability 1. In the other case the result will be V or H, with +45° polarization with probability 1.

4. With only V state as outcome, '+45°' would be the state of polarization during incidence.

5. The polarization state of the photon is 'H' if measured diagonally, if the resulting state is -45.

6. After the string of photon is transmitted, Bob asserts when the measurement result was "V" or "-45°," and both of them discard the remainder. A random bit string is generated using these results containing the information about Alice and Bob.

7. Both communicating parties share a part of the arbitrary string of bits, with the public to prevent eavesdropping. In the event of a high bit error rate, the protocol terminates. If not, they now have a safe and symmetric key that they can use to talk.

14.3.3   E91 Protocol

Quantum entanglement is a key concept in QKD. When one particle's property is measured, the opposite state on the entangled particle is observed instantly (Figure 14.6). This holds true no matter how far apart the entangled particles are separated. However, as the state that will be observed before measurement cannot be predicted, communication via entangled particles is not possible without first discussing the observations over a traditional channel. Ekert's protocol is based on quantum teleportation, a technique for communicating using entangled states and a conventional information channel.

Let's take a look at the quantum E91 protocol procedure in the steps below:

1. The source center chooses an EPR pair $|+=(1/2)(|00+|11)$ and sends the first particle $|+1$ to Alice and the second particle $|+2$ to Bob.

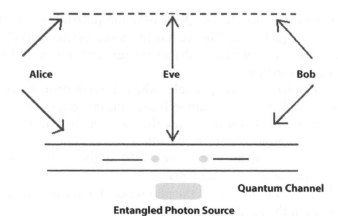

Figure 14.6 E91 protocol representation.

2. Alice measures in either direction: 0, 8, 4, whereas Bob takes a measurement in the direction: 8, 0, 8, 8. They keep track of measurement results and broadcast the methodology used to conduct the measurements via the traditional channel. Alice and Bob are both fully cognizant of the other's priority as a result. They classify the measurement results into two categories: decoy qubits G1 (measured using a different basis) and raw key qubits G2 (same measurement basis).

3. If eavesdropping occurs, the G1 group is used to identify it. They can calculate the test statistic S using the correlation coefficients between Alice and Bob's bases, which is comparable to the Bell test studies. As soon as Alice and Bob discover that S is inaccurate, they will infer that the quantum channel is unsecure and begin a new communication channel.

4. Given that Alice and Bob can acquire the same measurements, G2 can be used as the raw keys if the quantum link is secure. Both Alice and Bob conclude that the measurements |0 and |1 represent the traditional bits 0 and 1, respectively, resulting in the creation of their key sequence.

Modern communications rely heavily on key distribution. There could be no secure channel between people without it. Modern key distribution employs algorithms like RSA and Diffie-Hellman to generate a shared hidden key that allows two parties to communicate, typically over a symmetrically encrypted connection. The issue with these schemes is that they can't be proven to be safe. They can be broken with enough computing power. This isn't a problem with conventional computers because it's impossible; however, with the rise of quantum computers, these algorithms may soon be brute-forced, necessitating a new key distribution scheme.

14.3.4   SARG04 Protocol

SARG04 protocol's first phase is the same as BB84 protocol's first phase [11]. A pair of non-orthogonal states are announced by Alice that is different from the first phase. One of the bases is to encode Alice's bit instead of declaring them. Alice and Bob check to see if they have the same base for each bit. Only if Bob uses the correct basis, the exact state can be measured; otherwise, the bit will not be obtained [8].

14.4   Impact of the Sifting and Distillation Steps on the Key Size

BB84 is provably secure if an authenticated classical channel is used to communicate, the no-cloning theorem is true, the random number generators used are truly random, and the eavesdropper does not have physical access to the emitter and receiver's computers. It works by exchanging single photons between an emitter and a receiver. These photons' polarization is used to encode bit values, which is currently done in a fiber optic cable, but this may change in the future. The encoding is done using four polarization states (vertical, horizontal, and and) (for example, the vertical and states could be used to encode a 1). An eavesdropper's measurement could not distinguish between all four possible states (although it can determine if two states are orthogonal). Each of the incoming photons is filtered by the receiver. Filters are used to distinguish between the horizontal and vertical states that the emitter sends. The filter must be rotated to distinguish between the diagonal states (see Figure 14.7 and Figure 14.8). If a photon is sent through a filter with the wrong orientation, it will be deflected at random to one of the orientations for which the filter was designed. Because they don't have the filter configuration, it's impossible to know the states before the filter for the receiver and after the filter for the eavesdropper. The selection of which filter to use is made at random. After a large number of photons have been exchanged, the receiver sends the filter configuration to the emitter via a traditional secure channel, and the emitter indicates whether the filters are compatible or not. The value of the bits sent where the filter configuration was

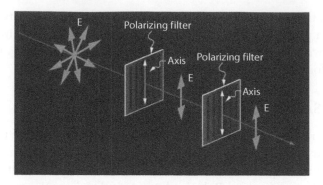

Figure 14.7 Polarization filters.

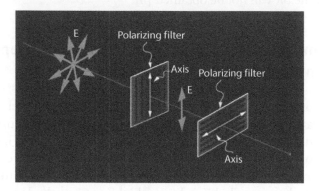

Figure 14.8 Polarization filters.

incompatible is then discarded by both sides, leaving both sides with a key that is roughly half the length of the number of photons sent (this process is called sifting the key) as shown in Figure 14.9. Because the eavesdropper has no way of knowing which bits were dropped and which were not, he is unable to obtain the key.

After that, key distillation is used to account for any errors that occurred as a result of equipment flaws or eavesdropper interference. All of these errors are assumed to be the result of an eavesdropper (worst-case scenario), and they are then corrected using a standard error correction protocol. We can also determine how much information the eavesdropper may have from this point. The eavesdropper's information on the key is then reduced using a privacy amplification protocol. The key is compressed at a rate determined by the amount of information obtained by the eavesdropper. Finally, there seems to be an authenticating phase to stop a man-in-the-middle attack. This is accomplished by using a traditional secure

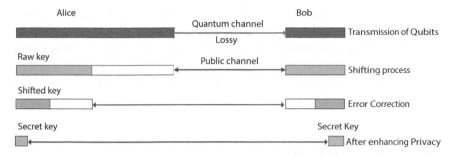

Figure 14.9 Impact of sifting and distillation steps on key size.

Alice's photon polarization	↔ ↗ ↕ ↔ ↖ ↗ ↕ ↕ ↗ ↔ ↖
Alice's bit sequence	0 0 1 0 1 0 1 1 0 0 1
Bob's basis	+ + × + × × × + × × +
Bob's measured polarization	↔ ↕ ↖ ↔ ↖ ↗ ↖ ↕ ↗ ↗ ↔
Bob's sifted measured polarization	↔ ? ? ↔ ↖ ↗ ? ↕ ↗ ? ?
Alice and Bob's bit sequence	0 0 1 0 1 0
Final key	0 1 1 0

Figure 14.10 The process of BB84 key distribution [12].

channel to compare a predetermined subset of keys. We now have a secure key suitable for symmetric encryption. This is illustrated in Figure 14.10.

The flaws with BB84 include the need for a secure channel for confirming information between the receiver and emitter, as well as the fact that the fiber optic cable used could be easily cut or blocked for a denial of service attack. Sending single photons is also difficult. This means that LASER pulses must be sent at a specific rate in actual implementations. A Poisson distribution, for example with = 0.2, will be used to distribute the number of photons. This means that most pulses have no photons, some have one, and some have several, but a photon is sent every 5 pulses on average. When a pulse has many photons, the unauthorized person can analyze the additional photons to learn the key without making any mistakes. Photon number splitting (PNS) is the term for this type of attack [14].

While BB84 has theoretical support, the most widely used QKD scheme is "Decoy State." Decoy state addresses the PNS problem by sending multiple qubits (photons) at different intensities at random intervals. The actual qubit (also referred to as a signal state) will be one of the decoys.

The emitter then announces which intensity levels correspond to each bit's signal state. An eavesdropper must measure photons and keep their error rate close to the equipment's natural error rate in order to successfully acquire information without being detected. This error rate, however, cannot be maintained due to changing photon-number statistics. Decoy State can now be used in the real world.

14.5　Cryptanalysis

The investigation of cryptographic techniques is known as quantum cryptanalysis. Even while computer programs are still rather new and in their infancy, it is anticipated that within a years they will grow to be sufficiently powerful to affect the cryptographic techniques currently used on our local computers, in the cloud, and elsewhere. So that we can be adequately prepared, we need to research their consequences and comprehend the needs for quantum resources. The various probabilities of Qubit are represented by the Bloch Sphere (Figure 14.11). Quantum gates and quantum bits, often known as qubits, are the two primary quantum resources. Any complex value between 0 and 1 can be represented by a qubit, q, can be defined as $|q\rangle = \alpha|0\rangle + \beta|1\rangle$ where α and β are complex probabilities, and $|0\rangle$ and $|1\rangle$ represent the computational basis states [13]. Quantum gates can act simultaneously on one or more qubits, a phenomenon known as quantum entanglement. Quantum gates can be used to mimic some classical gates, but some quantum gates cannot be modeled conventionally. One of these gates is the Hadamard gate, which, when used on a basis state, superpositionally places the qubit. We are aware of how quantum computers could be utilized to circumvent our present encryption techniques even without access to them.

Two potential algorithms that can break quantum cryptography are Grover's quantum search method (for block cyphers like AES and SHA) and Shor's quantum period finding algorithm (for RSA and Diffie-Hellman). The two algorithms that can be used to attack cryptography are most notable. They are Grover's quantum search method, which may be used against any technique, including block cyphers like AES or hash functions like SHA, and Shor's quantum period finding algorithm, which can only be used against public-key cryptography, such as RSA and elliptic curve Diffie-Hellman. The specific resource needs of these algorithms are always being studied, even though the cryptographic community is aware of their general impacts. We are aware of the following effects:

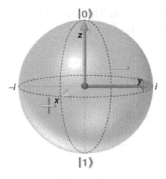

Figure 14.11 Bloch sphere [13].

1. Current public-key methods, including RSA, ECDH, ECDSA, etc., must be changed far in advance of the development of quantum computers because Shor's algorithm entirely destroys them.
2. Grover's technique essentially reduces key size in half, therefore to stay secure in the age of quantum computing a key of double the size should be used by algorithms like AES and SHA.

NIST made the AES a standard in 2002 [15]. Since then, it has become the standard for keeping sensitive information safe like government documents. Grover's algorithm uses a key half the size and provides AES-256 the same level of security as AES-128. But because of how Grover's algorithm must be used, there is some extra work to do. One of the goals of quantum cryptology right now is to reduce this extra work, and there are still many ways to do this.

14.6   Quantum Key Distribution in the Real World

ID-Quantique, MagiQ Technologies, QNu Labs, QuintessenceLabs, QRate, and SeQureNet are the only companies that offer QKD at the moment. Many large corporations, including Toshiba, IBM, Mitsubishi, HP, and NTT, have active research programs in this field. To summarize, there are a variety of QKD protocols, all of which have a similar basic structure but differ in their implementation. BB84 is very secure, but it's difficult to implement due to the challenge in producing single photons, and decoy-state is secure as well, but it uses decoy photons instead of filters. Such protocols are not widely used at the moment, but they will undoubtedly become more important in the future.

References

1. Forouzan, B.A., *Cryptography & network security*, McGraw-Hill Education, United Kingdom, 2008.
2. Bruss, D., Erdélyi, G., Meyer, T., Riege, T., Rothe, J., Quantum cryptography: A survey. *ACM Comput. Surv.*, 39, 2, 27 pages, 2007, Article 6, (June 2007), http://doi.acm.org/ 10.1145/1242471.1242474.
3. Rivest, R.L., Shamir, A., Adleman, L., A method for obtaining digital signatures and public-key cryptosystems. *Commun. ACM*, 21, 2, 120–126, 1978.
4. May, A., Computing the RSA secret key is deterministic polynomial time equivalent to factoring, in: *Advances in Cryptology—CRYPTO '04*. Lecture Notes in Computer Science, vol. 3152, pp. 213–219, Springer-Verlag, New York, 2004.
5. Singh, S., *The code book. The science of secrecy from ancient Egypt to quantum cryptography*, Fourth Estate, London, England, 1999.
6. https://quantumxc.com/blog/quantum-cryptography-explained/.
7. Shor, P., Polynomial-time algorithms for prime factorization and discrete logarithms on a quantum computer. *SIAM J. Comput.*, 26, 5, 1484–1509, 1997.
8. Grover, L.K., A fast quantum mechanical algorithm for database search. *Proceedings of the Twenty-Eighth Annual ACM Symposium on Theory of Computing*, 1996.
9. Vernam, G.S., Cipher printing telegraph systems for secret wire and radio telegraphic communications. *J. Am. Inst. Electr. Eng.*, 45, 109–115, 1926.
10. Bennet, C.H. and Brassard, G., Quantum cryptography: Public key distribution and coin tossing. *Proc. Int'l. Conf. Computers, Systems & Signal Processing*, CS Press, pp. 175–179, 1984.
11. Lopes, M., and Sarwade, N., On the performance of quantum cryptographic protocols SARG04 and KMB09. *2015 International Conference on Communication, Information & Computing Technology (ICCICT)*, 1–6, 2015.
12. Qiao, H. and Xiao-yu, C., Simulation of BB84 quantum key distribution in depolarizing channel, 2011.
13. https://www.pqsecurity.com/.
14. Scarani, V., Acín, A., Ribordy, G., & Gisin, N. Quantum cryptography protocols robust against photon number splitting attacks for weak laser pulse implementations. *Phys. Rev. Lett.*, 92, 057901, 2004.
15. Dworkin, M., Barker, E., Nechvatal, J., Foti, J., Bassham, L., Roback, E., Dray, J., Advanced Encryption Standard (AES), *Federal Inf. Process. Stds. (NIST FIPS)*, National Institute of Standards and Technology, Gaithersburg, MD, 2001, [online], https://doi.org/10.6028/NIST.FIPS.197 (Accessed June 25, 2022).
16. https://www.idquantique.com/

15

Security Issues in Vehicular Ad Hoc Networks and Quantum Computing

B. Veera Jyothi[1]*, L. Suresh Kumar[2] and B. Surya Samantha[3]

[1]Information Technology Department, Chaitanya Bharathi Institute of Technology,
Hyderabad, India
[2]Mechanical Department, Chaitanya Bharathi Institute of Technology,
Hyderabad, India
[3]Computer Science and Engineering Department, SRM University,
Andhra Pradesh, India

Abstract

Vehicular Ad Hoc Networks consist of a group of stationary or moving vehicles that are connected by wireless network. The Vehicular Ad Hoc Networks (VANET's) are created based on the principles of Mobile Ad Hoc Networks. The VANET's are the subset of MANET's which are used for intelligent transport systems. The VANET's are network of vehicles which warn the passengers, drivers and vehicles regarding road safety and traffic congestion besides infotainment. The On Board Unit (OBU), Road Side Unit (RSU), and Trusted Authority make up the VANETs (TA). Experience with the VANET varying network density brought on by fast moving automobiles. The network may face frequent or irregular node disconnections when there is heavy traffic or even bad weather. In such circumstances, the V2I infrastructure may provide the nodes with the appropriate guidance. Vast computational processing resources are integrated into VANETs to give real-time vehicle location, speed, and route information. In VANETs, security concerns and issues are particularly important because they guarantee the safety of both drivers and passengers. This is necessary to ensure safety and protection when designing crucial algorithms. Availability, authentication, integrity, secrecy, nonrepudiation, pseudonymity, privacy, mobility, data and location verification, access control, and key management difficulties are just a few of the security challenges that VANETs face.

*Corresponding author: veerajyothi_it@cbit.ac.in

Sachi Nandan Mohanty, Rajanikanth Aluvalu and Sarita Mohanty (eds.) Evolution and Applications of Quantum Computing, (249–264) © 2023 Scrivener Publishing LLC

Keywords: On board unit (OBU), quantum advantage, road side unit (RSU), trusted authority (TA), vehicular ad hoc networks (VANETs), VANET security, quantum internet

15.1   Introduction

The VANET's are network of vehicles which warn the passengers, drivers, and vehicles regarding road safety and traffic congestion besides infotainment [1]. The rapid growth of alliances combining automakers, numerous governmental organizations, and academia has proven the significance and potential influence of VANETs.

Examples include, among many others, the Advanced Safety Vehicle Program, the Vehicle Safety Communications Consortium, and the Car-to-Car Communication Consortium [2]. Although promoting traffic safety was the primary goal of VANETs, it has recently been more and clearer that these networks also provide new opportunities for Internet access, distributed gaming, and the quickly expanding mobile entertainment market.

15.2   Overview of VANET Security

This section summarizes the security issues and discusses recent VANET proposals that address them. As a foundation for the discussion of numerous security challenges that follow, the classification of assaults in the VANET is also offered.

15.2.1   Security of VANET

VANETs constantly endanger human life, in contrast to traditional networks where the main security issues are confidentiality, integrity, and availability, none of which are particularly pertinent to life safety. Important data cannot be altered or erased by an attacker [5]. VANET security, however, also includes the capacity to guarantee driver accountability while preserving driver privacy. A safe and, more crucially, timely transfer of information about the vehicles and the people within is required due to the potential for tragic events, such as car wrecks [6]. In the VANET, a security breach is quite likely.

On the VANET, security breaches are frequently serious and dangerous [3]. The dynamic nature of the vehicular network includes numerous quick vehicle arrivals and departures as well as frequent quick connecting times [4]. Due to the usage of wireless media, VANET is vulnerable to attacks that take advantage of wireless communication's open, broadcast, dynamic, and high mobility.

The following area is where VANET cryptographic attacks are categorized. Due to the unique properties of VANET, such as high mobility, changeable topology, brief connection durations, and frequent disconnections, there are extra security concerns beyond those that affect ordinary networks. There are security concerns with these many aspects, including certificate management, trust group creation, and position detection and protection.

15.2.2   Attacks are Classified

VANETs are vulnerable to numerous threats and assaults [7]. OBU does not encounter the barrier of a limited battery life like other mobile devices like smart phones and wearables because the vehicle itself is a sufficient supply of electricity [8]. As a result, we could incorporate a variety of CPUs and processors into the OBU to give the car workstation-level computing power. Sadly, this benefit is simply one of many that are provided [9]. Additionally, with this processing power, attacks that need a lot of computing and are challenging in traditional ad hoc networks can be launched.

Because of the distinctive characteristics of VANET, which also bring distinctive vulnerabilities and a variety of assaults that demand significant processing, it is required to categorize the attacks in VANET [10]. Figure 15.1 shows the classification and typical attacks. An attack is categorized

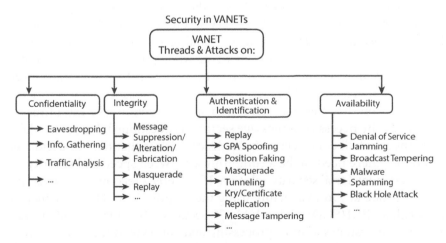

Figure 15.1 VANET attacks classification and examples.

based on the security criteria it attempts to violate. Threats to and attacks on Confidentiality, Integrity, and Availability are the main types [11]. Attacks against accountability and authentication fall under other areas.

15.3   Architectural and Systematic Security Methods

This section focuses on current suggestions that try to improve VANET security through methodical and architectural methods. Various attacks and accompanying cryptographic defenses are also covered in the debate.

15.3.1   Solutions for Cryptography

Due to limitations in the wireless technology employed in VANET, the network may be susceptible to security threats like eavesdropping, jamming, and interference [12]. Additionally, the Open System Interconnection (OSI) network model is referred to in the higher layers of the VANET protocol stack. As a result, vehicle networks acquire those weaknesses. Fortunately, VANET may also profit from the cryptographic defenses already in place against security breaches [13].

15.3.2   Framework for Trust Groups

Exchanging safety signals that inform nearby vehicles of hazardous scenarios and road conditions is one of the fundamental problems with VANET security [14]. These alerts fall within the periodic and event-driven safety message categories. The so-called periodic message is sent out to nearby vehicles on average several times every second and contains data like the location, speed, and direction of the sending vehicle [15]. On the other hand, event-driven alerts are only sent out when potentially dangerous circumstances, like accidents, occur nearby. Given that lives are in danger, event-driven alerts should be sent as soon as practical to every impacted vehicle. Given that message encryption and decryption take extra time on both ends, the necessity of message security is questioned. However, a false warning or a deliberate delay can also lead to risky situations like accidents. Therefore, there needs to be a compromise between speed and security.

As a standard trial security solution, IEEE 1609.2 recommends an asymmetric public key infrastructure using the Elliptic Curve Digital Signature Algorithm (PKI/ECDSA) for VANET security [16]. On the other side, ECDSA necessitates a lot of processing and can extend the time between safety messages. As a result, researchers have started creating symmetric

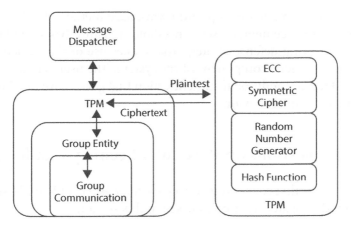

Figure 15.2 Architecture for the trust grouping framework and TPM.

cryptographic algorithms for different solutions. Consequently, security's strength is reduced. To reconcile the demands for speed and security, researchers create a hybrid solution that uses both symmetric and asymmetric cryptography techniques. TPM, group entity, message dispatcher, and group communication are the four main parts of this system, as depicted in Figure 15.2. Through the interactions that follow, all of these elements combine to produce the desired trusted group.

Asymmetric (ECC) and symmetric encryption, random number generation, and hash functions are all features of the TPM module [17]. The message dispatcher transmits the messages to it, and it receives them before sending the encrypted messages back fast and securely. Message signatures are also produced by the ECC module in addition to the hash function. The group entity consists of a group leader, usually the RSU, and the group's neighboring vehicular units. The leader generates one-time secret session keys and distributes them to its followers using the asymmetric ECC method. Using symmetric techniques to protect messages while retaining the robustness of asymmetric ones, the network's vehicles form trustworthy groups by banding together.

15.3.3 User Privacy Security System Based on ID

Authentication, integrity, and nonrepudiation should be the three main components of VANET security. Confidentiality should be offered in some specific instances in order to protect against attackers.

The suggested identity-based security framework for VANET can successfully address the issues with privacy and tractability [18]. To protect user privacy, the system employs a pseudonym-based method. To allow tracta-bility for law enforcement, it uses a threshold signature-based method. The privacy-preserving defense strategy that makes use of the authentication threshold is a crucial component of the system. The user's credentials will be revoked for any additional authentication that goes above the threshold, which indicates misbehavior.

15.4   Suggestions on Particular Security Challenges

The suggestions that concentrate on a particular aspect of VANET security, such as modeling attacks, are discussed in this section.

15.4.1   Content Delivery Integrity Metrics

One of the fundamental functions of VANET applications is content delivery. In order to improve safety and make travelling more enjoyable, it should give drivers fast and reliable information. The distribution of its material presents significant security difficulties because of the scattered, wireless, and open nature of the vehicle network. To gauge the success of VANET security mechanisms and give users confidence in utilizing and using the network, consistent security metrics are required.

The asymmetric profit-loss Markov (APLM) model used a black-box method to describe the gains and losses associated with data delivery, with gains defined as effective data corruption detection and losses as the receipt of tainted data [19]. The system's capacity to modify itself in response to profit and loss is recorded by the model using Markov chains. The model is asymmetrical in that it typically results in more losses for the system than gains.

The result of the optimization is VOR4VANET, a new integrity mecha-nism for VANET content delivery. By keeping track of each vehicle's per-formance history and using that information to determine its reputation, the new strategy benefits from device-centric techniques. Additionally, it is simple to install and functions locally on individual vehicles in a dispersed manner.

15.4.2   Position Detection

Numerous VANET applications, including navigation and weather fore-casting, are position-based. Vehicle positions in the VANET are regarded as sensitive information that can be used abusively by attackers. Users who wish to behave badly can even pretend to be in other positions. Dropping packets, injecting phoney packets, and replaying packets are examples of common position-based attacks. To stop position-based attacks, researchers suggest a revolutionary position detecting system. Their insight stemmed from the general requirement to create the topology for applications like the congestion alarm system.

By comparing what is heard and seen, the vehicle may then confirm the actual positions of the other cars. A new combo like this makes use of both ear and eye technologies [20]. The technique additionally adds a challenge-and-confirm verification process for distant cars to make up for the limitations of sight and auditory sensors. Four different types of observational sources are used in the proposed vehicle model; specifically, eye and ear device data as well as information about approaching (moving in the opposite direction) cars. A car will routinely broadcast its position and receive that information from its neighbors under the position detection technique.

The sender vehicle may be flagged as suspicious and unreliable if there is any inconsistency found during this cross-checking. Due of the local nature of this black listing, its implementation is effective. It is possible to achieve global positional security in addition to local positional security. Exchange of blacklists between nearby cars in an ad hoc manner is another method discussed for achieving location security on a broader scale.

15.4.3   Protective Techniques

To reconcile the high computational cost and low security of symmetric algorithms, VANET needs hybrid cryptography systems. Active defense methods must be used in addition to encryption's passive defenses. As required by the VANET's security protocols, the defensive mechanism makes use of game theoretic techniques and requires three steps for inputs. First, known and unknown opponents are discovered using ant colony optimization-based algorithms [21]. The model for a particular security issue is chosen in the second stage using Nash equilibrium. Using the game theoretic model from the first stage, the third stage enables the defensive mechanism to be built over traffic traces.

Figure 15.3 depicts such a structure.

Security, defensive probability, and dependability are the three factors used to evaluate the defensive system. The veracity of the source and the consistency of the message are what define reliability. Based on the effectiveness of the deployment of traffic management for both static and dynamic traffic conditions, the likelihood of a successful defense is

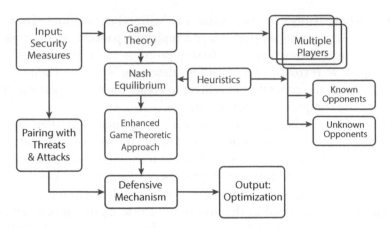

Figure 15.3 Flowchart for the defensive mechanism stage.

calculated. Finally, security takes into account both rural and urban traffic rates because there are much fewer cars in rural places than there are in metropolitan ones.

The simulation's findings show that the suggested defensive mechanism achieves more security and dependability when compared to the VANET's current defensive measures. The study's inventive use of game theory and colony optimization to fortify security precautions and proactively protect the vehicle network is its primary innovation.

Because VANET applications depend on delays and cannot use filtering techniques or other anti-jamming techniques used in IEEE 802.11 networks, VANET also poses special challenges to detect jamming and apply countermeasures [22]. There aren't many products on the market right now that integrate the data transfer and vehicle traffic models. It is unable to perform a more thorough analysis of how current commercial traffic simulators affect wireless signal propagation models and communication protocols because they lack a feedback mechanism.

For the development of defenses against Deny of Service attacks in the jamming style, the analysis of security metrics for VANET is used as a model. The hideaway approach was a brand-new class of defensive strategies created by the researchers to combat jamming. Simulations are used to compare the effectiveness of this new class to traditional channel surfing, also known as the retreat approach. The researchers combine attack/defense modules, traffic simulation, and VANET modules (OBU and RSU) into a simulation package. The major result shows that the efficiency of the hideaway strategy regularly beats that of traditional anti-jamming methods.

15.5   Quantum Computing in Vehicular Networks

The car industry has advanced over the last ten years; modern vehicles are more sophisticated, networked, and provide better driving experiences. The automotive sector must defend itself against an expanding and larger danger landscape since this change is being driven by advancements in computing and communication technology. Quantum-enhanced security is the recommended technique for protecting the core of any car's encryption, both now and in the future. Quantum technology's impact on vehicle security

Cars today have a wider range of in-vehicle technologies that depend on or demand over-the-air (OTA) connectivity in order to provide customers with the best services. Since the automotive sector wants to employ OTA services to create new revenue streams, V2X security is a major worry. Innovative goods. Quantum technology has boosted security to a level that can be trusted at the highest level, and this technology also ensures future-proof security that can survive new technological advances.

15.5.1   Securing Automotive Ecosystems: A Challenge

Both the automotive ecosphere itself and the communications networks connected to it are frequently attacked. The repercussions could be costly and harmful.

Several well-known cyber attacks against some of the major automakers in the world include the following:

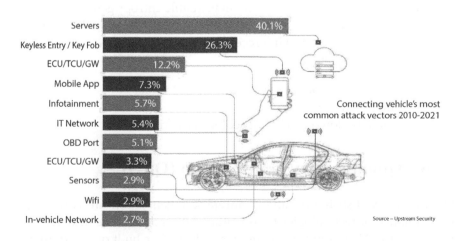

Figure 15.4 Security for automotive ecosystems.

Toyota operations were shut down as a result of a cyber attack, while Jeep was breached via the infotainment system. Tesla was compromised based on an attack on keys (Figure 15.4) [23].

Security for Automotive Ecosystems in the Quantum World it is crucial to deploy quantum-safe cryptographic solutions in order to future-proof car systems, vehicle-to-vehicle networks, vehicle-to-infrastructure networks, and back-end systems.

In order to safeguard data in motion across V2X ecosystems from both present and potential future attacks, IDQ offers a choice of quantum-safe security solutions.

15.5.2 Generation of Quantum Random Numbers (QRNG)

Strong key creation is crucial if you want to be sure that someone else cannot guess or figure out the security key. Therefore, it is crucial to use random numbers correctly. Quantum random number generation (QRNG), which swiftly strengthens pre-existing cryptographic methods and ensures that upcoming quantum resistant algorithms will continue to function correctly, is well suited for this function.

- Right away strengthen the encryption keys;
- Prevents communication with external hardware and programs;
- Prevents communication with clouds.

The IDQ Quantis QRNG chip is the ideal choice for inclusion into automotive HSMs. Along with a clear and dependable entropy generation technique, it provides a solid proof. It has DRBG post-processing that is NIST 800-90A/B/C compliant and has received AEC-Q100 approval.

Features and advantages:

- Provably random keys with the highest value;
- Immediately on;
- Low-cost, low-power, and ecologically friendly.

15.6 Quantum Key Transmission (QKD)

Quantum key distribution and quantum key generation are two of the most important technologies for quantum-safe security. The next generation of secure V2X communication networks will be built on top of them, and these networks will progressively use quantum-safe algorithms.

How safe a cryptographic system is will depend on how secure its keys are. These keys are essential for maintaining the confidentiality and integrity of data in motion, together with the authentication, non-repudiation, and access control of the parties engaged in the data exchange. To be regarded fully secure, keys need to be unique, truly random, and securely distributed.

Typically, QKD can be used to protect data transfer within the back-end infrastructure, which is a top target for attackers due to the enormous volumes of personal data that can be obtained simultaneously.

High entropy keys are generated and safely distributed over the network with the aid of QRNG and QKD. Vehicle communications are sufficiently encrypted to be protected from both ongoing and "hack now, break later" attempts. Quantum resistant algorithms (QRAs) can be introduced to vehicular communications without significantly altering the hardware or software once they become available.

15.7 Quantum Internet – A Future Vision

The future applications of the quantum internet are difficult to foresee, as is the case with any completely new technology.

For all of these applications, the ability of a quantum internet to transmit quantum bits (qubits), which are fundamentally distinct from classical bits, is essential. Qubits can simultaneously be both 0 and 1, unlike conventional bits, which can only have one of these two values (0 or 1). Qubits can also be entangled with one another, resulting in correlations over vast distances that are significantly stronger than those that can be achieved with classical information [24]. Additionally, copying a qubit is not possible and can be detected. Due to this characteristic, qubits are highly suited for security applications, but qubit transmission necessitates completely novel ideas and methods.

Applications that are essentially unattainable for the conventional internet will be made possible by a quantum internet. By leveraging quantum communication, a quantum internet could augment the current internet. However, some experts think that eventually all communication would take place over quantum channels.

15.7.1 Quantum Internet Applications

The quantum internet is anticipated to be incredibly advantageous. We are currently in the early stages of the development of the anticipated applications for the Quantum Internet [Castelvecchi] [Wehner].

Figure 15.5 Quantum internet applications.

Internet-based quantum applications (Figure 15.5). Safe access to distant quantum computers housed in the cloud is one use for a quantum internet. In particular, a straightforward quantum terminal that can only prepare and measure single qubits can connect with a distant quantum computer via a quantum internet without the latter being aware of the computation that was carried out.

15.7.2   Application Usage-Based Categorization

Applications can also be separated into three groups based on the functions they carry out. Applications can be divided into groups according to the following uses:

Quantum sensors are devices that use applications of quantum information technology to enable distributed sensors or Internet of Things (IoT) devices (e.g., clock synchronization).

Applications for quantum computing are ways to support remote quantum computing infrastructure using quantum information technology (e.g., distributed quantum computing).

Stages of a quantum internet's development (Figure 15.6). Each level is characterized by an increase in usefulness at the expense of an increase in technological complexity. Physics, computer science, and engineering must continuously collaborate in order to properly build and expand quantum networks. By outlining what we truly want to accomplish and offering guidance for protocol design, software development, and hardware implementations through experimental physics and engineering, the proposed stages of development will promote interdisciplinary dialogue [25]. The first multi-node quantum networks are anticipated to appear in the next

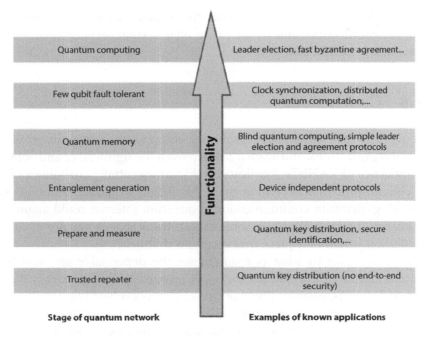

Figure 15.6 Stages of a quantum network.

years, despite the fact that it is difficult to predict exactly what would comprise a future quantum internet.

Similar to a traditional network, a particular quantum internet implementation may be customized for performance, distance, or both

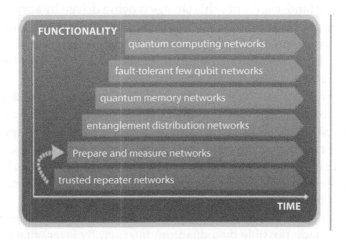

Figure 15.7 Phases of the quantum internet's development.

(Figure 15.7). A "network" is a state that transcends above moment in time communication, and its goal is to offer certain services to any end nodes that are connected to it.

15.8　Conclusions

The rapid growth of alliances combining automakers, numerous governmental organizations, and academia has proven the significance and potential influence of VANETs. Applications that are essentially unattainable for the conventional internet will be made possible by a quantum internet. By leveraging quantum communication, a quantum internet could augment the current internet. However, some experts think that eventually all communication would take place over quantum channels.

In comparison to what is required for the dependable and scalable implementation of complicated network protocols, whether across short or long distances, quantum network research has evolved but is still in its infancy. The creation of quantum repeaters, error-corrected teleportation, local quantum computation, and quantum memories are some of these lofty goals. However, there is a lot of action taking place on a global scale to achieve these goals.

Similar to a traditional network, a particular quantum internet implementation may be customized for performance, distance, or both. A "network" is a state that goes beyond point-to-point communication, and its goal is to offer certain services to any end nodes that are connected to it.

The automotive sector must defend itself against an expanding and larger danger landscape since this change is being driven by advancements in computing and communication technology. Quantum-enhanced security is the recommended technique for protecting the core of any car's encryption, both now and in the future. Quantum technology's impact on vehicle security.

Cars today have a wider range of in-vehicle technologies that depend on or demand over-the-air (OTA) connectivity in order to provide customers with the best services. Since the automotive sector wants to employ OTA services to create new revenue streams, V2X security is a major worry. Innovative goods. Quantum technology has boosted security to a level that can be trusted at the highest level, and this technology also ensures future-proof security that can survive new technological advances.

Applications that are essentially unattainable for the conventional internet will be made possible by a quantum internet. By leveraging quantum communication, a quantum internet could augment the current internet.

However, some experts think that eventually all communication would take place over quantum channels.

Quantum communication networks are still in their early stages. We have higher expectations as a culture because we can't imagine a world without networking and computing. We desire networks that can meet our computing needs and are quicker, more secure, and always available. Despite having a solid and established theoretical foundation in quantum mechanics, little is understood about quantum networks. A majority of science applications about how to really apply them.

References

1. Cacciapuoti, A.S., Caleffi, M., Tafuri, F., Cataliotti, F.S., Gherardini, S., Bianchi, G., Quantum internet: Networking challenges in distributed quantum computing. *IEEE Network*, 34, 1, 137–143, 2020.
2. Bhaskar, M.K., Riedinger, R., Machielse, B., Levonian, D.S., Nguyen, C.T., Knall, E.N., Park, H., Englund, D., Lončar, M., Sukachev, D.D., Lukin, M.D., Experimental demonstration of memory-enhanced quantum communication. *Springer Nat.*, 580, 7801, 60–64, 2020.
3. Aguado, A., Lopez, V., Lopez, D., Peev, M., Poppe, A., Pastor, A., Folgueira, J., Martin, V., The engineering of software-defined quantum key distribution networks. *IEEE Commun. Mag.*, 57, 7, 20–26, 2019.
4. Awschalom, D.D., Hanson, R., Wrachtrup, J., Zhou, B.B., Quantum technologies with optically interfaced solid-state spins. *Nat. Photonics*, 12, 516–527, 2018.
5. Castelvecchi, D., The quantum internet has arrived (and it hasn't). *Nature*, 554, 289–292, 2018.
6. Diamanti, E., Lo, H.-K., Qi, B., Yuan, Z., Practical challenges in quantum key distribution. *NPJ Quantum Inf.*, 2, 16025, 2016.
7. Broadbent, A. and Schaffner, C., Quantum cryptography beyond quantum key distribution. *Des. Codes Cryptogr.*, 78, 1, 351–382, 2015.
8. Reiserer, A. and Rempe, G., Cavity-based quantum networks with single atoms and optical photons. *Rev. Mod. Phys.*, 87, 1379–1418, 2015.
9. Mejri, M.N. and JalelBen-Othman, M.H., Survey on VANET security challenges and possible cryptographic solutions. *Veh. Commun.*, 1, 2, 53–66, April 2014.
10. Wilde, M.M., *Quantum information theory*, Cambridge Univ. Press, Cambridge, England, 2013.
11. Branciard, C., Cavalcanti, E.G., Walborn, S.P., Scarani, V., Wiseman, H.M., One-sided device-independent quantum key distribution: Security, feasibility, and the connection with steering. *Phys. Rev. A*, 85, 010301, 2012.

12. Caleffi, M., C.-A.S., Bianchi, G., Quantum internet: From communication to distributed computing!, in: *Proceedings of the 5th ACM International Conference on Nanoscale Computing and Communication, NANOCOM'18*, Association for Computing Machinery, New York, NY, USA, 2018.

13. Marcello, C.-A.S., Quantum switch for the quantum internet: Noiseless communications through noisy channels. *IEEE J. Sel. Areas Commun.*, 1, 1–14 2020.

14. Chakraborty, K., Rozpedek, F., Dahlberg, A., Wehner, S., Distributed routing in a quantum internet, *The SAO/NASA Astrophysics Data System*, 2019.

15. Chandra, D., Babar, Z., Nguyen, H.V., Alanis, D., Botsinis, P., Ng, S.X., Hanzo, L., Quantum topological error correction codes: The classical-to-quantum isomorphism perspective. *IEEE Access*, 6, 13729–13757, 2018.

16. Delteil, A., Sun, Z., Falt, S., Imamoglu, A., Realization of a cascaded quantum system: Heralded absorption of a single photon qubit by a single-electron charged quantum dot. *Phys. Rev. Lett.*, 118, 17, 177401–177437, 2017.

17. Deinhard, F. and Cappellaro, P., Quantum sensing. *Rev. Mod. Phys.*, 89, 3, 1–45, 2017.

18. Diamanti, E., Lo, H.-K., Qi, B., Yuan, Z., Practical challenges in quantum key distribution. *NPJ Quantum Inf.*, 2, 1, 16025, 2016.

19. Dahlberg, A., Skrzypczyk, M., Coopmans, T., Wubben, L., A link layer protocol for quantum networks, in: *Proceedings of the ACM Special Interest Group on Data Communication, SIGCOMM'19*, Association for Computing Machinery, New York, NY, USA, pp. 159–173, 2019.

20. Chen, X., Cheng, B., Li, Z., Nie, X., Yu, N., Yung, M.-H., Peng, X., Experimental cryptographic verification for near-term quantum cloud computing, arXiv:1808.07375v2 2019, 2018.

21. Perry, R.T., *Quantum computing from the ground up*, World Scientific Publishing Co., Singapore, 2012.

22. Yanofsky, N.S. and Mannucci, M.A., *Quantum computing for computer scientists*, 1st edition, Cambridge University Press, 11 August 2008.

23. Nielsen, M.A. and Chuang, I.L., *Quantum computation and quantum information*, Anniversary edition, Cambridge University Press, 9 December 2010.

24. Bernhardt, C., *Quantum computing for everyone*, Reprint edition, The MIT Press, 8 September, Cambridge, Massachusetts, 2020.

25. Hidary, J.D., *Quantum computing: An applied approach*, 1st ed., 2019 edition, Springer, 20 September, New York, 2019.

16

Quantum Cryptography with an Emphasis on the Security Analysis of QKD Protocols

Radhika Kavuri*, Santhosh Voruganti, Sheena Mohammed, Sucharitha Inapanuri and B. Harish Goud

Department of Information Technology, Chaitanya Bharathi Institute of Technology, Gandipet, Hyderabad, India

Abstract

Quantum computing is a fast-developing technology that uses the principles of quantum physics to solve issues that are too complicated for conventional computers. Even the most complex mathematical computations performed in conventional cryptographic algorithms can easily be hacked using quantum computers. Hence, cryptologists are recently looking into developing new quantum hard cryptographic algorithms that are secure against quantum computers. Quantum cryptography employs the inherent features of quantum physics in order to secure and transmit data in a way that cannot be intercepted. Quantum cryptography is emerging as a game changing technology in various domains including privacy preserving, secure online voting, banking, and manufacturing industries. This chapter covers basic terminology and concepts of quantum cryptography, trends in quantum cryptography, an in-depth overview of Quantum Key distribution protocols along with their vulnerabilities and future research foresights.

Keywords: Quantum cryptography, secure communication, quantum key distribution, BB84, BB92, E91, BBM92

Corresponding author: kradhika_it@cbit.ac.in

Sachi Nandan Mohanty, Rajanikanth Aluvalu and Sarita Mohanty (eds.) Evolution and Applications of Quantum Computing, (265–288) © 2023 Scrivener Publishing LLC

16.1   Introduction

In the definition of cryptography, "crypt" stands for secret and "-graph" for writing. Since cryptography uses codes and algorithms to protect data and secure communications, it can be thought of as hidden writing. Using quantum mechanical features to carry out cryptographic operations so that data cannot be hacked or intercepted, is termed as "Quantum Cryptography" [1, 2].

Quantum cryptography is a new, safer method of encryption. Quantum cryptography uses the ideas of quantum mechanics to encrypt messages, as opposed to conventional encryption, which requires intricate mathematical computations. Quantum cryptography is now significantly more secure possibly even impenetrable. In the chain of data security, cryptography is the most reliable link. Data can potentially be encrypted with quantum cryptography for longer lengths of time than with traditional cryptography. Beyond around 30 years, scientists cannot guarantee encryption using classical cryptography, digital records can be preserved for a centennial using quantum key distribution, but some stakeholders may need longer periods of protection. QKD [3] is capable of long-distance, secure transmission over a noisy channel.

The most renowned application of quantum cryptography is quantum key distribution, which offers a data secure resolution to the key exchange issue. The benefit of quantum cryptography is that it makes it possible to perform a number of different cryptographic operations that have been demonstrated or are hypothesized to be impractical when using exclusively traditional communication. For instance, it's challenging to duplicate data from qubits. The quantum state will change if the encoded data is read because of wave function breakdown. This could be used to identify spying during the distribution of quantum keys.

QKD, is the process of using quantum communication to share a key between two individuals without letting a third party know what that key is, even if the intruder can spy on all of the communication. The intruder will encounter inconsistencies if she attempts to uncover details about the key that has been established, which will draw the authorized party's attention. The key generation rate in reality has limits as transmission distances increases. A mechanism called quantum coin flipping is employed when there is no mutual confidence between the players. The participants exchange information by sending qubits through a quantum channel for communication.

16.2   Basic Terminology and Concepts of Quantum Cryptography

The basic concepts for understanding Quantum Cryptography are described below.

16.2.1   Quantum Cryptography and Quantum Key Distribution

These phrases are sometimes used synonymously since QKD is the most developed area of study in Quantum Cryptography [4]. However, the research that goes into quantum cryptography as a whole only has one application, which is quantum key distribution. Quantum cryptography also incorporates other techniques like quantum exchange of secrets and coin flipping.

16.2.2   Quantum Computing and Quantum Mechanics

Quantum computation can be thought of as a theory that uses quantum mechanics for its cryptography algorithms. The mathematical theory used to simulate how subatomic particles interact is known as quantum mechanics. Understanding quantum computation is necessary for post-quantum cryptography.

16.2.3   Post-Quantum Cryptography

Current cryptographic algorithms can easily be broken by Quantum computers, Post Quantum Cryptography algorithms use complex mathematical computations and thought as secure against cryptanalytic attack by Quantum computer.

16.2.4   Quantum Entanglement

The two atoms unusual connection to one another is referred to as quantum entanglement. It alludes to the phenomenon in which two particles interact and become entangled, linking their spin, position, and other attributes. Even if a particle is very far away from another particle, any change to one of them will have an impact on the other. According to quantum entanglement, the relationship between the transmitter and the receiver is entangled [5].

16.2.5   Heisenberg's Uncertainty Principle

According to Heisenberg's uncertainty principle, It is not possible to identify a particle's momentum even its exact location is known. However, even if the complete knowledge of a particle's momentum is known it is not possible to pinpoint its location. This rule states that it is not possible to confidently or accurately predict a position of particles or momentum [6].

16.2.6   Qubits

A qubit, also known as a quantum bit, is a fundamental quantum informational unit that is physically realized with a two-state device in quantum computing. It is the quantum equivalent of the traditional binary bit. A qubit, is a two-level quantum system that displays the characteristics of quantum mechanics. Examples are A single photon's polarization, where the two states can be understood as vertical and horizontal polarization, or the spin of an electron, where the two levels can be interpreted as spins up and down. A bit would need to be in one of two states in a classical system. The qubit can, however, exist in a coherent superposition of both states according to quantum mechanics [7]. Figure 16.1 shows the Qubits are quantum superpositions of two states, which correspond to the surface of a sphere. Conventional digital bits can only exist in one of two states left or right.

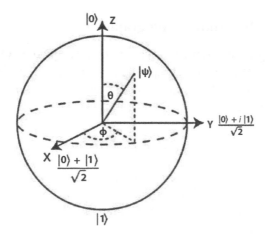

Figure 16.1 Quantum bits.

Table 16.1 The bit values for polarized photons.

Basis	0	1
Rectilinear basis		
Diagonal basis		

16.2.7   Polarization

The polarization of light is a possible medium for quantum information. The unbreakable units of light are called photons. One photon at a time can be generated by quantum researchers, and their polarization can be used to store quantum bits of information [1]. The bit values for polarized photons are shown in Table 16.1.

16.2.8   Traditional Cryptography vs. Quantum Cryptography

Table 16.2 depicts how traditional cryptography is different from Quantum cryptography.

Table 16.2 Comparison of traditional cryptography and quantum cryptography.

Parameter	Traditional cryptography	Quantum cryptography
Foundation	Mathematical calculations	Quantum mechanics.
Usage	Commonly employed	Advanced
Digital Signature	Yes	No
Bit Rate	influenced by processing speed	1 MBPS on an average
Bit Storage (in n-bit)	2n strings	One string
Scale	Millions of kilometers separate parties in the communication	Maximum communication is 10 miles
Testing	Rolled out and examined	Initial testing has not been completed
Upgrades	Necessary as processing power grows	It is based on law of physics
Medium Dependent	No	Yes
Cost	Low	High

16.3   Trends in Quantum Cryptography

In today's world of data sanctuary, Quantum Cryptography is one of the most prominent fields. The need for QKD has surged during the COVID-19 epidemic because many government and commercial entities use a hybrid protocol. Even before cyber-criminals knew that economic, military, airline and administrative entities were exchanging highly-sensitive data online. Additionally, the epidemic has enhanced the risk of sensitive data. These trends are opening up new markets for Quantum Cryptography [8, 9].

Current computerized world relies mainly on data safety, both during information storage and divulgence in areas such as net-banking, digitalized-government channels, and electronic-business. As quantum computers advance, the risk of breaching this security is potentially increasing. Ongoing Research & Development's investments are vital for industries in the QKD market proficient with vital assets and ensure long-term confidentiality in a broad range of use cases. Stakeholders are paying attention to new trends, recently Indian Space Research Organisation for the very first-time announced hack-proof demonstration of Quantum Communication in the free-space across a three hundred (300) meters in India [10]. Competitive rivalry in Quantum Communication in the free-space may lead to an agreement between the United States and China. Advanced cryptographic techniques for data safety gain prominence in nationwide Defense. Stakeholders in United States and China have begun a fierce competition in quantum data security.

Organizations in the QKD market are following the trends in live audio-visual conferencing using secure key encrypted signals. Reliable network infrastructure is expected to boost QKD technology adoption. Experts in digital (network and application) security and researchers are developing solutions and techniques that will increase industrial interest in QKD-enabled solutions.

16.3.1   Global Quantum Key Distribution Links

As cyber-security has large significance in applications like National Defense, there is a global demand for advanced cryptographic technologies. Most regions like North and South American, European, Russian, countries, etc., are ahead in implementing the advancements of QKD.

To secure quantum data Stakeholders in the United States and China have begun an intense competition. Through a single satellite called 'Micius', pairs of photons are transmitted to two ground stations distanced for about 1,120kilometers. A group of scientists, engineers, and technicians have gained attention for this new advancement. In contrast, United States, is growing rapidly its reliance on reliable data stream, which is generating new opportunities for organizations in the QKD market. As both US and China are interested in quantum communications in the free-space, it is expected that a feasible alliance to manage space rivalries will come into fruition. Table 16.3 shows the developments in the domain of quantum cryptography.

In April 2021, scientists at Moscow's Institute of Physics and Technology built the country's first domestic five-qubit circuit. In addition, the Russian Federation has openly assigned over $790 million to the progress of quantum technologies. People involved in the QKD market are capitalizing on assets in the end uses of both Information Technology and telecommunications. In South Korean a renowned wireless telecom operator -SK Telecom Co. Ltd, publicized a first-of-its-kind 5G smartphone 'The Galaxy

Table 16.3 Developments in quantum cryptographic trends.

Year	Development
1984 [11]	When the BB84 protocol was first introduced, it was characterized as using photon polarization states to transfer the information.
1991 [12]	The plan of Artur Ekert makes use of entangled photon pairs and E91protocol. Once the photons are distributed, Alice and Bob each receive one photon from each pair.
2005 [11]	Report on the condition of the first-ever network for quantum cryptography supported by US DARPA.
2009 [13]	Describe the QKQ network's SECOQC prototype, which is based on trusted repeater architecture, and which was developed in Vienna in 2008.
2009 [14]	Quantum network-based system that is user-focused and hierarchical.
2010 [15]	In 2010 saw the successful demonstration of a China-based urban all-pass Quantum Communication Network.
2014 [16]	Reports on the effectiveness of the Swiss quantum QKQ network in a city context in Geneva.
2016 [14]	In South Korea, the first commercial QKQ network went live in 2016.
2018 [16]	A 421 km secret key rate on the longest conventional QKQ one ultra-loss fiber was experimentally demonstrated in the United States.
2021 [29]	A ground-based quantum communication network that spans from Beijing to Shanghai. An integrated space-to-ground quantum communication network over 4,600 kilometers.

A Quantum', equipped with a chipset that generates quantum random number. Toshiba Corporation, a Japanese multinational conglomerate, plans to generate $3 billion by 2030 in revenue from Quantum Cryptography. Stakeholders are involving more on the enhanced cryptography technology for data security applications. By the end of 2030, the QKD market is expected to be worth 1.1 billion (USD). Table 16.3 mentions the developments in the field of Quantum Cryptography and Table 16.4 depicts Indian research organizations working on quantum cryptography.

Table 16.4 Indian research organizations working on quantum cryptography.

S. no.	Organization	Research areas
1	Tata Institute of Fundamental Research	The study of quantum events in superconducting circuits is the primary objective of the Quantum Measurement and Control Laboratory (QuMaC) at TIFR. Quantum simulations, new qubit designs, quantum restricted parametric amplifiers, and other topics are among the research areas.
2	IIT Madras	Research in these disciplines is being done in areas like QKD, secure communications systems, quantum detectors, etc. are all areas of research in these fields.
3	IISER Pune	In order to create cutting-edge computing systems and more practical uses like atomic clocks, precision sensors, GPS navigational equipment, geological mapping, and innovative materials, I-HUB seeks to harness quantum phenomena. I-HUB also supports technology incubation, human resource development, and translation.
4	THE BELAMY	The experimental program at this facility focuses on a variety of topics, including superconducting qubit devices, integrated photonic quantum networks, quantum sensors, and single-photon sources and detectors for quantum communications.

16.3.2   Research Statistics on Quantum Cryptography

The research and development (R&D) trends are introduced where the research investigates global "Quantum Cryptography" using a set of qualitative and quantitative metrics to achieve a better understanding of the state-of-art research in the field at the individual, institutional, national, global and levels.

For technical information and references, in 2004, the US Defense Advanced Research Projects Agency's DARPA Quantum Network project connected three Boston-area locations that were each around 10 kilometers apart to showcase the first metropolitan QKD network. A QKD network based on terrestrial fiber was used to achieve this. Using a QKD network to connect six points in Vienna City, the project developed in 2008 namely Secure Communication based on Quantum Cryptography, of the European Union showed that keys could be generated at a rate of about 1 kbps over a 30 km distance to support encrypted voice communication (phone lines).

In the context of interdisciplinary research, the survey provides a window into the most productive authors, keywords, characteristics of highly citied paper, research organizations as well as the top modes of research communication and broad research subject areas in all popular countries across the globe. The data analysis is based on the Scopus indexed database from the period 1992 to 2020, with a total of 10801 publications on Quantum Cryptography.

Under the assumption that years from today's state of Quantum Cryptographic development is likely to be within a realistic range. Out of the world's publication markets Scholarly journals held 59.61%. An average of citations per paper since publication is around 23.01 with the growth in research rate of 24.76% per year and an average of 305.46 citations per paper since publication as it contributes 4.03% of its highly cited papers. Nearly 29% of total output is accounted on the "Quantum Cryptography" projects funded by 100+ International financial firms and Multi-National Companies [28].

16.4   An Overview of QKD Protocols

QKD protocol aims to provide a distributed secret key that can be used to communicate securely connecting two distant parties via a shared communication route. The key generating process is undeniably secure against any attack that an eavesdropper could launch, which is the most crucial thing to keep in mind in this scenario. The principles of quantum mechanics ensure the protocol's security. As long as quantum mechanics is not refuted, one can be sure that the protocol will be secure forever. The QKD method uses the rules of quantum mechanics to guarantee absolute security on a transmission line. A quantum key distribution technique would typically be composed of two parts: The quantum transmission phase, which covers the first stage is where Alice and Bob communicate and calculate states of quantum. The creation of a pair of secure keys using the bit strings generated in the quantum phase occurs in the second phase, known as the traditional post-processing phase.

The purpose of QKD is to provide a method that enables Alice and Bob to produce secured private keys similar to one-time pads. The No-Cloning Theorem is used in QKD that states that no cubit can be copied. The fact that the key is continuously and randomly produced makes QKD nearly secure. As a result, both parties automatically share the key. Although there are many distinct types of QKD, in which the two primary categories are Prepare-and-Measure and Entanglement-based protocols.

16.4.1   Introduction to the Prepare-and-Measure Protocols

Quantum state measurements are the main focus of prepare-and-measure techniques. This kind of protocol can be used to identify eavesdropping and determine the amount of data that might have been intercepted. Entanglement-based protocols are built on coupled quantum states, which are formed when two objects are entangled with one another. Entanglement refers to the idea that measuring one object has an impact on another. With this approach, the other parties will be informed if an eavesdropper gains access to a previously trusted node and makes changes. The system will alter just by trying to observe the photons, which will enable the detection of an intruder. This is accomplished by employing quantum entanglement or quantum superpositions.

Discrete variable QKD (DV-QKD) and continuous variable QKD are two more categories of QKD (CV-QKD). A photon detector will be used to measure quantum states in DV-QKD in order to encode quantum information in variables. The BB84 protocol [17] is an illustration of a DV-QKD protocol. A laser's amplitude and phase quadrants are used by CV-QKD to encode quantum information before transmitting the light to a receiver.

16.4.2   The BB84 Protocol

The BB84 QKD technique was invented by Bennett and Brassard in 1984 [17]. It is the very first quantum cryptography protocol. The protocol is demonstrably secure under the following two assumptions:

(1) The fact that information gain may only be achieved at the cost of a signal disturbance if the two states being distinguished are not orthogonal;

(2) The presence of a public classical channel that has been verified. It is typically described as a technique for securely exchanging a secret key between parties for one-time pad encryption.

Each bit of the secret key is encrypted into the polarization state of a single photon using the BB84 protocol. The polarization state of a single photon cannot be measured without causing it to be destroyed, making this information "fragile" and inaccessible to the listener. The photon must be detected by any listener, say "Eve," who then has to either disclose herself or send the photon again. She will, however, inevitably send a photon with the wrong state of polarization. This will cause errors, which will make the eavesdropping obvious.

The protocol is then carried out as follows (Figure 16.2). Alice sends a series of pulses, each containing a single photon polarized in a different way. Alice encodes 1's as V-polarized photons and 0's as H-polarized photons. However, this only occurs in 50% of the cases. A diagonal polarization basis is used to encode the bits remaining cases. The 'D' polarization represents 0, while the 'A' polarization represents 1. Bob, uses a standard setup to measure the polarization. Using the HV basis, which is also referred to as "H," Bob can tell the difference between the H and V polarizations.

In 50% of the cases, Bob modifies his basis at random to AD, denoted as 'C.' After a predetermined number of bits have been transmitted, Bob publicly states the basis he employed for each bit. Then Alice describes which instances they used the identical bases in. Only the bits in which they utilized the same base remain after discarding the ones in which they used different bases.

After this process (key sifting), the length of the key is reduced twice, but what is left is random and coincides for Alice and Bob, check to see if there was any eavesdropping (Figure 16.2). To that end, they take a portion of the key and compare it. This procedure is also open to the public, but 10% of the results are discarded. The key would contain errors if the below-mentioned eavesdropping (Figure 16.3) occurred. The entire key is then discarded, and the procedure is repeated. Figure 16.4 illustrates how to send 8 bits of a secret key. Only four bits remain after key sifting.

It is not necessary to use polarization; the bits can also be encoded into the phase of single photons. The advantage of polarization is that it is well conserved during light propagation through the atmosphere. The longest transmission distance is now 1200 km from a satellite to a ground station. A critical question is how to generate single photons. One method is to use light emitted by single atoms, molecules, diamond color centers, or quantum dots. However, this requires a significant amount of effort and does not provide 'on demand' photons; when emission and collection efficiency

Operations on Alice's Side:

1. Two random bits:

$a = (a_1, a_2, a_3 \ldots \ldots a_{4n}) \leftarrow$ key bit,

$b = (b_1, b_2, b_3 \ldots \ldots b_{4n}) \leftarrow$ basic bit: 0=C, 1=H

2. Alice Prepares a state $|\psi\rangle A = \overset{4n}{\underset{i=1}{\otimes}} |\psi_{a_i b_i}\rangle A$,

each qubit is in one of the four states:

$|\psi_{00}\rangle_A = |0\rangle$,

$|\psi_{10}\rangle_A = |1\rangle$,

$|\psi_{01}\rangle_A = 1/\sqrt{2}(|0\rangle + |1\rangle)$ and

$|\psi_{11}\rangle_A = 1/\sqrt{2}(|0\rangle + |1\rangle)$

Operations at Bob's Side

1. Bob receives the state $\varepsilon(|\psi\rangle_A \langle\psi|$ where $|\psi\rangle_A \overset{4n}{\underset{i=1}{\otimes}} |\psi_{a_i b_i}\rangle_A$

2. Bob calculates bit strings from the state bits.

$a^1 = (a_1^1, a_2^1, a_3^1 \ldots \ldots a_{4n}^1)$ and $b^1 = (b_1^1, b_2^1, b_3^1 \ldots \ldots b_{4n}^1)$

Figure 16.2 Working of BB84 Protocol.

Eavesdropping in BB84 Protocol – *Intercept and Resend*

1. The '$4n$' qubits Alice sends are intercepted by Eve.

2. Eve selects the measurement basis at random (C or H).

In '$2n$' instances: correct guess → correlated bits

In '$2n$' instances: incorrect guess → random result

3. With same basis Alice measures, prepares each qubit, and sends it to Bob.

4. Bob uses a randomly chosen basis to measure the qubits.

5. Sifting step: a and a^1 of length $2n$

In 'n' instances: while Bob and Alice both select the same basis, Eve's basis is different

Figure 16.3 BB84 – Eavesdropping.

Key bit:	0	1	1	1	0	0	1	1	1	0
Alice's basis:	C	C	H	C	C	H	H	C	H	H
Alice's state:	$\|\psi_{00}\rangle$	$\|\psi_{10}\rangle$	$\|\psi_{11}\rangle$	$\|\psi_{10}\rangle$	$\|\psi_{00}\rangle$	$\|\psi_{01}\rangle$	$\|\psi_{11}\rangle$	$\|\psi_{10}\rangle$	$\|\psi_{11}\rangle$	$\|\psi_{01}\rangle$
Eve's basis:	H	C	C	H	C	H	C	H	C	H
Eve's state:	$\|\psi_{01}\rangle$	$\|\psi_{10}\rangle$	$\|\psi_{10}\rangle$	$\|\psi_{01}\rangle$	$\|\psi_{00}\rangle$	$\|\psi_{01}\rangle$	$\|\psi_{10}\rangle$	$\|\psi_{11}\rangle$	$\|\psi_{10}\rangle$	$\|\psi_{01}\rangle$
Bob's basis:	H		H	H	C	C	H	C	H	C
Bob's result:	0	1	0	0	0	0	1	1	0	0
Sifting:	✗	✓	✓	✗	✓	✗	✓	✓	✓	✗
Key bit:		1	0		0		1	1	0	
P.E.:			✗				✓	✓		

Figure 16.4 Sending 8 bits of a secret key in BB84.

are taken into account, these emitters remain probabilistic. In practice, weak coherent states are still used.

16.4.3   B92 Protocol

Bennett's B92 protocol, proposed in 1992, employs two non-orthogonal states, such as H for 0 and D for 1. Alice sends 0 or 1 bits, but 0 in the 'H' basis and 1 in the 'C' basis, and she again chooses the basis at random [18]. Bob also selects the basis at random. If he gets V polarization in the 'H' basis, it can't be H, so he writes '1' down. However, if he obtains H on this basis, it could be D, so he declares that the result is inconclusive and discards this bit. The same thing happens if Bob uses the 'C' basis and gets D: it could be D, but it could also be H. As a result, the outcome is inconclusive, and the bit is discarded. Only if Bob obtains A in the 'C' basis does he write '0' because it cannot be D. The B92 protocol is relatively lesser complex than the BB84 protocol, and as we will see later, it can be used with continuous-variable states. However, it is thought to be less secure than BB84.

16.4.4   Six State Protocol (SSP)

One variation of DV-QKD protocol called the six-state protocol is more robust in the presence of a noisy channel as compared to BB84 [19]. In SSP protocol, an eavesdropper needs to select the right basis from 3 possible bases, SSP causes a higher probability of errors against the attempts made by an eavesdropper, making faults easier to detect. Higher dimensional systems have proven to offer greater security. A six-state protocol can be constructed without the need of quantum computer by using specialized optical technologies. The SSP's 3 conjugate bases are depicted in Figure 16.5.

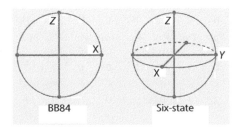

Figure 16.5 The three conjugate bases of SSP.

To send a qubit string to Bob via the secure quantum channel, Alice randomly generates one, encodes it using one of three bases, and does so. One of the bases will likely be used one-third of the time. Bob chooses a random base from a pool of three after receiving the string of qubits to measure each qubit's state. Using a conventional, unsecure, but authenticated channel, Alice and Bob exchange information while discarding measurements, with Bob using a different basis for measuring the qubit's state than Alice did for encoding. States of qubits when the measurement basis was the same as the encoding basis used to calculate the secret key.

16.4.5 SARG04 Protocol

The SARG04 protocol [20] is robust against PNS attacks [21], in which an eavesdropper might change a better transmission line to a noisy one as shown in Figure 16.6. As a result, an eavesdropper can eliminate some of the losses, which are referred to as accessible loss. The inaccessible loss could be due to detector inefficiencies or minimal transmission losses. The eaves dropper then tries to launch an attack over this improved transmission medium.

The SARG04 protocol employs the same quantum states as BB84 protocol. The main distinction is in terms of post-processing phase during which a secure key is generated from a single or 2 photon parts. This protocol uses encoding of classical bits into pairs of non-orthogonal states which cannot be distinguished deterministically.

SARG04 Protocol: Different sifting than BB84

1. Alice's state: $|\psi_{00}\rangle$

2. After Bob's measurement, she announces $\{|\psi_{00}, |\psi_{01}\rangle\}$ and records 0 as the secret key.

3. This can be valid or invalid:

   a. If Bob chooses basis C, then he gets $|\psi_{00}\rangle$, but if the communicated state has been $|\psi_{01}\rangle$, this result is also possible. Hence, the bit is **invalid.**

   b. If Bob chooses basis H,

   result $|\psi_{01}\rangle$ → the bit is **invalid** and

   result $|\psi_{11}\rangle$ → the bit is **valid** and Bob records 0.

Figure 16.6 Sifting in SARG04.

16.4.6   Introduction to the Entanglement-Based Protocols

The entanglement-based protocols allow two parties to create a secret key together even while the entangled photon source may be in the custody of an attacker. In entanglement, It is possible for the quantum states of two (or more) distinct objects to link together to the point that they can only be characterized by a combined quantum state and not as independent items. The entanglement-based QKD can be more resilient to environmental changes, can tolerate larger channel loss, and can make the analysis of the cryptographic key simpler [22]. E91 protocol and BBM92 protocol are the two main entanglement-based protocol types now in use.

16.4.7   The E91 Protocol

Quantum teleportation, the method of exchanging information via entangled states with the aid of a conventional information channel, is the base of Ekert's protocol best known as E91. Ekert presents a channel in which a solitary source produces pairs of entangled elements, which may be polarized photons [23]. Figure 16.7 illustrates the process of E91 protocol.

The process can be shown in Figure 16.8.

16.4.8   The BBM92 Protocol

Bennett, Brassard, and Mermin proposed BBM92 protocol [24] which involves entangled photon pairs that represent an entanglement-based variation of the BB84 protocol. It's crucial to recognize how BB84 and Eckert's

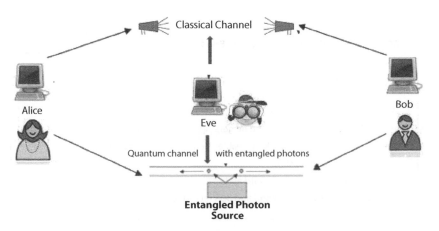

Figure 16.7 Ekert's protocol.

---

1. The EPR pair (Entangled Bell State shown in figure 8.1) $|\varphi+\rangle=(1/\sqrt{2}$)
   $(|00\rangle+|11\rangle))$ is selected by the source Centre, and $|\varphi+\rangle_1$ is sent to Alice
   (first particle) and $|\varphi+\rangle_2$ is sent to Bob(second particle).

Figure 8.1 Bell state.

2. Alice does a measurement from $\{0, \dfrac{\pi}{8}, \dfrac{\pi}{4}\}$ randomly selected directions,
   whereas Bob does a measurement from the directions $\{-\dfrac{\pi}{8}, 0, \dfrac{\pi}{8}\}$.

3. They broadcast the measurement basis that they employed and record
   the measurement result through the conventional path.

4. Alice and Bob are now aware of one another's choices.

5. They split the measurement data into the decoy qubits: 'D' group and
   raw key qubits: 'R' group where a different measurement basis is used in
   D and the same measurement basis in R.

6. The 'D' group is used to sense the eavesdropping by calculating the test
   statistic 'E', the correlation coefficients of Alice's and Bob's bases.

7. When there is a discrepancy in the value of 'E', which indicates the
   presence of an eavesdropper, inferring that the quantum channel is
   insecure, Alice and Bob will break off their present connection and start
   a new one.

8. Given that Bob and Alice could both get the same measurements, 'R' can
   be used as the raw keys if the quantum channel is secure.

Figure 16.8 Working of E91 protocol.

protocol are comparable. We are essentially left with BB84, if Bob and Alice didn't do Eckert's entanglement check and Alice was the source. According to Bennet and Brassard [BBM92], the variations of BB84 could be adjusted to employ an entangled photon source rather than Alice as the source [25, 26]. Alice and Bob exchange a photon from an entangled photon pair, for which they each measure the polarization state in one of two non-orthogonal bases that were randomly selected i.e., either H = 0° and V = 90° or the +/-basis i.e., + = +45° and − = −45°. Figure 16.9 shows BBM92 protocol implementation with Entangled Photon Source (EPS), Single Photon Counting Module (SPCM), PC (Polarization Controller), and PBS (Polarizing Beam Splitter). Optical connections are represented by black arrows, whereas electrical wires are represented by blue and red arrows.

Following a measurement run in which Alice and Bob measured incoming photons for a predetermined amount of time, they publicly

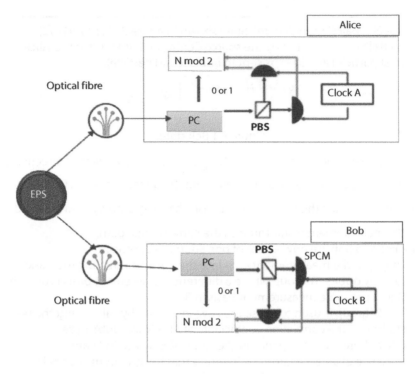

Figure 16.9 BBM92 protocol.

communicated over a traditional channel the basis in which each photon was measured. They each save their measurement results whenever they measure on the same basis since they should be anti-correlated and they can create a secret key from them. Any measurements that Alice and Bob made using different bases should be discarded because the findings won't be correlated. This process is termed as sifting.

16.5 Security Concerns in QKD

QKD is absolutely secure as it is assumed that Eve cannot break physics rather than that she cannot solve complex mathematical problems [27]. The man-in-the-middle attack, in which Eve acts to be Alice to Bob and Bob to Alice at the same time, is still possible using the QKD protocols. Under any key distribution mechanism, such an attack cannot be stopped without Alice and Bob first authenticating one another. Further, there are certain inherent issues with employing quantum states to transmit information, some of which are related to quantum theory itself and some of which are practical issues with equipment effectiveness that have an impact on protocol security. In this section, we discuss about such issues related to QKD.

With Noisy Channels
In actual systems, if Alice and Bob find that their measurements are not completely correlated, it can be challenging for them to identify whether the disparity was brought on by employing noisy, poor equipment or by an observer measuring the photons while they were being disturbed.

PNS Attack
It is currently impractical for technology to consistently produce and detect single photons in addition to noise. In contrast, practical systems frequently employ a laser that produces a modest amount of coherent light. However, generating numerous photons makes the photon number splitting (PNS) attack, a new type of attack, possible. In PNS, Eve divides each bit transmission into a single photon or a limited number of photons for measurement and lets the rest go to Bob. By doing this, Eve would be able to measure her photons without interfering with Bob's photon measurements.

Denial of Service
The point-to-point structure of QKD limits future expansion and opens the door to a denial-of-service attack: if Eve is unable to collect crucial information, cutting the physical link will prevent Alice and Bob from doing the same, which might be just as useful for Eve's objectives.

The Distance
The length of a channel has a detrimental effect on quantum characteristics like polarization. Since quantum transmissions cannot be amplified, the channel's losses will eventually be so enormous that readings from detectors won't be able to tell them apart from dark count rates. Lossy channels, which pose problems for QKD systems by limiting long-distance data transfer and introducing security flaws, are unfortunately unavoidable.

Rate of Key Distribution
Another barrier to the practical application of QKD systems is the exponentially decreasing rate at which key material can be transferred over long distances.

Authenticated Classical Channel
Between Alice and Bob, a fully authenticated classical channel must be employed in order to perform the standard post-processing steps and guard against MIM attacks. The overall security of the QKD system is limited to the security of the traditional authentication procedure, which may only be computationally secure rather than unconditionally secure.

Quantum Theory

Since the formulation of quantum theory more than a century ago, numerous experimental findings have been made that support its predictions. Even so, it might not be enough to compel. Some well-established physics theories are currently being aggressively challenged by researchers, most notably the Standard Model of particle physics, which is being actively questioned in spite of experimental results that are remarkably accurate.

Side Channel Attacks

This take place when it is possible to indirectly obtain useful information from the system, perhaps by introducing errors or by performing CPU power analysis. The development of QKD technology has not benefited from ongoing studies into this kind of data leakage because it is still in its infancy.

Key Management

To be effective, quantum key distribution must be a part of a larger key management strategy that addresses key generation, storage, maintenance, and destruction over the course of the key's useful life.

16.6   Future Research Foresights

16.6.1   Increase in Bit Rate

In comparison to conventional encryption, the bit rates attained in quantum cryptography experiments are significantly lower. Quantum key distribution (QKD) performance and utility can only be enhanced in next-generation secure networks with larger bit rates over longer distances. The future application of QKD to far bigger scale networks will be made possible by the increase in bit rate. Since users in such networks must share the key, higher bit rates are crucial. Additionally, implementing a one-time pad, it will enable high bandwidth unconditionally secure communications and increase the range of individual lines.

16.6.2   Longer Distance Coverage

Today's quantum cryptography can only safely connect two points that are around 100 km apart, drastically restricting its usefulness. Research is concentrating on making QKD more affordable and practical as well as working on expanding its range and the transmission rate of the encryption key in order to produce a commercially viable alternative to conventional cryptography.

16.6.3 Long Distance Quantum Repeaters

According to experimental research, the quantum key essentially satisfies the needs of the local area network, and the safety distance is roughly 100 km. Quantum repeaters, on the other hand, are a need if you wish to accomplish greater distance distribution. The development of quantum repeaters has the potential to address global communication issues and advance the replacement of existing communication technologies.

16.6.4 Device Independent Quantum Cryptography

If the security of a quantum cryptography protocol does not depend on the veracity of the quantum devices being utilized, the protocol is said to be device-independent. Device-independent quantum key distribution (DIQKD) is the practice of distributing secret keys via unsecure networks utilizing untrusted hardware. Therefore, scenarios including flawed or even malevolent devices must be taken into account in the security analysis of such a protocol.

16.6.5 Development of Tools for Simulation and Measurements

As they can help researchers gain key insights at a minimal cost, simulations are a crucial tool for the study of quantum cryptography. Working with simulations can yield information that can guide future study towards the creation of new communication protocols as well as the development of real hardware systems.

16.6.6 Global Quantum Communication Network

Future widespread practical applications of quantum communication technology are possible. Similar to how national quantum networks from various nations can be linked, a global quantum communication network can be created if universities, institutions, and businesses work together to standardize relevant hardware and protocols.

16.6.7 Integrated Photonic Spaced QKD

For quantum applications, integrated quantum photonics makes use of conventional integrated photonic technologies and apparatus. Chip-scale integration has become essential for scaling up and converting laboratory demos into practical technologies, just like in classical photonics. The creation of monolithically integrated, hybrid integrated, or heterogeneously integrated quantum photonic integrated circuits is at the heart of integrated quantum photonics research.

16.6.8   Quantum Teleportation

In quantum teleportation, a spin state (qubit) is sent between observers without physically moving the involved particle thanks to the characteristics of quantum entanglement. The particles themselves aren't really teleported; instead, the information that each particle's state encodes is transferred by having that particle's state destroyed on one side and extracted on the other. The method is not instantaneous since it requires traditional communication between observers, which takes time. The value of quantum teleportation rests in its capacity to transmit quantum information over arbitrary long distances without subjecting quantum states to environmental thermal decoherence or other negative effects. A "quantum internet" that functions by transferring data between nearby quantum computers using quantum teleportation may one day be made possible with the help of quantum teleportation.

References

1. Alvarez, D. and Kim, Y., Survey of the development of quantum cryptography and its applications. *2021 IEEE 11th Annual Computing and Communication Workshop and Conference (CCWC)*, pp. 1074–1080, 2021.
2. Jasoliya, H. and Shah, K., An exploration to the quantum cryptography technology. *2022 9th International Conference on Computing for Sustainable Global Development (INDIACom)*, pp. 506–510, 2022.
3. Shor, P.W., Algorithms for quantum computation: Discrete logarithms and factoringin, in: *Proceedings 35th Annual Symposium on Foundations of Computer Science*, pp. 124–134, 1994.
4. Sehgal, S.K. and Gupta, R., A comparative study of classical and quantum cryptography. *2019 6th International Conference on Computing for Sustainable Global Development (INDIACom)*, pp. 869–873, 2019.
5. Moizuddin, M., Winston, J., Qayyum, M., A comprehensive survey: Quantum cryptography. *2017 2nd International Conference on Anti-Cyber Crimes (ICACC)*, pp. 98–102, 2017.
6. Jain, A., Khanna, A., Bhatt, J., Sakhiya, P.V., Kumar, S., Urdhwareshe, R.S., Desai, N.M., Development of NavIC synchronized fully automated

inter-building QKD framework and demonstration of quantum secured video calling. *Optik*, 252, 168438, 2022.

7. Liao, S.K. *et al.*, Satellite-to-ground quantum key distribution. *Nature*, 549, 43–47, 2017.

8. Cao, Y., Zhao, Y., Wang, Q., Zhang, J., Ng, S.X., Hanzo, L., The evolution of quantum key distribution networks: On the road to the qinternet. *IEEE Commun. Surv. Tutorials*, 24, 2, 839–894, 2022.

9. Kundu, N.K., Dash, S.P., Mckay, M.R., Mallik, R.K., Channel estimation and secret key rate analysis of MIMO terahertz quantum key distribution. *IEEE Trans. Commun.*, 70, 5, 3350–3363, 2022.

10. D'Oliveira, R.G.L., Cohen, A., Robinson, J., Stahlbuhk, T., Médard, M., Post-quantum security for ultra-reliable low-latency heterogeneous networks. *MILCOM 2021 - 2021 IEEE Military Communications Conference (MILCOM)*, pp. 933–938, 2021.

11. Sharma, P., Agrawal, A., Bhatia, V., Prakash, S., Mishra, A.K., Quantum key distribution secured optical networks: A survey. *IEEE Open J. Commun. Soc.*, 2, 2049–2083, 2021.

12. Aji, A., Jain, K., Krishnan, P., A survey of quantum key distribution (QKD) network simulation platforms. *2021 2nd Global Conference for Advancement in Technology (GCAT)*, pp. 1–8, 2021.

13. Zhang, H., Ji, Z., Wang, H., Wu, W., Survey on quantum information security. *China Commun.*, 16, 10, 1 36, Oct. 2019.

14. Cao, Y., Zhao, Y., Wang, Q., Zhang, J., Ng, S.X., Hanzo, L., The evolution of quantum key distribution networks: On the road to the qinternet. *IEEE Commun. Surv. Tutorials*, 24, 2, 839–894, Secondquarter 2022.

15. Padamvathi, V., Vardhan, B.V., Krishna, A.V.N., Quantum cryptography and quantum key distribution protocols: A survey. *2016 IEEE 6th International Conference on Advanced Computing (IACC)*, pp. 556–562, 2016.

16. Fernández-Caramés, T.M., From pre-quantum to post-quantum IoT security: A survey on quantum-resistant cryptosystems for the Internet of Things. *IEEE Internet Things J.*, 7, 7, 6457–6480, July 2020.

17. Bennett, C.H. and Brassard, G., Quantum cryptography: Public key distribution andcoin tossing. *Proceedings of IEEE International Conference on Computers, Systems, and Signal Processing*, IEEE, pp. 175–179, 1984.

18. Cangea, O., Oprina, C.S., Dima, M.-O., Implementing quantum cryptography algorithms for data security. *ECAI 2016 - International Conference – 8th Edition Electronics, Computers and Artificial Intelligence*, Ploiesti, Romania, 30 June -02 July, 2016.

19. Bechmann-Pasquinucci, H. and Gisin, N., Incoherent and coherent eavesdropping in the six-state protocol of quantum cryptography. *Phys. Rev. A*, 59, 4238–4248, 1999.

20. Scarani, V. *et al.*, Quantum cryptography protocols robust against photon number splitting attacks for weak laser pulse implementations. *Phys. Rev. Lett.*, 92, 5, 057901, 2004.

21. Lütkenhaus, N. and Jahma, M., Quantum key distribution with realistic states: Photon-number statistics in the photon-number splitting attack. *New J. Phys.*, 4, 1, 44, 2002.
22. Ma, X., Fung, C.-H.F., Lo, H.-K., Quantum key distribution with entangled photon sources. *Phys. Rev. A*, 76, 012307, 2007.
23. Kaszlikowski, D., Oi, D., Christandl, M., Chang, K., Ekert, A., Kwek, L., Oh, C., Quantum cryptography based on qutrit Bell inequalities. *Phys. Rev. A*, 67, 012310, Published 21 January 2003.
24. Bennett, C.H., Brassard, G., Mermin, N.D., Quantum cryptography without Bell's theorem. *Phys. Rev. Lett.*, 68, 557, 1992.
25. Houshmand, M. and Hosseini-Khayat, S., An_entanglemen based quantum key distribution protocols. *8th International ISC Conference on Information Security and Cryptology*, 27 October 2011.
26. Bruss, D., Erdelyti, G., Meyer, T., Riege, T., Rothe, J., Quantum cryptography: A survey. *ACM Comput. Surv.*, 39, 2, 27 pages, Article 6, June 2007.
27. Haitjema, M., A survey of the prominent quantum key distribution protocols, December 2, 2007.
28. Gupta, B.M., Dhawan, S., Mamdapur, G.M., Quantum cryptography research: A scientometric assessment of global publications during 1992-2019. *Sci. Technol. Lib.*, 40, 1–19, 2021.
29. Chen, Y.A., Zhang, Q., Chen, T.Y., Cai, W.Q., Liao, S.K., Zhang, J., Chen, K., Yin, J., Ren, J.G., Chen, Z., Han, S.L., An integrated space-to-ground quantum communication network over 4,600 kilometres. *Nature*, 589, 7841, 214–219, 2021.

17

Deep Learning-Based Quantum System for Human Activity Recognition

Shoba Rani Salvadi[1]*, Narsimhulu Pallati[2] and Madhuri T.[1]

[1]Information Technology, Chaitanya Bharathi Institute of Technology, Gandipet,
Telangana, India
[2]Computer Science &Engineering, Chaitanya Bharathi Institute of Technology,
Gandipet, Telangana, India

Abstract

People's daily activities and communications with their living settings are becoming increasingly important to better comprehend through human activity recognition (HAR), a fiercely debated topic in ubiquitous computing environments. Social communication has always relied heavily on human behavior. In order to better understand human behavior, it is important to look at how people interact with each other. In a variety of applications, such as human-intelligent video surveillance, the identification of human behavior is a significant difficulty. Extraction and learning data are critical to the evaluation algorithm. Numerous imposing outcomes, including neural networks, came from the triumph of deep learning. In order to get superior outcomes, quantum computing is used in the deep learning model. ORQC-CNN (Optimized Random Quantum Circuits with Convolutional Neural Networks) model is used to identify the HAR. The architecture that consists of a series of quantum classified layer is shown as an analogy to the classical CNN. Artificial gorilla troops optimizer (AGTO) for ORQC-CNN parameter update is presented using variational quantum methods. According to a network complexity analysis, the proposed model outperforms its predecessor exponentially.

Keywords: Convolutional neural network, artificial gorilla troops optimizer, deep learning, human activity recognition, random quantum circuits

**Corresponding author*: reddymallashobarani2@gmail.com

Sachi Nandan Mohanty, Rajanikanth Aluvalu and Sarita Mohanty (eds.) Evolution and Applications of Quantum Computing, (289–312) © 2023 Scrivener Publishing LLC

17.1 Introduction

Health care, interactive gaming, sports, and general-purpose monitoring schemes are just a few of the many applications for HARs that have risen to prominence in the recent decade [1]. In addition, the ageing population has become a major issue in the world today. The number of people over the age of 65 is predictable to rise from 461 million to 2 billion by the year 2050, according to current projections. This enormous growth will have far-reaching social and health-care implications for those involved. HAR is proving to be an effective tool for monitoring the bodily, useful, and cognitive health of senior citizens at home [2]. In both controlled and uncontrolled environments, Human activity is the goal of HAR. However many applications HAR algorithms have, the complexity and variety of daily activities, as well as intra- and inter-subject variability for a single activity, the tradeoff between performance and privacy, competence on embedded and moveable devices, and the struggle of data annotation remain significant challenges [3]. HAR algorithms can be trained and tested using data from two basic sources: sensor arrays, both surface-mounted and in-wall, Sensors in the environment, such as temperature sensors or video cameras, might be referred to as ambient sensors. Personal devices such as smartphones and smart watches [4, 5], as well as specialist medical equipment, can incorporate embedded sensors [6–9]. There are various privacy and computational concerns when gathering video data from cameras in HAR applications [10]. Many researchers have turned to various ambient and embedded sensors, with depth pictures, as a substitute to video cameras because of their rich contextual information.

The use of Deep Learning (DL) approaches in HAR research has exploded, leading to improved recognition accuracy [11] and image segmentation [12]. Classic Machine Learning (CML) replicas may be more suitable for HAR applications because of the short quantity of the dataset, smaller dimensionality of the input data, and the availability of expert information in articulating the problem. The growing usage of sensors devices, particularly in health and well-being applications, can be linked to an increased interest in HAR [13]. The sensors and devices are needed to collect data before developing HAR-based applications (device identification). This is the second phase in determining the specifics of the data gathering process. The final stage is to pick and train a machine learning model on annotated data using a supervised learning approach (model selection and training) [14]. It's important to keep in mind that, the model selection might also affect the preprocessing data stage. Last but not least, the model is put through its paces by measuring its performance in terms of several activity recognition metric (model evaluation) [15]. Due to the lack of a consistent metric in this study, we employ accuracy as the only comparative metric. AUC, F1, and receiver operating physiognomies (ROC) curves are more representative metrics when dealing with uneven data, however they aren't often included in research articles. An HAR is provided by reviewing each phase of the process using this workflow as an example. since with other sensors is on the rise [16].

Quantum computing (QC) [17] has demonstrated the importance of the QC field in solving intractable issues with classical analogues, and QC's expansion and advancement in machine learning (ML) have both contributed to this development; QC has also had a significant impact on near-term quantum computers in the field of machine learning [18]. Methods utilizing quantum neural networks (QNNs) have recently come to light [19]. The hybrid classical-quantum technique is the focus of this investigation. There are new quantum convolutional layers in CNNs that can estimate the kernel in high-dimensionality using quantum circuits. Another paper by [20] provided a quantum kernel algorithm with Quantum Circuit Learning (QCL) is a new hybrid approach based on quantum circuits suggested by [21]. Large dataset clustering, regression, and classification are all part of QCL's scope of work.

So, the goal of this research is to integrate the advantages of the quantum layer (ORQC) with CNN to create a new proposed hybrid quantum (ORQC-CNN) model. It is the goal of this model to increase the CNN's ability to identify HAR situations.

The following are the work's primary contributions:

1. The ORQC-CNN model for HAR prediction is a new hybrid CNN model that incorporates image processing.
2. The parameters of the RQC are determined using AGTO, and the RQC-CNN perfect is evaluated on two publically available datasets in terms of several metrics.
3. The chapter has five major sections, where the study of related works is presented in Section 17.2. The brief description of research work is provided in Section 17.3. The validation analysis is given in Section 17.4 and finally, the scientific contribution is depicted in Section 17.5.

17.2   Related Works

Deep learning model based on LSTM proposed by Li, Y. [22]. An inertial sensor's residual block is used to determine the forward and backward dependencies of feature sequences extracted from MEMS inertial sensors. Features are then sent into Softmax, which completes recognition of human activity. The model's optimum parameters are determined through experimentation. It has been combined into a single dataset that includes the six most common human movements of sitting and ascending and descending stairs. The suggested perfect is evaluated using our own data and two publicly available datasets, WISDM and PAMAP2. Based on the results of our experiments with the datasets WISDM and PAMAP2, we can estimate that the projected model has an accuracy of 96.35%, 97.32%, and 97.15%.

An action categorization system that combines 3D skeleton data and deep learning is proposed by Basak, H., [23] in their paper. The skeletal data is used to extract four dissimilar kinds of features: The depth-stacked pictures with distance and velocity coding were fed into an Inception-ResNet-modified Convolutional Neural Network model. Similarly, the encoded pictures into the same network. It is then necessary to remove non-informative or misleading features from the feature representation, which is done using an Ant Lion Optimizer-inspired metaheuristic, after the models have been trained, and to minimize their dimensionality. After being tested on three publicly available HAR datasets, the suggested DSwarm-Net model was found to outperform existing models on both UTD-MHAD, and NTU RGB+D 60.

A DL model inspired by Google's Inception-ResNetconstruction, Ronald, M. [24] proposes iSPLInception, which not only attains high predicted accuracy but also utilizes less device resources. Model performance is evaluated using four public HAR datasets from the UCI machine learning repository such as the UCI HAR using smartphones dataset, the Daphnet frozen gait dataset, and the PAMAP2 physical activity monitoring dataset. Performance of the suggested model is associated to that of previous DL constructions that have been proposed recently to solve the HAR problem.

Using a combination of a CNN and a LSTM network, Khan, I.U. [25] creates a hybrid model for activity recognition that makes use of both the CNN and the LSTM. The Kinect V2 sensor was used to capture data from 20 subjects, resulting in a new demanding dataset that contains data from 12 different classes of human physical activity. Traditional deep learning models are studied extensively to find the best answer for HAR. The CNN-LSTM method achieves an accuracy of 90.89%, demonstrating the model's suitability for HAR.

Jaouedi's Gated Recurrent Neural Networks model (GRNN) is a novel technique to human action recognition based on a hybrid deep learning model [26].

The projected technique is tested using data from UCF Sports, UCF101, and KTH. We got an average accuracy rate of 96.3% when we ran our tests on the KTH dataset. Nafea, O., [27] provides a new method for capturing characteristics at various resolutions using convolution neural networks (CNN) and BiLSTM. A number of sensors, accelerometers, and gyroscopes are employed in this proposed methodology, which is based on data from the University of California, Irvine (UCI). As a result of these findings, it can be concluded that the method under consideration is beneficial in improving HAR. This method was found to be more accurate than prior methods, attaining a higher WISDM dataset score than a lower UCI dataset score (98.53% vs. 97.05%).

17.3   Proposed Scheme

The projected ideal working flow is defined in Figure 17.1.

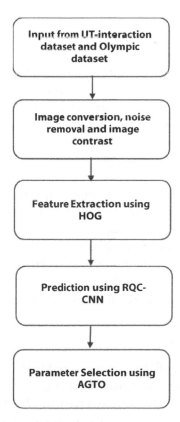

Figure 17.1 Working flow of proposed ideal.

Figure 17.2 Activities from UT- Dataset 1: shaking hands, pointing, punching, hugging, kicking, and assertive.

Figure 17.3 Sample images of olympic dataset.

17.3.1   Datasets Description

These six classes of human-to-human encounters are documented in the UT-interaction dataset: shake hands, point, embrace, drive, kick, and strike [28]. Twenty video streams, each lasting approximately one minute, were made available for testing. At least one execution is required for each contact, resulting in an average of eight human encounters in each film. More than 15 various wardrobe scenarios are shown in the video clips, which are viewed by a large number of responders. Throughout the film, the photos were shot at a resolution of 720 x 480 and 30 fps. Interaction classes include handshaking, hugging, pointing, kicking, and pushing. The UT-interaction dataset is illustrated in Figure 17.2.

Throughout the film, events such as the long jump (720×480), pole vault (30 frames per second), triple jump (720×480), and vault (30 frames per second) may be seen in the Olympic sports dataset [28]. Examples of photographs from the sports dataset are exposed in Figure 17.3.

17.3.2   Pre-Processing

All training and testing photos are equalized to 3232 in the first stage. For this reason, color photos are transformed to greyscale before being used in any feature extraction techniques. As a result of this conversion, each image requires fewer computations to process. Low-pass filters are then used to eliminate the noise from the photos. Preventing artefacts and incorrect key points in the feature extraction techniques is the goal of this work. Final step: sharpen the image's edges with an edge sharpening filter. After the image has been improved, the following step is to extract features from it.

17.3.3   Feature Extraction

HOG, a local feature descriptor, is employed in this chapter to extract valuable features from photos depicting human activity. The distribution of gradient directions is used as a feature in the HOG descriptor. Intensity gradients and edge paths can be used to describe local information in picture components; hence this descriptor was created to capture that information. Using this approach, the gradients in specific areas of an image can be computed. The first step is to divide the image into an 8x8 grid. The Sobel operator is then used to determine the gradient's amplitude and direction for each pixel in each cell. This is followed by the computation of an 8-bin histogram of gradient orientations in each cell. Histogram bins are established by the quantized directions, and the votes (the values that go into the bins) are chosen according to magnitudes. Each cell's 8-bin histogram is generated by adding the votes in each bin. The general lighting of a picture affects the gradients of an image, thus they are normalized to make them more resistant to changes in lighting. A 16-cell window is utilized to create 22 blocks of large size for this purpose. Sliding this window by one cell creates a neighbor block with two overlapping cells that are identical to the present block. Consequently, each block includes four histograms with eight bins, which may be combined to produce a vector of length 4*8=32, before being normalized with the L2 norm. Finally, all the 32x1 HOG descriptors are vector for the entire image. 8-1*8-1*32=1568 is the length of this vector. When it comes to human activity recognition, HOG has two distinct benefits. The first benefit is that the gradient directions may be computed from the difference between the local intensities. The shift and partial affine deformation contribute to the second advantage, which is the ability to withstand deformation. Because of this, changes in the histogram values are largely inconsequential.

17.3.4   Preliminaries

The quantum bit, quantum gates, and the construction of CNN are covered in this section.

17.3.4.1   Quantum Computing

Quantum mechanics is used to process information in QC. QC allows us to solve complicated problems more quickly and efficiently than we could with classical computing. As in traditional computing, the quantum bit (qubit) is used to store and process data. Linear superposition refers to the ability of a qubit to be in either one or both states at the same time. As a Hilbert space state vector, the qubit serves as the qubit's primary representation.

$$|\psi| = \begin{pmatrix} \theta \\ \delta \end{pmatrix} = \theta |o| + \delta |1| \qquad (17.1)$$

where θ and δ are the likelihood amplitudes that are characterized by complex numbers and $|\theta^2| + |\delta^2| = 1$.

A quantum gate is a unitary transformation, according to the postulates of quantum physics. Assuming, we can conclude that U is unitary. Quantum gates can be divided into gates based on the number of qubits. The Hadamard gate, or square root of the NOT gate, is the most commonly used gate in one-qubit gates. Using the Hadamard gate, two qubits can be in a superposition state. One-qubit gates, such as Pauli gates, are also available. Second, two-qubit gates, such as the controlled NOT and swap gate, operate on 4 4 unitary matrices. The final type of multiple-qubit gate is the Toffoli and swap gate, both of which operate on 2n2n unitary matrices.

$$UU^\dagger = U^\dagger U = I \qquad (17.2)$$

17.3.4.2   Convolutional Neural Networks

Inspired by convolution, CNN created a convolutional (Conv) layer. With the input image, a multilayer perceptron (MLP) is formed by a series of hidden layers that predict labels over a layer of output information. Based on CNN ideas, such as ResNet50 and VGG-19, other models have been built.

17.3.5   Proposed ORQC-CNN Model

With the suggested ORQC-CNN model, medical pictures will benefit from enhanced CNN performance, while HAR will be predicted more

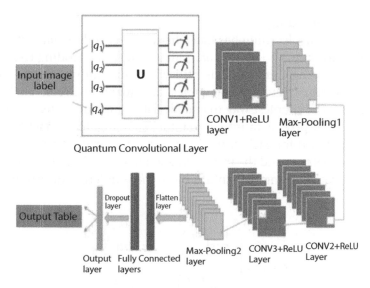

Figure 17.4 Block diagram for proposed ORQC-CNN model.

accurately. There are two aspects to this model: one is the quantum part, which is used in the quantum Conv layer suggested by the authors [29]. Secondly, there's the more traditional CNN component. There is a single quantum Conv layer in the model, and two max-pooling levels, followed by two FC layers. Figure 17.4 provides the architecture of proposed model.

This section explains each of the model's layers.

17.3.5.1   Quantum Convolutional Layer

Although conventional convolution can produce complex kernels, quantum convolution can produce kernels that may be difficult to process classically. The convolution action in quantum convolution is performed utilizing small random quantum circuits (RQCs). Initialization of the quantum penny Lane gadget mimics that of a four-qubit system. In order to use the RQC, an image must be divided into (2 by 2) squares. The RY gate encodes each (2 x 2) a quantum state. In different areas of the image, the encoding procedure is repeated. Convolution with a kernel size of (2x2) and a stride of 2 is compatible with this technique. Qubits (layers) in the RQC are arranged in two-by-two squares. It is necessary to compute the expectation values. There are four output channels (each with a single pixel) for these values. Phases one through three of the quantum convolution layer are: encoding, RQC, and decoding.

17.3.5.1.1   Encoding

Quantum machine learning has had a hard time encoding data into quantum code until now. In Lloyd *et al.*, [30] a variety of encoding techniques are addressed. Angle encoding is utilized in this study to convert input data into quantum state rotation angles. In a quantum circuit, angle rotation gates are the simplest way to encode data. Quantum gates are used to encode classical pixel data into a quantum state due to the fact that only one gate is needed for each entry. There are three types of Pauli matrices: the rotation matrices and the transformation matrices. Three rotation gates are used to rotate a single quantum bit in three different directions: X, Y, and Z.

$$
R_x(a) = \begin{pmatrix} \cos\left(\dfrac{a}{2}\right) & -i\,\sin\left(\dfrac{a}{2}\right) \\ -\sin\left(\dfrac{a}{2}\right) & \cos\left(\dfrac{a}{2}\right) \end{pmatrix}
\tag{17.3}
$$

$$
R_y(a) = \begin{pmatrix} \cos\left(\dfrac{a}{2}\right) & -\sin\left(\dfrac{a}{2}\right) \\ \sin\left(\dfrac{a}{2}\right) & \cos\left(\dfrac{a}{2}\right) \end{pmatrix}
\tag{17.4}
$$

17.3.5.1.2   Random Quantum Circuits

A quantum circuit is a collection of quantum unitary operations (also known as gates) and measurements that are linked together via wires (Qubits). In the same way that the classical Conv layer applies to the input image, the quantum Conv layer consists of quantum kernels. Images are broken down into small, localized regions by using RQCs in the quantum convolution process. The advantage of using a convolution is that it just requires a small number of quantum bits and only a shallow quantum circuit depth.

17.3.5.1.3   Measurement

The decoding phase is another name for the measuring phase. It is the process of decoding that involves converting quantum data into a classical form. It's possible to measure things using Pauli matrices [31]. The Pauli-Z gate is utilized for decoding in the RQC-CNN model.

17.3.5.2   Convolutional Layer

CNN's feature extraction process relies heavily on the Conv layer, which is the most important layer in CNN. Images are processed in this layer by performing a convolution operation. An image's dot product is computed using convolution between small local regions and kernels.

$$(F * K)(i, j) = \sum_m \sum_n K(m,n)F(i - m, j - n) \qquad (17.5)$$

A convoluted feature map can be created by performing a convolution on the input feature, F, and the kernel or filter, K. Next comes the ReLU function alteration, which inserts activation values into the model network. For all negative numbers, the function returns 0 and returns the supreme value for all positive values. The following formula can be used to define the ReLU function.

$$ReLU(x) = max(0, x) \qquad (17.6)$$

where x is an input price.

17.3.5.3   Max-Pooling Layer

Using the Max-pooling layer, the most significant and valuable features are prioritized. Small zones have been created based on the number of strides taken. Each small location's maximum value was used to create pooled feature maps. In CNN, the flatten layer is used to connect two sections by transforming the max-pooled feature map into a 1-D array before the classification stage begins.

17.3.5.4   Fully Connected Layer

There are two layers in a CNN: FC and FC2. Following the flattening layer, the FC layers apply weights to forecast classes, where weights are optimally selected by AGTO algorithm, which is explained in the below section. After the FC layer, the dropout layer is used to reduction the model's overfitting. Figure 17.4 depicts the RQC-CNN model's flowchart: Quantum Conv layer, conventional Conv layers with ReLU function (three

Table 17.1 Layer summary.

Layer	Type	Units	Kernel size	Input size	No. of parameters
1	Quantum Conv	4	2X2	$(32 \times 32 \times 1)$	--
2	Conv2D	16	2X2	$(16 \times 16 \times 4)$	136
3	MaxPooling2D	--	2X2	$(16 \times 16 \times 4)$	--
4	Conv2D	16	2X2	$(8 \times 8 \times 4)$	528
5	Conv2D	32	2X2	$(8 \times 8 \times 32)$	2080
6	MaxPooling2D	--	2X2	$(8 \times 8 \times 8)$	--
7	FC1	300	--	(288)	700
8	FC2	100	--	(300)	100
9	Output	--	--	(100)	202

maxpooling and two FC), and a softmax activation layer are applied to the proposed HQ-CNN model's nine layers. The RY rotation gate, RQCs, and PauliZ gate make up the three sections of the quantum Conv layer. In the 2D CNN, the three classical Conv layers are coupled with the max-pooling layer and employed. After each max-pooling layer, a dropout layer with a dropout rate of 0.2 is applied, followed by another dropout layer. For the first and second FC layers, the model use 300 and 100 neurons, respectively. The RQC-CNN model has 119 645 parameters. Table 17.1 illustrates the suggested RQC-CNN model's summary layers.

17.3.6 Parameter Selection Using Artificial Gorilla Troops Optimization Algorithm (AGTO)

In this section, introduce a new metaheuristic procedure dubbed AGTO, which is inspired by the group behaviors of gorillas and explains the two phases of examination and exploitation in detail using special mathematical processes. The AGTO method makes use of five different operators to replicate gorilla behavior in order to perform optimization operations (exploration and exploitation).

Migration to an unfamiliar location to increase AGTO exploration has been carried out using three distinct operators. Two gorillas moving to the other side of the enclosure increases the balance between exploration and exploitation. Namely migration towards a known site. Although only one operator is employed during exploration, this greatly enhances search performance. The phase transition procedure for exploration and exploitation is carried out using a different manner in AGTO.

17.3.6.1   Exploration Phase

It was decided to employ a parameter known as p to determine the method of migration to an unknown area. When rand p, the first mechanism is selected. In contrast, if rand is less than 0.5, the gorilla will use the approach strategy. Rand >= 0.5 selects the instrument for migrating to a well-known place. The AGTO algorithm has a great deal of flexibility based on the techniques it employs. To mimic the three mechanisms that were used during the exploration phase, Equation (17.7) was utilized.

$$GX(t+1) = \begin{cases} (UB-LB) \times r1 + LB, & rand < p, \\ (r_2 - C) \times X_r(t) + L \times H, & rand \geq 0.5, \\ X(i) - L \times (L \times X(t) - GX_r(t)) + r_3 \times (X(t) - GX_r(t)) & rand < 0.5 \end{cases}$$

(17.7)

According to Equation t+1, GX(t+1), The gorilla is currently located at X(t). Rand, r 1, r 2, r 3, and r 4 are examples of random values that range from 0 to 1. p must be set prior to the optimization operation in order to compute the probability of selecting a migration mechanism for an unknown location with a range of 0–1. The upper and lower bounds of the variables are vital to know. Group X r, one of the gorillas, was picked at random from the entire population and is also known as GX r. Each phase's positions are represented in a random selection of five candidate roles. C, L, and H are designed using Equations (17.8), (17.9), and (17.10).

$$C = F \times \left(1 - \frac{It}{MaxIt}\right)$$

(17.8)

$$F = \cos(2 \times r_4) + 1$$

(17.9)

$$L = C \times l$$

(17.10)

Equation (17.8) uses Equation (17.9) to determine F using the current iteration's iteration value, MaxIt as the total number of iterations. According to Equation (17.8), but this interval diminishes in the latter stages. Equation (17.10) is used to calculate L, where l is a random number between -1 and 1. The silverback's leadership is simulated using Equation (17.10). It is possible that the silverback gorilla's early experiences as a leader of a group are insufficient, but he eventually gains enough experience to be able to make the proper judgments for the group's well-being.

As an example, H is calculated using Equation (17.11), whereas Z is intended using the same equation, where Z is a random number in the problematic dimensions.

$$H = Z \times X(t) \tag{17.11}$$

$$Z = [-C, C] \tag{17.12}$$

During the exploration phase, the position of search agent vectors shifts. A group operation is carried out at the end of the examination phase. Assuming that $GX(t) = X(t)$ is less expensive at the end of exploration, then it is the $X(t)$ solution to employ as the $X(t)$ solution. This phase's best solution is therefore referred to as a "silverback."

17.3.6.2   Exploitation Phase

Competition for adult females and follow-the-silverback are applied in AGTO's exploitation phase. A silverback gorilla is the leader of a troop, in charge of all decisions and movements, and responsible for leading the troop to food sources. Moreover, the group's safety and well-being are the sole responsibility of the silverback, and all of its gorillas follow his orders. There is a chance that the silverback gorilla will succumb to his old age and die, leaving the blackback gorilla in charge of the group, or other male gorillas may challenge the silverback gorilla in order to take control and rule the group themselves. The C value in Equation (17.8) can be used to select either Follow as explained with the two methods utilized in the exploitation phase. A silverback mechanism is selected if C W, while adult females' Competition is picked if C W. W is a pre-optimization parameter that must be set before the procedure can begin.

17.3.6.3   Follow the Silverback

The silverback and the other male gorillas in the group are both young and healthy since the group is still forming, and they closely follow the silverback. To find food, they travel to various locations at the direction of Silverback, who gives them orders. Group mobility can also be influenced by members of the group. It is used when the C W value has been chosen. This phenomenon can be simulated using Equation (17.13).

$$GX(t + 1) = L \times M \times (X(t) - X_{silverback}) + X(t) \tag{17.13}$$

$$M = \left\{ \left| \frac{1}{N} \sum_{t=1}^{N} GX_i(t) \right|^g \right\}^{\frac{1}{g}} \tag{17.14}$$

$$g = 2^L \tag{17.15}$$

$X(t)$ denotes the gorilla's position, while X silverback denotes the silverback gorilla's location in equation (17.13) (best solution). Equation (17.10) is used to calculate L and Equation (17.11) to calculate M. For each possible gorilla in Equation (17.14), $GX_i(t)$ is the vector location of that gorilla during that iteration. N is the total gorilla population. Equation (17.15), in which L is also determined, is also used to predict g.

17.3.6.4   Competition for Adult Females

The exploitation if C W. When adolescent male gorillas reach puberty, they compete violently with other males in their group for the choice of adult females. Fights between members of the gang sometimes linger for days. This phenomenon can be simulated using Equation (17.16)

$$GX(i) = X_{silverback} - (X_{silverback} \times Q - X(t) \times Q) \times A \tag{17.16}$$

$$Q = 2 \times r_5 - 1 \tag{17.17}$$

$$A = \beta \times E \tag{17.18}$$

$$E = \begin{cases} N_1, & rand \geq 0.5 \\ N_2, & rand < 0.5 \end{cases} \qquad (17.19)$$

As seen in Equation (17.16), X silverback (the best answer) represents the current position of the silverback gorilla whereas X(t) represents the current gorilla position. Equation (17.17) shows that Q simulates the collision force. For the sake of Equation (17.17), r 5 can take on any value between 0 and 1. Equation (17.18) is used to construct a coefficient vector that indicates the level of violence in a conflict. For example, in Equation (17.18), the pre-optimization parameter is, and E is utilized to mimic the effect of violence on solution dimensions by applying Equation (17.19). Random normal distribution values and the problem dimensions will be used if rand 0.5, but if rand 0.5, E will be a random normal distribution value. Additionally, the random number generator uses the term "random" to describe a number between 0 and 1.

It is decided to utilize the GX(t) solution instead of the X(t) solution once a group formation operation has been completed, and if the cost of GX(t)X(t), it is considered the X(t) solution. The silverback solution is then chosen from amongst everyone in the group.

17.3.7   Computational Difficulty

The AGTO algorithm's computational difficulty is influenced by several steps, including startup, fitness evaluation, and vulture updating. The initialization stage has a computational complexity of O because there are N gorillas (N). However, there are two distinct phases to the computing complexity of the method for updating itself. Ultimately, the optimum solution is achieved at each stage and is equal to $O(TN) + O(TND) + 2$. T is the maximum number of iterations, and D is the size of the problems that need to be addressed. Consequently, the AGTO algorithm's computing complexity has increased.is $O(N \times (1 + T + TD) \times 2)$.

17.4   Results and Discussion

Raspberry Pi3 with 1.2 GHz processor, and 4 GB RAM can be used to create the following model. Python 3.8.8 and Tensorflow 1.7 are used to implement the human activity recognition model.

17.4.1   Performance Measure

Now, use the performance indicator to get accurate information about the proposed system's efficiency because it is defined as a regular dimension of results and results that can be measured. In addition, the process of reporting, acquiring, and analyzing data on a group's or individual's activities serves as an indicator of effectiveness. Table 17.2 shows the confusion metric used to evaluate the classifier for binary data, which may be explained as follows:

When we say something is "really positive," we mean something that has been appropriately labeled as such. The FP then implies that the classified true positive is erroneously negative. TN and FN are both examples of actual negatives that were mistakenly labeled as positive.

The mathematical of ACC, F-m, PR, and RC are denoted in the Eq. (17.20), (17.21), (17.22), and (17.23).

$$Accuracy = \frac{TN + TP}{TP + TN + FN + FP} \times 100 \tag{17.20}$$

$$F - measure = \frac{2TP}{(2TP + FP + FN)} \times 100 \tag{17.21}$$

$$Precision = \frac{TP}{(FP + TP)} \times 100 \tag{17.22}$$

$$Recall = \frac{TP}{(FN + TP)} \times 100 \tag{17.23}$$

Table 17.2 Confusion matrix.

	Predicted positive	**Predicted negative**
Actual positive	True Positive (TP)	False Positive (FP)
Actual Negative	False Negative (FN)	True Negative (TN)

17.4.2   Performance Analysis of Dataset 1

Table 17.3 and Figure 17.5 presents the comparative analysis of proposed model with existing techniques in terms of various metrics.

In this comparison analysis, the proposed technique reaches the better performance value of 94.13% accuracy and better F-measure value of 98.97%, where other techniques have low performance than the proposed technique. In the analysis of precision, the auto-encoder achieved 78.14%, RNN achieved 70.91%, LSTM achieved 64.17%, CNN achieved 91.94%, and proposed model achieved 96.84%. These same models achieved recall of 89.92%, 72.69%, 86.66%, 95.61% and proposed model achieved 97.24%.

Table 17.3 Comparative analysis of proposed technique.

	Parameter evaluation			
Methodology	**Accuracy (%)**	**Precision (%)**	**Recall (%)**	**F-measure (%)**
Auto-encoder	88.67	78.14	89.92	80.72
RNN	72.33	70.91	72.69	75.17
LSTM	80.24	64.17	86.66	68.28
CNN	76.86	91.94	95.61	95.78
ORQC-CNN	**94.13**	**96.84**	**97.24**	**98.97**

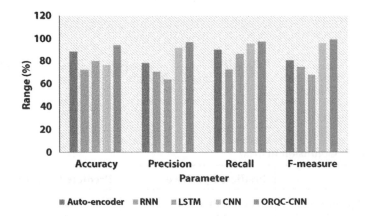

Figure 17.5 Graphical description for dataset 1.

17.4.3 Performance Analysis of Dataset 2

Table 17.4 and Figure 17.6 presents the comparative analysis of proposed model with existing techniques for sports dataset.

In the below table represent that the comparative analysis of proposed technique. In this comparison analysis, the proposed technique reaches the better performance value of 96.87% accuracy and better F-measure value of 95.15%. But, the other techniques have achieved low performance than the proposed technique.

Table 17.4 Comparative analysis of proposed technique.

Methodology	Parameter evaluation			
	Accuracy (%)	Precision (%)	Recall (%)	F-measure (%)
Auto-encoder	78.14	89.92	80.69	88.67
RNN	70.82	72.42	75.17	72.21
LSTM	64.17	86.66	68.01	80.24
CNN	91.94	95.61	95.65	76.86
ORQC-CNN	96.87	97.24	98.97	95.15

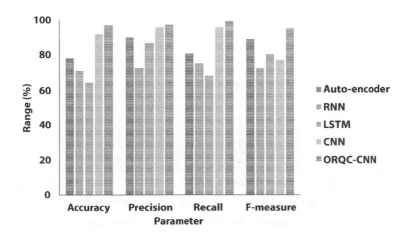

Figure 17.6 Graphical description for dataset 2.

17.4.4   Comparison

Table 17.5 and Figure 17.7 presents the comparison analysis of proposed AGTO with various DL techniques in terms of accuracy, precision, recall and F-measure.

In the below table represent that the comparative analysis of proposed classifier with feature selection technique. In this comparison analysis, the proposed technique reaches the better performance value. In this

Table 17.5 Comparative analysis of proposed AGTO with various classifiers.

Optimization	Classifiers	Parameter evaluation			
		Accuracy (%)	Precision (%)	Recall (%)	F-measure (%)
Without AGTO	LSTM	89.14	87.56	89.75	90.23
	CNN	89.47	88.12	90.57	90.27
	RQC-CNN	90.24	91.47	92.89	93.41
With AGTO	LSTM	94.47	95.14	95.68	95.27
	CNN	95.78	96.79	96.74	96.49
	RQC-CNN	96.57	97.48	97.69	98.35

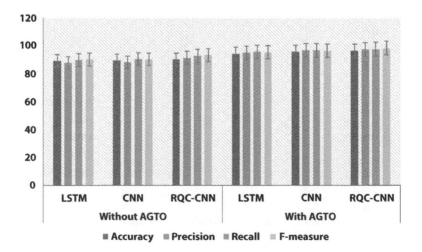

Figure 17.7 Comparison of proposed AGTO with different classifiers.

comparison analysis, optimization techniques are used. In the without optimization technique, the model reaches the better accuracy of 90.24% and better F-measure value of 93.41%. In other with optimization technique level, the proposed have better performance of better accuracy of 96.57% and better F-measure value of 98.35% respectively. In the comparison, optimization technique can give better performance than without optimization.

17.5   Conclusion

In order to get superior outcomes, quantum computing is used in the research work for the HAR process. ORQC-CNN (Optimized Random Quantum Circuits with Convolutional Neural Networks) model is used to identify the HAR. The architecture that consists of a series of quantum classified layer is shown as an analogy to the classical CNN. AGTO for ORQC-CNN parameter update is presented using variational quantum methods. Analysis of network complexity shows that compared to its classic version, this model gives exponential acceleration; 96.57% better accuracy and a superior F-measure value of 98.35% were found in the experiment analysis using optimization technique level. When compared to a system without an optimization approach, a system with an optimization technique can perform better.

References

1. Antunes, R.S., Seewald, L.A., Rodrigues, V.F., Costa, C.A.D., Gonzaga, Jr., L., Righi, R.R., Maier, A., Eskofier, B., Ollenschläger, M., Naderi, F., Fahrig, R., Bauer, S., Klein, S., Campanatti, G., A survey of sensors in healthcare workflow monitoring. *ACM Comput. Surv.*, 51, 2, 1–37, Jun. 2018.
2. Wang, Y., Cang, S., Yu, H., A survey on wearable sensor modality centred human activity recognition in health care. *Expert Syst. Appl.*, 137, 167–190, Dec. 2019.
3. Lara, O.D. and Labrador, M.A., A survey on human activity recognition using wearable sensors. *IEEE Commun. Surv. Tutor.*, 15, 3, 1192–1209, 3rd Quart., 2013.
4. Liu, Y., Nie, L., Liu, L., Rosenblum, D.S., From action to activity: Sensor-based activity recognition. *Neurocomputing*, 181, 108–115, Mar. 2016.
5. Zeng, M., Nguyen, L.T., Yu, B., Mengshoel, O.J., Zhu, J., Wu, P., Zhang, J., Convolutional neural networks for human activity recognition using mobile

sensors, in: *Proc. 6th Int. Conf. Mobile Comput., Appl. Services*, pp. 197–205, 2014.

6. Uma Maheswari, V., Aluvalu, R., Chennam, K.K., Application of machine learning algorithms for facial expression analysis, in: *Machine Learning for Sustainable Development*, vol. 9, p. 77, 2021.

7. Kanjo, E., Younis, E.M.G., Ang, C.S., Deep learning analysis of mobile physiological, environmental and location sensor data for emotion detection. *Inf. Fusion*, 49, 46–56, Sep. 2019.

8. Neverova, N., Wolf, C., Lacey, G., Fridman, L., Chandra, D., Barbello, B., Taylor, G., Learning human identity from motion patterns. *IEEE Access*, 4, 1810–1820, 2016.

9. Kantipudi, M.V.V., Moses, C.J., Aluvalu, R., Kumar, S., Remote patient monitoring using IoT, cloud computing and AI, in: *Hybrid Artificial Intelligence and IoT in Healthcare*, pp. 51–74, Springer, Singapore, 2021.

10. Donahue, J., Hendricks, L.A., Guadarrama, S., Rohrbach, M., Venugopalan, S., Darrell, T., Saenko, K., Long-term recurrent convolutional networks for visual recognition and description, in: *Proc. IEEE Conf. Comput. Vis. Pattern Recognit.*, Jun. 2015, pp. 2625–2634.

11. Miller, D.D. and Brown, E.W., Artificial intelligence in medical practice: The question to the answer? *Am. J. Med.*, 131, 2, 129–133, 2018.

12. Vania, M., Mureja, D., Lee, D., Automatic spine segmentation from CT images using convolutional neural network via redundant generation of class labels. *J. Comput. Des. Eng.*, 6, 2, 224–232, 2019.

13. LeCun, Y., Bengio, Y., Hinton, G., Deep learning. *Nature*, 521, 7553, 436–444, 2015.

14. Wang, L., Qiao, Y., Tang, X., Action recognition with trajectorypooled deep-convolutional descriptors, in: *Proc. IEEE Conf. Comput. Vis. Pattern Recognit.*, Jun. 2015, pp. 4305–4314.

15. Liu, J., Shahroudy, A., Xu, D., Wang, G., Spatio-temporal LSTM with trust gates for 3D human action recognition, in: *Computer Vision—ECCV*, B. Leibe, J. Matas, N. Sebe, M. Welling (Eds.), pp. 816–833, Springer, Cham, Switzerland, 2016.

16. Voulodimos, A., Doulamis, N., Doulamis, A., Protopapadakis, E., Deep learning for computer vision: A brief review. *Comput. Intell. Neurosci.*, 2018, 1–13, Feb. 2018.

17. Arute, F. *et al.*, Quantum supremacy using a programmable superconducting processor. *Nature*, 574, 7779, 505–510, 2019.

18. Dunjko, V. and Briegel, H.J., Machine learning & artificial intelligence in the quantum domain: A review of recent progress. *Rep. Prog. Phys.*, 81, 7, 074001, 2018.

19. Farhi, E. and Neven, H., Classification with quantum neural networks on near term processors. Preprint arXiv:1802.06002, 2018. https://arxiv.org/pdf/1802.06002.pdf

20. Havlíček, V., Córcoles, A.D., Temme, K., Harrow, A.W., Kandala, A., Chow, J.M., Gambetta, J.M., Supervised learning with quantum-enhanced feature spaces. *Nature*, 567, 7747, 209–212, 2019.
21. Mitarai, K., Negoro, M., Kitagawa, M., Fujii, K., Quantum circuit learning. *Phys. Rev. A*, 98, 3, 032309, 2018.
22. Li, Y. and Wang, L., Human activity recognition based on residual network and BiLSTM. *Sensors*, 22, 2, 635, 2022.
23. Basak, H., Kundu, R., Singh, P.K., Ijaz, M.F., Woźniak, M., Sarkar, R., A union of deep learning and swarm-based optimization for 3D human action recognition. *Sci. Rep.*, 12, 1, 1–17, 2022.
24. Ronald, M., Poulose, A., Han, D.S., iSPLInception: An inception-ResNet deep learning architecture for human activity recognition. *IEEE Access*, 9, 68985–69001, 2021.
25. Khan, I.U., Afzal, S., Lee, J.W., Human activity recognition via hybrid deep learning based model. *Sensors*, 22, 1, 323, 2022.
26. Jaouedi, N., Boujnah, N., Bouhlel, M.S., A new hybrid deep learning model for human action recognition. *J. King Saud Univ.-Comput. Inf. Sci.*, 32, 4, 447–453, 2020.
27. Nafea, O., Abdul, W., Muhammad, G., Alsulaiman, M., Sensor-based human activity recognition with spatio-temporal deep learning. *Sensors*, 21, 6, 2141, 2021.
28. Gochoo, M., Akhter, I., Jalal, A., Kim, K., Stochastic remote sensing event classification over adaptive posture estimation via multifused data and deep belief network. *Remote Sens.*, 13, 5, 912, 2021.
29. Hemdan, E.E.-D., Shouman, M.A., Karar, M.E., Covidxnet: A framework of deep learning classifiers to diagnose COVID-19 in X-ray images. Preprint arXiv:2003.11055, 2020. https://arxiv.org/ftp/arxiv/papers/2003/2003.11055.pdf
30. Lloyd, S., Schuld, M., Ijaz, A., Izaac, J., Killoran, N., Quantum embeddings for machine learning. Preprint arXiv:2001.03622, 2020. https://arxiv.org/pdf/2001.03622.pdf
31. Takeuchi, Y., Morimae, T., Hayashi, M., Quantum computational universality of hypergraph states with pauli-x and z basis measurements. *Sci. Rep.*, 9, 1, 1–14, 2019.

18

Quantum Intelligent Systems and Deep Learning

Bhagaban Swain[1] and Debasis Gountia[2]*

[1]Department of Computer Science & Engineering, Assam University, Silchar, Assam, India
[2]Department of Computer Science Application, OUTR University, Bhubaneshwar, Odisha, India

Abstract

Quantum computing can provides better solutions to many complex problems, and thus quantum technology can help to improve machine-learning problems. This chapter discuses about quantum machine learning algorithm for the quantum data like quantum support vector machine (QSVM), quantum principal component analysis (QPCA) and quantum neural network (QNN). For learning from classical data in in the noisy intermediate scale quantum (NISQ) computer, quantum variational classifier with a classical optimizer to train a parameterized quantum circuit is discussed.

Keywords: Quantum machine learning, QPCA, quantum feature map, variational quantum classifier, QNN

18.1 Introduction

Machine Learning is a powerful component in the field of data science. Machine learning algorithms tells how to learn from data and improve the learning accuracy gradually. Machine learning has wide area of applications like in health care, computer security, speech and natural language processing, robotics and machine automation etc. In recent years, both in

Corresponding author: dgountia@outr.ac.in

Sachi Nandan Mohanty, Rajanikanth Aluvalu and Sarita Mohanty (eds.) Evolution and Applications of Quantum Computing, (313–326) © 2023 Scrivener Publishing LLC

theory and practice quantum computing has rapidly advanced. Quantum Computing algorithms like database search, Prime factorization, quantum cryptography has a potential advantage as compared to its classical counterpart. There are many papers addressing to boost the performance of machine learning systems utilizing quantum devices and methods. The field of quantum computing where machine-learning problems are solved using quantum computer is called quantum machine learning. Quantum machine learning uses quantum computer for training machine learning models by the help of quantum data and quantum algorithms. Machine learning, in general, being divided into four paradigms depending on whether the data used is generated by a quantum system (Q) or a classical system (C) and the computing device is quantum (Q) or classical (C). The conventional approach of machine learning where classical system model is used for machine learning task. In conventional machine learning, CC (classical data with classical system) and QC (quantum data with classical system) are the two approach of machine learning. The CC approach of machine learning is done in classical computer using classical data. The QC approach discuss about the conventional machine learning solves the quantum problems where data generated by quantum experiment and the quantum data is converted into classical object or classical data and then the classical machine learning model is applied. Other two approach of machine learning, CQ (classical data and quantum Computer) and QQ (quantum data and quantum computer), where quantum machine and quantum machine learning algorithms are used in the machine learning task is called quantum machine learning. In this chapter these two types quantum machine learning CQ and QQ will be discussed.

In machine learning using quantum data and quantum machine learning algorithm (QQ) discussion about quantum principal component analysis which gives the idea about dimensional reduction of input quantum data. Quantum support vector machine for data classification will also be discussed. Lastly in QQ, quantum neural network will be discussed.

In the quantum machine learning for classical data (CQ), mainly variational quantum classifier, will be discussed. In CQ approach of machine learning, the first thing is to encode the classical data into quantum data, which is called quantum feature map. Various data encoding techniques for classical data to quantum data will be discussed starting from Pauli's feature map to other ansatzs. Various variational quantum circuits for the classification of the quantum data will be discussed. This chapter will also discuss how the variational quantum classifier in data encoding phase can provide efficient way of kernel matrix calculation for the use in either quantum SVM or SVM for classification.

18.2   Quantum Support Vector Machine

A support vector machine (SVM) [1] is a basic supervised machine learning algorithm that classify unknown data by creating hyper-planes trough a training data set. Let's consider a training data set $M = \left\{ \left(\vec{x}_j, y_j \right) : \vec{x}_j \in R^N, y_j = \pm 1 \right\}_{j=1}$ ... For data in one class $y_j = 1$ is considered and for $y_j = -1$ data in another class is consider. In the training, two parallel hyper-planes are created. one hyper-plane (positive) is the boundary for one class of data and another hyper-plane (negative) is the boundary of other data class having no data points between the two hyper-planes. These two hyper-plane are separated by maximum distance is $\dfrac{2}{|\vec{w}|}$. If a data point $\vec{x}_j$ is inside the boundary of positive hyper-plane then equation ω will be satisfied and if it is inside the boundary of negative hyper-plane then equation $\vec{\omega} \cdot \vec{x}_j + \omega_0 \geq 1$ will be satisfied. The offset of the hyper plane is given by $\omega_0 / |\vec{w}|$. In the training process the hyper-plane parameters are obtained and a new unknown vector $\vec{x}$ is classified in which side of the hyper-plane by evaluating the function

$$f(\vec{x}) = sgn(\vec{\omega} \cdot \vec{x} + \omega_0) \tag{18.1}$$

The data point $\vec{x}$ will be assigned in positive class if $f(\vec{x}) = 1$ or will be assigned in negative class if $f(\vec{x}) = -1$. The value of ω_0 and ω is determined for a given set of training data $\vec{x}_j$ by introducing real numbers β_j. ω can be expressed in terms data points $\vec{x}_j$ as

$$\vec{\omega} = \sum_{j=1}^{M} \beta_j x_j \tag{18.2}$$

ω_0 and α_j can be determined by solving the linear equation

$$F \begin{pmatrix} \omega_0 \\ \beta_1 \\ \vdots \\ \beta_M \end{pmatrix} = \begin{pmatrix} 0 \\ y_1 \\ \vdots \\ y_M \end{pmatrix} \tag{18.3}$$

where, $y_i = f(x_i) = \pm 1$, and F is a $(M + 1) \times (M + 1)$ matrix given by

$$F = \begin{pmatrix} 0 & 1 & \cdots & 1 \\ 1 & & & \\ \vdots & & K + \dfrac{I_M}{\gamma} & \\ 1 & & & \end{pmatrix} \tag{18.4}$$

Here, K is the kernel matrix having elements

$$K_{ij} = \vec{x}_i \cdot \vec{x}_j \tag{18.5}$$

is kernel matrix of M × M dimension and γ is a fixed constant which for assuring the existence of the solution of the linear equation (18.3) and the result is a binary classifier for new data $\vec{x}$

$$y(\vec{x}) = sign(\textstyle\sum_{i=1}^{M} \beta_i K(\vec{x}_i, \vec{x}) + \omega_0) \tag{18.6}$$

if $y(\vec{x}) = 1$ then the data $\vec{x}$ is positive class and if $y(\vec{x}) = -1$ the data $\vec{x}$ point in negative class. The SVM discussed above is for classical data in classical computation.

For classification of quantum data in quantum computer the quantum support vector machine (QSVM) can be used [2]. The data set used in the QSVM is the quantum data and is stored quantum memory. In QSVM, the training-data taken from quantum memory [3] in the form of quantum state $|\vec{x}_j\rangle = \dfrac{1}{|\vec{x}_j|} \sum_{i=1}^{N} (\vec{x}_j)_i |i\rangle$ the quantum state $|\vec{x}_j\rangle$ which is the quantum analogous of the classical training data $\vec{x}_j$. For training the QSVM, a quantum oracle is used. The training data oracle is stared from the initial state $1/\sqrt{M} \sum_{j=1}^{M} |j\rangle$. The training-data oracles and the training data given to the training set register create the parallel state $|\chi\rangle = 1/\sqrt{N_x} \sum_{j=1}^{M} |\vec{x}_j| |j\rangle |\vec{x}_j\rangle$, with $N_\chi = \sum_{j=1}^{M} |\vec{x}_j|^2$. This process trains the training data oracle with the help of training set register. The density matrix of the training data oracle discarding the training set register will be $tr_2\{|\chi\rangle\langle\chi|\} = \dfrac{1}{N_x} \sum_{i,j=1}^{M} |\vec{x}_i||\vec{x}_j| \langle\vec{x}_i|\vec{x}_j\rangle |i\rangle\langle j| = \dfrac{K}{trK}$. The kernel matrix is obtained up to a constant factor, i.e., trK from the reduced density matrix of the training data oracle. Using quantum method kernel matrix can be efficiently calculated which is computationally hard in classical method.

In QSVM, the hyper-plane parameters are determined by the quantum state $|\beta,\vec{\alpha}\rangle$. The quantum algorithm for solving linear system of equations [4, 5], can be used to determine the hyper-plane $|\beta,\vec{\alpha}\rangle = F^{-1}|\vec{y}\rangle$.

Let $|v_i\rangle$ be the Eigen-states of F with corresponding eigenvalues λ_i. then $|\tilde{y}\rangle$ can be formally expanded as $|\tilde{y}\rangle = \sum_{i=1}^{M+1}\langle v_i|\tilde{y}\rangle|v_i\rangle$. With a register for storing an approximation of the eigenvalues (initialized to $|0\rangle$), phase estimation [6] generates a state which is close to the ideal state storing the respective eigenvalue:

$$|\tilde{y}|0\rangle \rightarrow \sum_{i=1}^{M+1}\langle v_i|\tilde{y}\rangle|v_i\rangle|\lambda_i\rangle \rightarrow \sum_{i=1}^{M+1}\frac{\langle v_i|\tilde{y}\rangle}{\lambda_i}|v_i\rangle \qquad (18.7)$$

The hyper-plane can be written as,

$$|\beta,\vec{\alpha}\rangle = \frac{1}{\sqrt{C}}(\beta|0\rangle + \sum_{k=1}^{M}\alpha_k|k\rangle) \qquad (18.8)$$

where $C = \beta^2 + \sum_{k=1}^{M}\alpha_k^2$ once the hyper-plane $|\beta,\vec{\alpha}\rangle$ is determined then the training of the QSVM is complete. To classify an unknown state of $|\vec{x}\rangle$ the query state is formed from the state $|\vec{x}\rangle$ as

$$|\vec{x}\rangle = \frac{1}{\sqrt{N_{\tilde{x}}}}\left(|0\rangle|0\rangle + \sum_{j=1}^{M}|\vec{x}||j\rangle|\vec{x}\rangle\right) \qquad (18.9)$$

with $N_{\tilde{x}} = M|\vec{x}|^2 + 1$. Similarly the training-data oracle from the state $|\beta,\vec{\alpha}\rangle$ as:

$$|\tilde{v}\rangle = \frac{1}{\sqrt{N_{\tilde{u}}}}\left(\beta|0\rangle|0\rangle + \sum_{j=1}^{M}\alpha_j|\vec{x}_j||j\rangle|\vec{x}_j\rangle\right) \qquad (18.10)$$

ith $N_{\tilde{u}} = \beta^2 + \sum_{j=1}^{M}\alpha_j^2|\vec{x}_j|^2$. By overlapping the quantum states $|\tilde{v}\rangle$ and $|\tilde{x}\rangle$ will classify the state, i.e., $y(\vec{x}) = \text{sign}(|\tilde{v}\rangle\langle\tilde{x}|)$.

If the expectation value $|\tilde{v}\rangle\langle\tilde{x}|$ is greater than 0, the classification of the vector $|\tilde{x}\rangle$ will be in positive class, otherwise it will be negative class. The QSVM discussed here is also experimentally realized by [7] for classification of handwritten images.

18.3   Quantum Principal Component Analysis

Principal component analysis (PCA) is a dimension reduction technique where a high dimensional data often lies in a lower-dimensional space and can be projected in to lower dimension. In PCA, the fewer dimensions that retain the trend and pattern of the original data is kept. These lower dimensions are called principal components [1, 8]. The dimension reduction techniques are used in many machine learning applications like, Support vector machine, clustering and other machine learning algorithms for which there are classical algorithms and applications in the literature. Similarly, in quantum machine learning, there are quantum data, which are in high dimensional Hilbert space but can be well expressed in lower dimensional Hilbert space. So, a quantum state from high dimension can be represented to few low dimensional mutually orthogonal unit vectors called the quantum principal components analysis (QPCA) that maximally preserve the data variance.

Let us here discuss the QPCA [9] where a d-dimensional quantum system are there and a state can be expressed as a low-rank density matrix $\rho = \sum_i \lambda_i |\lambda_i\rangle\langle\lambda_j|$ where $\langle\lambda_i|\lambda_j\rangle = \delta_{ij}$. Create n copies of the density matrix ρ. consider any density matrix σ which is nth order in time t. Applying the swap operator $e^{-iS\Delta t} = \cos(\Delta t)I - i\sin(\Delta t)$ to the system $\rho \otimes \sigma$ and taking the partial trace of the first system we will get as

$$tr_p e^{-iS\Delta t} \rho \otimes \sigma e^{iS\Delta t} = tr_p(\cos(\Delta t)I - i\sin(\Delta t)S)\rho \otimes \sigma(\cos(\Delta t)I$$
$$+ i\sin(\Delta t)S) = (\cos^2\Delta t)\sigma + (\sin^2\Delta t)\rho - i\sin\Delta t[\rho,\sigma]$$
$$= \sigma - i\Delta t[\rho,\sigma] + O(\Delta t^2) \tag{18.11}$$

with n copies ρ by repeated infinitesimal application of swap operator to $\rho \otimes \sigma$ one can construct $e^{-i\rho n\Delta t}\rho \otimes \sigma e^{i\rho n\Delta t}$. As $n\Delta t = t$ and with the Suzuki Trotter quantum simulation theory we can write $e^{-i\rho n\Delta t} \otimes \sigma e^{i\rho n\Delta t} = e^{-i\rho t}$. Again for positive semi definite low rank matrix ρ, the quantum matrix inversion algorithm [21, 22] can also be used to construct the operator $e^{-i\rho t}$. As we know in quantum phase estimation algorithm $e^{-i\rho t}$ with varying time to any state $|\psi\rangle$ with initial ground state $|0\rangle$ can compute the eigen values, i.e., $e^{-i\rho t}|\psi\rangle|0\rangle = \sum_i r_i|\chi_i\rangle|\hat{r}_i\rangle$, where $|\chi_i\rangle$, and $\hat{r}_i$ are respectively corresponding eigen vectors (principal components), and the estimates of the eigenvalues of ρ and r_i is the eigenvalue of $|\psi\rangle$.

If ρ is taken as initial state then quantum phase estimation algorithm will give $\sum_i r_i|\chi_i\rangle\langle\chi_i| \otimes |\hat{r}_i\rangle\langle\hat{r}_i|$ and hence the eigen values and eigen vectors can be obtained by sampling this. Once all the eigen values and its corresponding eigen vector is available we can use the principal eigen values and eigen vector as per our requirement.

18.4   Quantum Neural Network

The neural network model based on the principle of quantum mechanics is called quantum neural network (QNN). In QNN, the qubit is used as quantum neuron [10]. The unitary operator acting on the corresponding input and output qubits layer act as perceptron [11] in a particular layer of the network. The parameters of the unitary operator incorporate the weights and biases of the network. The quantum neural network proposed by [12] is efficient one because the training algorithms does not depends on the on the depth of the network rather depends on the width of the individual layers. Here we are discussing the quantum neural network algorithm [12]. The initial layer of the QNN is in any unknown quantum mixed state and can be represented as ρ^{in} in density matrix form. The output layer of the QNN and hidden layers l is in the ground state and is represented by ket notation as $|0 \cdots 0\rangle_{out}$ and $|0 \cdots 0\rangle_l$ respectively before the perceptron is applied. The perceptron from one layer to another layer is initially an *arbitrary* unitary matrix applied to the m qubits in first layer to n qubits second layer. If there are L *hidden* layers then there will be $L + 1$ unitary matrix acting as perceptron. Let U^1 be the unitary operator as perceptron form initial layer to first hidden layer and U^2 the unitary operator first hidden layer to second hidden layer and so on. Let U^{out} is the unitary operator from last hidden layer to output layer. The unitary operator U is also an unitary operator consist of perceptron unitary in each layer, i.e., $U \equiv U^{out}U^L U^{L-1} \cdots U^1$. The output layer qubit is mapped form the input layer qubit as:

$$\rho^{out} \equiv tr_{in,hid}\left(U\left(\rho^{in} \otimes |0 \cdots 0\rangle_{hid,out} \langle 0 \cdots 0|\right)U^\dagger\right) \qquad (18.12)$$

Again, if there are n qubits in $l - 1$ and m qubits in l layer then unitary matrix U^l is the tensor product of m unitary matrix each unitary matrix is the n qubits of the $l - 1$ layer acting on a qubit in the l layer. These unitary matrix generally don't commute so order of operation is maintained. U^l can be written as $U^l = U_m^l U_{m-1}^l \cdots U_2^l U_1^l$ and is shown in the figure below. The structure of the feed forward neural network can be represented as:

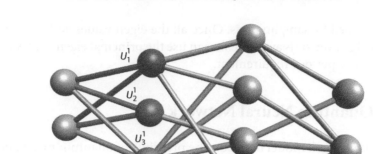

$$\rho^{out} = \mathcal{E}^{out}\left(\mathcal{E}^L\left(\mathcal{E}^2\left(\mathcal{E}^1\left(\rho^{in}\right)\right)\cdots\right)\right) \tag{18.13}$$

where all the $\mathcal{E}^l$'s is the sequence of *completely positive* layer-to-layer transition maps. The action of $\mathcal{E}^l$'s from $l-1$ to l can be written as

$$\mathcal{E}^l(\rho^{l-1}) \equiv tr_{l-1}\left(\prod_{j=m_l}^1(\rho^{l-1}\otimes|0\cdots0\rangle_l\langle0\cdots0|)\prod_{j=1}^{m_l}U_j^{l\dagger}\right) \tag{18.14}$$

The parameters of the perciptron matrix U_j^l can be updated by using quantum back propagation algorithm according to the equation $U \to e^{i\epsilon K}U$, where the matrix K is given as

$$K_j^l = \eta\frac{2^{m_{l-1}}}{N}\sum_{x=1}^N tr_{rest}M_j^l \tag{18.15}$$

where the trace is over all qubits that are not affected by U_j^l, η is the learning rate and

$$M_j^l = \left[\prod_{\alpha=j}^1 U_\alpha^l\left(\rho_x^{l-1}\otimes|0\cdots0\rangle_l\right)\prod_{\alpha=1}^j U_\alpha^{l\dagger},\prod_{\alpha=j+1}^{m_l}U_\alpha^{l\dagger}\right.$$
$$\left.\left(\mathbb{I}_{l-1}\otimes\mathcal{F}^{l+1}\left(\cdots\mathcal{F}^{l+1}\left(|\psi_x^{out}\rangle\langle\psi_x^{out}|\right)\cdots\right)\right)\prod_{\alpha=m_l}^{j+1}U_\alpha^l\right] \tag{18.16}$$

$\mathcal{F}^l$ is the adjoint channel to $\mathcal{E}^l$, i.e. the transition channel from layer $l+1$ to layer l. To compute the value of K_j^l at a particular layer only the density matrix of the adjacent layers are required. At time of training if the input quantum state is $|\psi_x^{in}\rangle$ and its corresponding output is $|\psi_x^{out}\rangle$ but the quantum network output is ρ_x^{out}. Then the cost function is

$$C(s) = \frac{1}{N} \sum_{x=1}^{N} \langle \psi_x^{out} | \rho_x^{out} | \langle \psi_x^{out} \rangle \tag{18.17}$$

which provides the stopping criteria for the algorithm.

The algorithm for the QNN is summarized below:

1. **Initialization:** All the perceptron matrix U^l for all j and l are chosen randomly
2. **Feedforward:** For every training data $|\psi_x^{in}\rangle$ and its corresponding output state $|\psi_x^{out}\rangle \left(|\psi_x^{in}\rangle, |\psi_x^{out}\rangle \right)$ and every layer l, perform the action of E^l from $l-1$ to l as per mentioned in equation (18.13).
3. **Update the network:**
   3a. Calculate the parameter $_j K^l$ at a particular layer l to a particular neuron j as per the formula given in equation (18.15).
   3b. Update each unitary $_j U^l$ at a particular layer l to a particular neuron j according to $_j U_j^l \rightarrow e^{i\varepsilon K_j^l} U_j^l$
4. **Calculate cost:** Calculate the cost function after applying perceptron in each layer up to the output layer for a particular input $|\psi_x^{in}$ according to equation (18.17).
5. **Repeat:** Until the cost function reaches its maximum value repeat steps 2 to 4.

18.5   Variational Quantum Classifier

The Variational Quantum Classifier (VQC) is a kind of quantum neural network which consist of quantum circuit and can be implemented in a noisy intermediate-scale (NISQ) quantum computer with real world classical data. Different types of variational circuits are used in literature [13–16] for variational quantum classifier. The quantum circuit here is a variational quantum circuit or parameterized quantum circuit. These parameters of the quantum circuit will be optimized during the training process from labeled data to classify new data samples. The working of variational quantum classifier follows four steps and is explained below:

1. Load data onto the Quantum Computer.
   In classical machine learning [1], the data is generally mapped non-linearly onto a higher dimensional space in where a better kernel can be found to classify efficiently. In

case of quantum computing the available data may in classical form which need to be converted into quantum data so that quantum computer can process it. Thus input x from an input set X into a quantum state that is described by a vector $|\varphi(x)\rangle$ and which lives in Hilbert space F. This procedure of input encoding fulfills the definition of a feature map $\varphi : X \to F$, which we call a *quantum feature map*. The quantum feature map is a state preparation circuit $U_\varphi(x)$ that applied on the ground state or vacuum state $|0...0\rangle$ of a Hilbert space F as $U_\varphi(x)|0...0\rangle = |\varphi(x)\rangle$ and convert the classical state x into quantum state $|\varphi(x)\rangle$. The circuit is called $U_\varphi(x)$ the *feature-embedding circuit*. In general a quantum feature map or feature embedding circuit is a quantum circuit that mapped data from one space to another Hilbert space. Different quantum embedding circuits such as basis embedding and amplitude-embedding are simplest form of quantum embedding circuit whereas ZFeatureMap, ZZFeatureMap, PauliFeatureMap, [18–20] are some complicated quantum embedding circuits used in the literature that can create quantum data in entangled quantum state.

2. Quantum Variational Circuit: The circuit $W(\vec{\theta})$ which is responsible for classification. The circuit $W(\vec{\theta})$ *is* a parameterized circuit by a set of variables θ applied on the quantum state created by quantum feature map and the parameter of the circuit is optimized during training. We decompose W into

$$W = W_L \ldots U_\ell \ldots W_1, \qquad (18.18)$$

Where, each W_ℓ is either a single qubit or a two-qubit quantum gate. The parameters of this variational circuit are then trained in the classical optimization loop until it classifies the data points correctly. This is the learning stage of the algorithm and accuracy of the model can vary based on the variational circuit one chooses.

3. Measurement and Assigning a Binary Label: Measurement of the output at the end of the wire is also called expectation value. From these expectation values, the cost of the circuit can be calculated with some classical post-processing.

4. Classical Optimization Loop: The parameters of the quantum variational circuit are updated using a classical optimization routine once the measurements are ready. This is the

classical loop that trains our parameters until the cost function's value decreases. Commonly either COBYLA, SPSA or SLSQP optimizers are used. Variational quantum classifier algorithm is summarized below:

1. Encode input data $\{x_i\}$ into some quantum state $|\phi(x_i)\rangle$ by applying a unitary input gate $U_\phi(x_i)$ to initialized qubits $|0...0\rangle$

2. Apply a θ-parameterized unitary $|\psi_{out}(x_i, \theta)\rangle$ to the input state and generate an output state $|\psi_{out}(x_i, \theta)\rangle = W(\vec{\theta})|\phi(x_i)\rangle$

3. Measure the expectation values of $|\psi_{out}(x_i, \theta)\rangle$ with respect to some observable. In case qubit system subset of Pauli operators $\{B_j\} \subset \{I, X, Y, Z\}^{\otimes N}$ is used. Evaluate the output $y_i = y(x_i, \theta)$ by some output function f as $y(x_i, \theta) \equiv f(B_j(xi, \theta)$

4. By turning the circuit parameter θ by minimizing the cost function $L(f(x_i), y(x_i,\theta))$ of the teacher $f(x_i)$ and the output y_i.

5. Performance can be checked with test data set once the training is over using step 2 and 3 above with set of trained data set.

18.6   Conclusion

We have presented the ability of quantum computers to use in machine learning task. The QPCA method to reduce the dimension of quantum data by a quantum computer is explained. The quantum version of support vector machine is discussed which can also be used to evaluate the kernel efficiently. The quantum generalizations neural network is discussed where unitary matrix operation is formulated as perceptions and qubit (qudit) as neuron. Also an efficient quantum algorithm to train the quantum neural network is discussed. To handle classical data into quantum computer the concept of quantum feature map as a parameterized circuit is explained. The quantum circuit version of neural network called the quantum variational classifier is also discussed.

References

1. Mitchell, T.M., *Machine learning*, International Edition, McGraw-Hill Series in Computer Science. McGraw-Hill, Maidenhead, U.K., 1997.

2. Rebentrost, P., Mohseni, M., Lloyd, S., Quantum support vector machine for big data classification. *Phys. Rev. Lett.*, 113, 130503, Sep 2014.
3. Giovannetti, V., Lloyd, S., Maccone, L., Quantum random access memory. *Phys. Rev. Lett.*, 100, 160501, Apr 2008.
4. Harrow, A.W., Hassidim, A., Lloyd, S., Quantum algorithm for linear systems of equations. *Phys. Rev. Lett.*, 103, 150502, Oct 2009.
5. Pan, J., Cao, Y., Yao, X., Li, Z., Ju, C., Chen, H., Peng, X., Kais, S., Du, J., Experimental realization of quantum algorithm for solving linear systems of equations. *Phys. Rev. A*, 89, 022313, Feb 2014.
6. Nielsen, M.A. and Chuang, I.L., *Quantum computation and quantum information*, Cambridge University Press, Cambridge, England, 2000.
7. Li, Z., Liu, X., Xu, N., Du, J., Experimental realization of a quantum support vector machine. *Phys. Rev. Lett.*, 114, 140504, Apr 2015.
8. Bishop, C.M., *Pattern recognition and machine learning (Information science and statistics)*, Springer-Verlag, Berlin, Heidelberg, 2006.
9. Lloyd, S., Mohseni, M., Rebentrost, P., Quantum principal component analysis. *Nat. Phys.*, 10, 9, 631–633, Sep 2014.
10. Abbas, A., Sutter, D., Zoufal, C., Lucchi, A., Figalli, A., Woerner, S., The power of quantum neural networks. *Nat. Comput. Sci.*, 1, 6, 403–409, Jun 2021.
11. Schuld, M., Sinayskiy, I., Petruccione, F., Simulating a perceptron on a quantum computer. *Phys. Lett. A*, 379, 7, 660–663, 2015.
12. Beer, K., Bondarenko, D., Farrelly, T., Osborne, T.J., Salzmann, R., Scheiermann, D., Wolf, R., Training deep quantum neural networks. *Nat. Commun.*, 11, 1, 808, Feb 2020.
13. Mitarai, K., Negoro, M., Kitagawa, M., Fujii, K., Quantum circuit learning. *Phys. Rev. A*, 98, 032309, Sep 2018.
14. Schuld, M. and Killoran, N., Quantum machine learning in feature hilbert spaces. *Phys. Rev. Lett.*, 122, 040504, Feb 2019.
15. Farhi, E. and Neven, H., Classification with quantum neural networks on near term processors. *Quantum Physics*, 2018.
16. Wan, K.H., Dahlsten, O., Kristjánsson, H., Gardner, R., Kim, M.S., Quantum generalisation of feedforward neural networks. *NPJ Quantum Inf.*, 3, 1, 36, Sep 2017.
17. Havlíček, V., Córcoles, A.D., Temme, K., Harrow, A.W., Kandala, A., Chow, J.M., Gambetta, J.M., Supervised learning with quantum-enhanced feature spaces. *Nature*, 567, 7747, 209–212, Mar 2019.
18. Schuld, M., Sweke, R., Meyer, J.J., Effect of data encoding on the expressive power of variational quantum-machine-learning models. *Phys. Rev. A*, 103, 032430, Mar 2021.
19. Huang, H.-Y., Broughton, M., Mohseni, M., Babbush, R., Boixo, S., Neven, H., McClean, J.R., Power of data in quantum machine learning. *Nat. Commun.*, 12, 1, 2631, May 2021.

20. Schuld, M., Supervised quantum machine learning models are kernel methods. *Quantum Physics*, 2021.
21. Cai, X.-D., Weedbrook, C., Su, Z.-E., Chen, M.-C., Gu, M., Zhu, M.-J., Li, L., Liu, N.-L., Lu, C.-Y., Pan, J.-W., Experimental quantum computing to solve systems of linear equations. *Phys. Rev. Lett.*, 110, 230501, Jun 2013.
22. Pan, J., Cao, Y., Yao, X., Li, Z., Ju, C., Chen, H., Peng, X., Kais, S., Du, J., Experimental realization of quantum algorithm for solving linear systems of equations. *Phys. Rev. A*, 89, 022313, Feb 2014.

Index

Printed and bound by CPI Group (UK) Ltd, Croydon, CR0 4YY

27/10/2024

14580129-0004